This Is Assisted Dying by Stefanie Green - Cdn Memoir - Team 4

Transfer Date	Name	Email	Phone
October 1	Helen Muratori	hsmuratori@gmail.com	905-227-4~
November 1	Brenda Dolha	brenda.dolha@icloud.com	905-650-5135
December 1	Louise Couchman	louise.couchman@icloud.com	289-213-7047
January 1	Nancy Cain	nancycain12@gmail.com	289 567 0393
February 1	Linda Thatcher	lrthatcher@sympatico.ca	905-931-4144
March 1	Ann Milligan	milligan.ann@gmail.com	905-933-4344
April 1	Dianne Marshall	dmarsh@live.ca	905-685-7678
May 1	Margo Standish	margostandish@gmail.com	905-688-1653
June 1	Vicky Guertin	vickyguertin@aol.com	905-984-5885
July 1	Denise Bradden	denisebradden@gmail.com	905-892-9293

THIS IS
ASSISTED
DYING

A DOCTOR'S STORY OF EMPOWERING PATIENTS
AT THE END OF LIFE

STEFANIE GREEN, MD

SCRIBNER

New York   London   Toronto   Sydney   New Delhi

Scribner
An Imprint of Simon & Schuster, Inc.
1230 Avenue of the Americas
New York, NY 10020

First Scribner hardcover edition March 2022

SCRIBNER and design are registered trademarks of The Gale Group, Inc., used
under license by Simon & Schuster, Inc., the publisher of this work.

For information about special discounts for bulk purchases, please contact Simon
& Schuster Special Sales at 1-866-506-1949 or business@simonandschuster.com.

The Simon & Schuster Speakers Bureau can bring authors to your live event. For
more information or to book an event, contact the Simon & Schuster Speakers
Bureau at 1-866-248-3049 or visit our website at www.simonspeakers.com.

Interior design by Wendy Blum

Manufactured in the United States of America

3   5   7   9   10   8   6   4

Library of Congress Cataloging-in-Publication Data has been applied for.

ISBN 978-1-9821-2946-0
ISBN 978-1-9821-2951-4 (ebook)

For my patients, who have each left an indelible mark
And for all the members of CAMAP, upon whose shoulders I stand

PROLOGUE

WHAT IF YOU COULD DECIDE, at the end of your life, exactly when and where your death would happen? What if, instead of dying alone, in the middle of the night, in a hospital bed, you could be at home at a time of your choosing? You could decide who would be in the room with you, holding your hand or embracing you as you left this Earth. And what if a doctor could help ensure that your death was comfortable, peaceful, and dignified? What if you could plan a final conversation with everyone you love? You might never look at death the same way again.

I knew from the first moment I met him that Ed was an eccentric man. When he opened the door to his apartment, I was struck by the variety of handmade jewelry on his body: a row of bracelets, several necklaces, and multiple earrings. A small statue of the Buddha surrounded by various colored crystals sat on the floor behind him, and a strong smell of incense wafted out of the completely unfurnished space. I had been offering assisted deaths—providing medication and helping people to end their lives—for several months by then, and I had met some fascinating individuals, the courageous pioneers and the truly desperate, but still, Ed stood out.

I got to know Ed and his story over several months while visiting him in various residences, or sometimes in the hospital, in Victoria, British Columbia, Canada. At sixty-eight, Ed was proud to say he had never held a job and had "lived the life of a free spirit." He told me he had seen the world, chased his dreams, and had few, if any, regrets.

Like more than 65 percent of the people I work with, Ed had terminal metastatic cancer. His cancer had developed over four years, and never once had he consented to active medical treatment, avoiding chemotherapy, surgery, and radiation. His disease had progressed as expected and now was causing symptoms he couldn't avoid. Ed's pain was reasonably controlled, but his increasing need for narcotics, his deep fatigue, and his frequent, urgent trips to the restroom were severely limiting his ability to move around independently, which made it all but impossible for him to venture outside. Life confined within four walls was not a life for Ed. He was articulate in his explanation of the loss of meaning in his everyday experience, the dwindling of sand in his hourglass. He was a true believer in reincarnation, he told me, and was eager to move on to his next life.

Ed was also the first person to tell me he wanted to die alone.

When I arrived on the day of his scheduled death, he was in a small private hospital room, a surprising choice for where he wanted to die, and we chatted for a while first. He seemed ready, eager to proceed, tired of waiting. After a few minutes, he excused himself to go to the washroom and returned wearing a full clown suit: tie-dyed pants and T-shirt, a colorful clown wig, and a red nose. He told me he hadn't been sure if he was going to use the nose or not, but in the end, he'd decided to go for it. Despite all our previous conversations, I'd never realized Ed was an amateur clown. I asked him why he'd chosen to wear the clown suit on this day, and he told me he wanted to go out laughing. He figured this was his best bet.

I called for the nurse, and as Ed was having his IV started, I excused myself to go see his friend Maggie, who he had asked to wait in the quiet sitting area nearby. About ten years his junior, she was sad but coping. I wanted to explain to her what would be happening even though she wasn't going to be in the room with us, but before I got started, I mentioned that Ed had put on his clown suit.

"Oh, good," she said, "he felt sure that would make him smile." I saw a small, shy grin. "You should tell him a joke."

I was open to the idea but at a bit of a loss for content.

"He helped me through a tough time a while back," Maggie explained. "We've known each other over twenty years. He taught me the basics of how to be a clown." She smiled broadly at the memory. "We even worked a few events together. I was terrible at it, but it wasn't really about the clowning—it was about the friendship."

Then she told me his favorite joke.

I headed back into Ed's room, where everything was in place. He was resting on top of the bedsheets, quite colorfully laid out. He was ready, he told me, and the nurse confirmed that all was in order from his perspective too.

The nurse, a middle-aged man dressed in hospital greens, was a veteran in his profession, and as he finished packing up his IV supplies, he paused to look me in the eye. These were still early days in assisted dying, and I wasn't sure what might be going on in his mind. Across the bed from him, I replanted my feet, lifted my chin (perhaps only metaphorically), and readied myself for a possible lecture about how he couldn't condone the work I was doing. But the nurse spoke quietly and explained it was the first time he'd been involved in a case of assisted dying. He wanted to thank me for my work. He believed having this option was important, that it was long overdue, and he was glad he could contribute in some way. I exhaled. I suspected he may have witnessed many deaths over the years that he might not have described as "good," and his brief, unexpected remarks sparked a feeling in me of relief and being supported. I thanked him for his words and work, and he left Ed and me alone.

"Are you sure you're ready?" I asked Ed.

"Yes, I am certainly ready," he replied. He was looking straight up at the ceiling: not nervous, not sad, but not smiling.

"All right, then, I will begin."

I was standing next to the bed on Ed's left with the medications neatly lined up on the bedside table. Eight syringes in all; the middle two were quite large and filled with a milky-white substance. The bright blue plastic tackle box I carried them in was on the floor next to my foot. I administered the first dose of medication through the IV catheter in his arm. Often around this time, I will guide my patient to a cherished memory, if appropriate. On this occasion, however, I leaned over and spoke close to his ear.

I asked, "Ed, why don't cannibals ever eat clowns?"

He turned his face toward mine with a big smile, and without missing a beat, he delivered his favorite punch line:

"Because they always taste a little funny."

We were nose to nose and both grinning from ear to ear, and as he turned his head back to a comfortable position, I heard him chuckle. Then he closed his eyes and fell asleep.

———

Ed's death—and my ability to legally assist him—was made possible by a Supreme Court of Canada decision, known as the *Carter* decision, which struck down the blanket prohibition of assisted dying and was followed by a change in the law that took place on June 17, 2016. On that day, the Parliament of Canada legalized what it termed "medical assistance in dying," or MAiD, which allows doctors and, uniquely, nurse practitioners to assist someone in ending their life under certain specific circumstances.

Under the new legislation, patients have a choice of two methods of assistance—either a self-administered drink with a health care practitioner standing by to make sure all goes smoothly; or, much more commonly, medication that is delivered by the clinician through an IV, as I had offered Ed. Participants have to be eligible for government-funded health care (essentially, Canadian residents or citizens); over eighteen; capable of making their own health care decisions; and suffering from a "grievous and irremediable condition." There have since been changes to what this entails, but at the time, for someone to be eligible for MAiD, their suffering had to be intolerable, their decline irreversible, and their natural death "reasonably foreseeable." This did not mean they were required to have a terminal illness or a prognosis that specified the limited time they had remaining. There was no need to quantify how much longer a patient might live if they *didn't* receive MAiD; it could be days or weeks for some, months or even years for others. It meant only that they were on a trajectory toward a natural death due to their serious and incurable illness. But the person must already be in an advanced state of decline, and they must make their request voluntarily and under no sense of coercion.

Assisted dying in some form or another is now available in many countries around the world, although it's known by different names in different jurisdictions.

In the United States, the most common term is "assisted suicide" (or physician-assisted suicide), in which a person can take his or her own life with a doctor providing the medications with which to do so. This term is meant to emphasize the essential element that the death is *self-administered*. The medication involved exists primarily as a drink, a somewhat foul-tasting liquid mixture of barbiturates, and in 2016, when I began working in the field, this form of assisted dying was legal in the Netherlands, Belgium, Luxembourg, Switzerland, Canada, and five American states.

Here in Canada, we offer both the self-administered drink and another option, which involves a health care professional administering the medications via an intravenous (IV). Many describe this second option as euthanasia. The term "euthanasia" originates from the Greek *eu*, meaning good or well; and *thanos*, meaning death. The modern understanding and use of the term define it as the administration of a lethal medication, *by a health care professional*, at the explicit request of a competent adult, with the goal of relieving further pain and suffering. The key difference between assisted suicide and euthanasia, then, is in who administers the medication—the patient or the health care professional. Euthanasia—that is, an assisted death carried out by a health care professional—is not available in the

U.S. but is legal in Canada, Belgium, the Netherlands, Luxembourg, and Colombia.

Although "euthanasia" is still the preferred term in Europe for voluntary, legalized, medically assisted dying, Canada consciously chose to use the term "medical assistance in dying," or MAiD, in part to avoid negative connotation. Outdated phrasing, such as someone "committed suicide," implies a crime was involved. And the word "euthanasia" was purposely and inaccurately used by those in the eugenics movement around the turn of the twentieth century to describe the killing of "unwanted" or "undesirable" persons, including the physically disabled or mentally impaired, as part of the pursuit of genetic purity. It was then adopted by the Nazis during World War II and used euphemistically for their killing campaign. Detractors of assisted dying will sometimes default to this terminology in order to evoke that repugnant history. Not only does the use of "MAiD" avoid any association with past atrocities, it's also designed to be an umbrella term that includes *both options*, clinician-assisted suicide and voluntary euthanasia. The MAiD terminology has been written into Canadian law, is used widely, and has been accepted to mean the legalized, compassionate end-of-life care provided by Canadian physicians and nurse practitioners in specifically outlined, safeguarded circumstances.

———

When MAiD became law, I found myself at a crossroads. I had been practicing medicine for over twenty years, trained as a family physician, and focused on maternity and newborn care. As a maternity doctor, I prepared women and their families for birth and the profound transition that a new baby would bring to their lives, and I delivered their babies and helped them through those first chaotic months. But when the law changed, I changed course with it, learning everything I could about this newly emerging field so that I could support people with their final wishes and their transition at the other end of life.

At both "deliveries," as I call them, I am invited into a most intimate moment in people's lives. Although Ed chose to die alone, the majority of my patients are surrounded by loved ones. I've been witness to their extraordinary final conversations, the whispered words of love between husbands and wives, the tearful goodbyes of mothers and children, the final advice between grandparents and grandchildren. I've seen people attend their own living wakes where friends and family gather to toast them before they go. When a person knows the hour and date of their death, they can plan their final words and actions with profound intention.

This book is a chronicle of my first year providing assisted dying in and around Vancouver Island, BC, a region that has turned out to have the highest percentage of assisted death, not just in the province or in the country but worldwide. It's also the place I call home, along with my husband, son, and daughter. Through the stories of the patients I have helped, I hope to show what I do, how it works, what I've seen, and what I've learned. Time and again, I've witnessed the power that having the right to choose the time and manner of death affords people. Patients are so grateful that they can have a frank discussion about death and dying. And I have learned that hearing one is eligible for this care is therapeutic in and of itself: I see the relief on my patients' faces. The fear of an unknown ending is replaced by a semblance of control. Instead of feeling helpless, people feel empowered, something their illness may have denied them for months or even years. For many, it can be a way out of intolerable suffering at the very end of life. For others, it is a way to reduce some of their fears and fully reclaim the time they have left, to live their final days with a startling amount of purpose.

I also hope to give some insight into how it feels to do this work—to facilitate a person's final wishes and to administer the medications that bring about death. When I began, it was all very new, so new that the ink on the relevant paperwork was barely dry. A small group of like-minded colleagues and I built a process and developed protocols as we went along. We figured out how to determine who was eligible for assisted dying. We learned how to talk with people facing the end of their lives, and we learned how to talk to their family members. For my part, I stumbled while trying to find the right balance between personal boundaries, safety, and responsibilities. At the beginning, I had to ask myself: Was I comfortable providing this care? How public should I be about my work? Would I encounter any backlash? As time went on and I became more immersed in my new role, I had to assess, when it was literally a matter of my patient's life and death, whether I was allowed to impose some limits on my availability. How about those patients whom I couldn't assist because they weren't eligible under the law? Exactly what was my responsibility to them—and to myself? My work in MAiD also led me to ask some fundamental questions: Was I devoting the right amount of time and energy to the people who mattered most to me? Was I having the conversations I needed to have before it was too late?

Most of the time I just hope I helped; sometimes I simply couldn't. Much of my work has been to bear witness, often to scenes of breathtaking poignancy and sorrow. Although my job is to assist in death and dying, I believe that through this work, I have been privileged to see the best of life and living.

Part 1

BEGINNINGS

CHAPTER 1

JUNE IN VICTORIA, BRITISH COLUMBIA, means long days of sunshine. Perched on the southernmost tip of Vancouver Island, the city lies just southwest of mainland Canada and north of Washington State. Sometimes referred to as the Garden City, it's an oasis of lush, abundant greenery surrounded by the vast Pacific Ocean. The famously mild climate means it is home to elite athletes and retirees alike: one set rigorously scheduled, the other newly set free, both sharing the multiple walking and cycling paths that crisscross this city by the sea. On most June days, while out for a walk, I can look up and spot several bald eagles. I bump into far too many deer, and often I stop to watch the otters dipping in and out of sight along the water's predominantly undeveloped West Coast edges.

On this particular day, June 6, 2016, I'm not as attuned to my natural surroundings. I'm preoccupied with the proposed Canadian legislation known as Bill C14, which is working its way through the various layers of governmental process but, as a result of ongoing parliamentary debate, is not yet firmly in place. This technicality certainly isn't going to stop suffering patients from asking for help. Despite not yet having a law to regulate the practice, as of this date, medically assisted dying is no longer criminal in Canada. Which means that on this momentous Monday morning, I am free to begin my work.

My first ever consultation in my new field of practice is with Peggy, a ninety-four-year-old woman who was given my name and number by the local chapter of Dying With Dignity Canada (DWDC), a national advocacy group that is part of the larger right-to-die movement. I'd contacted them a few weeks earlier to let them know I would be offering this service. When Peggy initially called, she told my office manager that she was suffering from terrible osteoarthritis and had neurologic pain in her legs. She'd said she was simply fed up with living like this, that she wanted to die. I arranged to meet Peggy on the morning of June 6, a few days after that initial phone call, and by the time I lift the heavy knocker on the door to her condominium, I am pretty certain she is one of the first legal consultations for MAiD, or medical assistance in dying, in Canada.

I have no idea what to expect as I stand in front of her solid oak door. For the majority of my career, I have been a family doctor, specializing in maternity and newborn care. I haven't practiced general medicine or cared for a patient over the age of fifty in over thirteen years. More to the point, perhaps, I have never spoken with anyone who has so clearly expressed a wish to die. Would a caregiver be there too? Would we meet in Peggy's living room or in her bedroom? Peggy's voice was fairly strong when we spoke earlier on the telephone to confirm her appointment, but I can't quite picture who or what might await me behind that door. Just how infirm is she going to be? I am ashamed to realize I'm concerned about how I might react to what I see. Everything feels unfamiliar; I'm at someone's home instead of in my office. I'm greeting an elderly person instead of a newborn. A new bag weighs awkwardly on my back. Even the old photo on my hospital ID badge looks like someone else. After twenty-one years of medical practice, I feel like a student once again: eager for experience, fearful of my limitations, and curious as to what I might encounter next. I let the heavy knocker fall.

"Dr. Green, thank you so much for coming. I'm Peggy. Won't you please come in?"

She is not nearly as unwell as I'd expected. Tall and lean, Peggy is wearing a comfortable dress and low heels. Though she walks with a distinct limp, she holds the wall instead of using a cane, and she insists on serving us both tea before settling down on her living room couch for our meeting.

Peggy's view of the city is spectacular. Her spacious apartment is high up on a hilltop, and I can see all the way over to the downtown waterfront. The glass-fronted dining room hutch holds porcelain figurines and pieces of fine bone china, and three large, rustic wood bookshelves are crammed full of travel guides and novels.

Peggy serves tea and begins telling me about herself. Born in Germany in the early 1920s, Peggy lived with her family in Hamburg and was in high school by the time World War II began. She shares detailed stories of chaos and bombings, of family disruption, and of the loss of many close friends. "My story is long and twisted, but I have no regrets, and despite my share of sadness, I also have many wonderful memories."

She describes emigrating to Canada at age twenty-two, marrying a local man, and starting a family of her own, struggling to raise a child with special needs but fulfilled with a teaching career and a plethora of volunteer activities. Her daughter grew up to become independent, but I learn her husband died suddenly and unexpectedly after a small accident seven years ago.

"I have outlived everyone I know, my daughter no longer needs me, and I am in constant, steady pain. I am unable to contribute to society, so I know my time is over. I am certain I am ready to move on."

Peggy could talk all day, and I would happily listen. But I have not been summoned here for a social call. Despite the fact that I like Peggy and understand why she feels ready to die, I realize not long into our conversation that she is likely ineligible for my services.

I am aware that the proposed Canadian law is strict in its definition of eligibility. Among the requirements for MAiD, a person must have a "grievous and irremediable" illness—"grievous" meaning extremely serious and causing a significant decline in function; "irremediable" meaning it cannot be cured. This includes the necessity that the patient's suffering is intolerable and that a natural death is reasonably foreseeable. These criteria are about to become enshrined in our law, and like them or not, they have been put in place in an attempt to protect the vulnerable.

There's no doubt Peggy is experiencing pain, but she isn't exactly dying. I am hard pressed to think of what might ultimately cause her death other than her advancing age, which means that her death isn't "reasonably foreseeable," as the eligibility criteria demand. And she doesn't appear to be in an advanced state of decline as she serves me tea and cookies.

I feel an unanticipated burden and wonder how often this will happen, that someone will ask me to help them but I will find they do not meet all medical or legal criteria. I'm worried I will disappoint Peggy when I tell her I won't be able to assist her, but there's no comfort in false hope, so I speak frankly and try to explain: "I'm so sorry, Peggy. I understand your reasons for inviting me here today, but under the current law, you aren't eligible to have an assisted death. I see that you are suffering, but your death isn't 'reasonably foreseeable,' as the law requires, so I can't move forward with your case."

She takes it well, tells me she isn't at all surprised, and after exchanging a few more pleasantries, I get up, say my goodbyes, and go.

On the drive back to my office, I reflect on what has just happened. I've learned a lot by listening to Peggy. In the course of two hours and with very little prompting, she shared with me what was most important to her in life and why. I learned why she was asking for an assisted death, what resources might make a difference to her if she had access to them right now, and how she was or wasn't coping in the meantime. I was reminded that the act of listening can be therapeutic in itself. But as I think about future appointments, I realize that unless I assume some control over the conversation, my visits could easily last a very long time. Moving forward, I'll need to better triage my appointments, guide the course of the conversation, and find out more about community resources for the elderly so that I can direct people to access the help they need, if they haven't already done so.

"How'd it go?" my office manager, Karen, asks as I walk through the door.

"Enlightening," I offer.

Karen has been my office manager for nearly thirteen years. She is so much more than a manager, however. She is the voice and the frontline face of my medical practice. When I switched course from maternity care to assisted dying, there was no question she would come with me. A few years older than I am, Karen lives in the neighborhood, wants the job more than she needs it, and is as loyal to the patients and the practice as I am.

"I'd forgotten how interesting older people can be," I tell her.

Karen smiles at me as the phone rings: It's a fax coming in on line two. "She was super-chatty with me on the telephone," Karen says. "She didn't sound that sick."

"No, she's not actually eligible."

I turn my head and watch as my reliable old fax machine whirs into action. When it falls silent, I walk over and pull off the single sheet of paper that's come through. I notice it's from a colleague's office.

Thanks for seeing this seventy-four-year-old gentleman with end-stage liver failure. He's been following the news carefully and is eager to make a request for an assisted death. I hear you'll be providing this service in Victoria—courageous! I look forward to your assessment. Summary of his file is below.

I read it twice to myself before sharing it with Karen. We look at each other for a short moment before I break the silence. "His name is Harvey. I'm going to need a chart."

While Karen goes about making one for Harvey—demographics on the front sheet, blank request forms we might need tucked away in the back—I pick up the phone and dial his number. His wife, Norma, answers.

Since Harvey isn't mobile, I agree to meet them in a few days at their home. This will give Harvey the benefit of a planned visit from his palliative care doctor beforehand and give me enough time to gather and review all of Harvey's medical records. I spend the rest of the afternoon speaking with Harvey's liver specialist and learning how to connect remotely from my office to the hospital electronic record system.

———

Three days later, I stand in my bathroom brushing my teeth and practicing what I will say to Harvey. I go over how I want the conversation to begin, the tone I want to set. My plan for this second consultation is to orchestrate things from the start rather than letting them randomly progress, as I did with Peggy.

As I turn off the water, I hear the familiar sounds of my home. There's the drone of the Nespresso machine in the kitchen: My husband, Jean-Marc, is having his second coffee. Once an astrophysicist, he is now pursuing a path as an artist and entrepreneur. I hear the clicking nails of our dog, Benji, as he scurries outside to chase a squirrel. My son, Sam, seventeen, is probably still in bed; he has his music turned down low, but the steady beat of hip-hop reverberates through the walls. And I can hear the footsteps of my daughter, Sara, padding down the hallway, then the familiar creak of the fourth step: She's heading downstairs for breakfast. She has a final exam this morning, and like any typical fifteen-year-old, she's not likely to be particularly chatty.

I climb in the car and drive over to Harvey's home, continuing to rehearse. When I arrive at the house, I walk up to the entrance, open the screen, and knock firmly on the wooden door behind. A man in his seventies with a bushy gray mustache opens the door and offers me a sad smile as he extends his hand. "Hi, Dr. Green, thanks for coming. I'm Rod, Harvey's brother-in-law. Come on in."

I cross the threshold and am ushered directly upstairs to an open dining area and living space, where I see two people sitting together on a couch, a man in a bathrobe and a woman sitting close beside him. The woman stands up without moving toward me. "Hello, Doctor, thank you for coming," she says, smiling. "We spoke on the phone, I'm Norma."

With short dark hair, a bright blue blouse, dark slacks, and a long chunky necklace, Norma is clearly of the generation who still dresses for the doctor. Her hands fidgeting in front of her, she appears slightly nervous, or maybe just awkward. I can hardly blame her as I recognize traces of the same feeling within myself. I push my nerves aside and begin. "Good to meet you, Norma, please sit, be comfortable. I'll come join you."

"My sister and brother-in-law are here too," she adds as I walk into their living space. "Patty might join us in a bit, but Rod will probably stay out in the backyard."

She sits back down, and I turn my attention to the man I've come to see. Dressed in gray pajamas and covered with a warm fleece blanket, Harvey looks at least fifteen years older than his wife. I notice his protuberant, fluid-filled abdomen and papery, yellowed skin, signs that his liver failure is advanced. I see his frail hands and his gaunt, unshaved face. He likely has only weeks left to live.

"Good to meet you," I say as I reach out to give Harvey's left hand a short squeeze. It is cool and bony, mottled with purple, and has little musculature left for support, but he holds on a little tighter and just a moment longer than I expect, slowly shifting his gaze to look me straight in the eye before letting go. It's as if his movements are just a few seconds behind his intentions. Norma is sitting on his right, holding his other hand. I sit down directly in front of Harvey on a sturdy dining room chair that someone previously brought over, and I ready myself to begin what I have been practicing all morning.

"I'd like to start by breaking the first rule of medical school."

Norma looks at Harvey, who musters a sly grin, intrigued, but doesn't say anything, which I take as an invitation to continue.

"In medical school, they taught me that when I meet a new patient, I should sit down, be quiet, and let them speak first . . . good advice as a rule. But I want to start by telling you two things about myself."

I am so focused on what I'm planning to say next that I barely notice the woman who silently walks into the room carrying a pad of paper and a pen. She sits down on the love seat to my right. I assume this is Norma's sister, Patty, but I don't ask. What exactly is the etiquette around these personal meetings? Would Harvey want her to be present for this assessment? Should I interrupt and introduce myself? My instinct tells me that Harvey should remain my priority, so I continue my introduction undistracted. If he doesn't mind her attending, then neither, I decide, do I.

"The first thing I want to tell you is that I am pretty direct," I say.

I notice Norma looking straight at me; so is the woman I presume is Patty. I suspect Patty is primarily here to support Norma, who is clearly here to support Harvey, who is egging me on with a slow, wobbly nod.

"We're going to talk about death today, and we're going to talk about dying," I continue. "We're going to talk about *your* death, and we're going to talk about *assisted* dying. We're also going to talk about what's important to you. I'm going to talk about these things quite frankly. I'm not going to use euphemisms or talk about 'passing over meadows.'"

I pause for just a moment and lower my voice, speaking more familiarly, addressing Harvey directly, as if no one else is in the room. "It's like using anatomically correct terms. I want to be as clear as possible. You okay with that?"

I am relieved to see Harvey is smiling.

"Yes, that's exactly what I hoped for," he says. "No more *bull*shit." His voice is a bit gravelly, but this last word comes out strong, emphatic, the emphasis on the first syllable. "We're going to get along just fine," he adds.

Norma seems slightly embarrassed but not entirely surprised that Harvey is swearing, and she chuckles a little, breaking the tension. I notice a tear slipping from her eye while she quietly bats at him, admonishing him for his language. She is playful in her chiding, and Harvey puts his other hand over hers but keeps his eyes on me, not wanting to miss what I might say next. His face looks more relaxed than when I first entered the room just a few minutes ago. A small smile is re-creating deep laughter lines by his eyes. I sense him settling in; I see the tension I wasn't aware of leaving his face.

"The second thing I want to tell you is that I grew up in Nova Scotia—perhaps not quite so interesting, but where I come from, in my family, we speak fast." I pause. "I know I am a fast talker, but I've lived out here on the West Coast for long enough now that I think I've sufficiently slowed down. Sometimes when I get talking, I speed back up. My point is, if I'm talking too fast, I won't be offended if you or anyone else asks me to repeat myself or slow down. Okay?"

"Okay." Harvey says it with meaning, but I notice he's a little unsteady. His head wobbles, and despite the interest I see in them, his eyes are sunken and watery. I am reminded why I am here.

My plan is to summarize his medical history as much as possible, to not waste precious time on the minutiae I can gather from his records. I'm going to ask some questions and answer some others, but mostly I want to set up a knowledge exchange. I want to explain how assisted dying works, and I hope to find out what motivated Harvey to ask for it. The official requirements are rolling around in my head: the federal eligibility criteria, the provincial regulatory guidelines, the documentation necessities. I am keenly aware that I'll need to elicit the answers to a myriad of questions I am just beginning to learn to ask, so I've made a cheat sheet of sorts and tucked it away inside the chart I'm now holding in my hand. But I don't look at it. I prefer to let the conversation unfold a little more naturally.

I quickly get down to the essentials. "Why do you want to die?"

Harvey smirks as if he's been anticipating this question. Like a kid who's sure he has the correct answer, he blurts out his response. "I don't!"

I wait, say nothing.

"I'd rather live. I've had a great life, a great run. But it seems I no longer have much say in the matter."

It's my turn to nod, and it encourages him to continue.

"I've got great friends, great kids, we're blessed with family all around us. I know I'm lucky. I've been married to this gal here for fifty-two years . . ." He trails off, holds Norma's hand in his, and shakes it at me a bit. He swallows some emotion before continuing, his voice slightly hoarse. "Fifty-two years this past weekend," he says. "I really wanted to make it to fifty-two years . . . and I did." He's quieter now, his energy already drained. "Now I'm ready. I'd go for more if I could, but I know I can't."

Harvey is straightforward with me about his wishes. He knows he is dying, that it will not be long, but he wants to control the how and the when.

"I want Norma and the kids with me at the end," he says with a flash of spirit, "here, in my home, in my own bedroom."

He pauses for a moment, then tells me he wants it to be quick and comfortable. He doesn't want anyone to sit vigil by his bedside; doesn't want to drop in and out of consciousness with pain medications. He is clear of mind in this moment and wants to make sure he is heard.

"I know my options, I know what I'm asking of you. I've had a lot of good times—good memories with fantastic friends and all—but I want my family's faces to be the last thing I see. Can this new law really help, Doc?" he asks me. "Can you make this possible, please?"

"I'm so sorry it's come to this, Harvey. I think we all understand you are dying. Unfortunately, I cannot change this. I can probably help you, though, yes." It's obvious to me that, unlike Peggy, Harvey ticks off every box of eligibility. He is capable of making his own decisions. He is making a voluntary request, and he certainly has a grievous and irremediable condition. I check off the criteria in my head.

Patty hasn't moved a muscle or even uttered a sound. Norma has a tense, wide smile I expect she's been wearing a lot these past few weeks. Throughout our conversation, she has been restless, but something changes when she hears this last sentence. The fidgeting stops and she exhales. Harvey is listening carefully now, working hard to remain focused.

"But there is another option, as you know," I continue. "We have outstanding palliative care here in Victoria . . . we're very lucky that way. The team's been taking very good care of you, from what I've read: supporting you at home, managing your pain."

"Yes, yes, they've been wonderful," he agrees.

"Why not continue to let them take care of you?" I ask. "They can manage your symptoms, keep you comfortable, and allow your illness to simply take you in its own short time."

I am required to ensure that Harvey is aware of the option of palliative care, though I know he is already under their service.

"You could have a comfortable, natural death here at home, or in the hospice unit, if you prefer. Your decision to stop treatments, to not have any more paracentesis, means you probably only have a few short weeks left to live. I know you know that." I touch his knee while I say this, pausing just a little to recognize the gravity of the situation. I lower the volume of my voice. "You will likely get weaker, sleepier, over the course of the week. We can support you through that. Why have an assisted death at all?"

I am curious about his choice, his rationale. Why isn't his current plan of care enough?

"No, Doc, no thanks," he says. "I really don't want that. The palliative folks have been superb, but I've been holding out for my anniversary and for this law of ours to change. And now it finally has. I want to do it my way. I want to have my friends over this weekend, have one last bash, maybe even sneak a sip of a beer . . ." He smiles at the thought, and I see the playful, defiant little boy in him. "And then I want to go. I've seen friends linger on at the end . . . in bed . . . out of their minds. I'm not interested in putting either myself or my family through that. I know my life is over, but I want to be in charge of how it happens."

For the next hour and a half, Harvey and Norma tell me about his life, how he immigrated to Canada from the UK when he was a teenager. He worked hard, held several jobs at a time, and eventually started a construction company of his own. He retired four years earlier with a proud legacy, the respect of his peers, and a history of giving back generously to the community. Harvey is known for his skill in woodworking, his eye for detail, and his fiercely independent spirit. And he's deeply devoted to his family. I realize he wants an assisted death so he can feel the same way in death that he does in life: self-made.

My mind turns to what needs to happen next. Harvey will need to sign an official request form, and Norma assures me it will be completed by the end of the day. They are aware it will need to be witnessed by two independent people, neither of whom provide medical or personal care to Harvey or could benefit in any way from his death. Once the form is signed and dated, a mandatory ten-day reflective period can begin. The law also requires a second clinical opinion, so I will call a local colleague to see if he is available. Given that this is my first time, my plan is to go back to my office, reread the new provincial guidelines, and double-check every step in preparation for his death.

The next few days are busy. Harvey gets his second opinion, and the other doctor agrees that he is eligible. As is expected with his liver failure, Harvey continues to decline cognitively. If he declines too much, too quickly, he won't be able to give his final consent immediately before the procedure, which is required. Because the other doctor and I agree this risk is imminent, we are allowed to shorten the ten-day waiting period. I explain the situation to Harvey, and he chooses a reasonable date three days out. Although he can elect to take his final medications by mouth, he decides on the intravenous option, so I start to focus on the practicalities. I reach out to several pharmacists and find one who is willing to prepare and provide the medications.

Dan owns the pharmacy in my office building and also happens to be the father of one of my son's good friends. After I explain what I am looking for, he agrees to help. We spend an afternoon reviewing the provincial prescription, decide he will draw up the medications for me to create multiple prefilled syringes, and we design a method to label and secure them for transport. I speak to everyone who could possibly be involved—the family physician, Harvey's family members, the health authority, the College of

Physicians and Surgeons of British Columbia (CPSBC), legal counsel, and the second physician assessor. I am well aware that when the procedure is complete, I won't need to notify the coroner, but I call him anyway, in advance, to be 100 percent certain we are following protocol, and we verify our mutual procedures. I learn about an experienced nurse practitioner named Jessica who has already received permission from the health authority to support community MAiD procedures. I contact her and find out she can source any required IV catheters and provide the skills to site them. I have heard that Jessica's expertise in this realm is unsurpassed no matter the size of the vein she is working with, or the scarring left behind from chemotherapy. This is a great relief to me, as I haven't started an IV in over a decade.

True to his word, three days before his scheduled death, Harvey and Norma host an open house for friends and neighbors to celebrate his life and give everyone a chance to say goodbye. Meanwhile, I review all the practicalities and guidelines. I am keenly aware that if I get anything wrong, there could be significant ramifications; I could be liable for criminal charges. The words "up to fourteen years in prison" keep flashing in the back of my mind. No one yet has a sense of the mood of the prosecutors. Are they waiting to meticulously comb through each case and make an example of a clinician who makes a mistake? Might they instead stand by and seek only to confirm we were all working to the best of our abilities, always acting in good faith? I'm not willing to leave anything to chance.

Harvey isn't just my first assisted death. His is the first MAiD death to proceed on Vancouver Island and among the first in all of Canada. I am aware that I need to get this right—for myself, for the MAiD program, but most important, for Harvey.

CHAPTER 2

AS A CHILD, I HAD only a vague idea of death. No one in my immediate family died when I was young, so my earliest encounters with an end of life involved a canary and a few small gerbils. The notion that people could cease to exist was, for me, the stuff of storybooks. I understood it happened and the theoretical consequences when it did, but it was something that happened to others. I was stuck in the "now," the present tense of childhood, without much sense of what came before or after.

I was the youngest child of Jewish parents—my father owned a restaurant, my mother was home while I was young and worked part-time in property management for her parents as they began to age. My maternal grandparents were pillars of the close-knit Jewish community of Halifax. We were not particularly observant but kept a kosher home, and the culture and traditions of Judaism were woven into the fabric of my life through holiday celebrations, attendance at Hebrew school several days a week following my regular school day, and my absolute favorite—summer camp. Judaism wasn't something I chose, but it provided a tremendous sense of community and belonging, and a moral compass I did not question.

One of my earliest memories of someone dying in my community happened when I was a teenager. I don't know who it was calling that Sunday morning or how she got my name. She was an elderly woman from the synagogue whose family name I recognized but whose face I couldn't quite picture, and she was asking if I had a few hours free, might I be willing to help? She didn't elaborate except to say that someone, a man I didn't know, had died. The funeral, she informed me, was happening at one p.m., and they needed help at his house for the shiva, the seven-day mourning period in Jewish tradition where family and friends gather to offer condolences and support. I was to meet another woman at the house of the deceased and do whatever it was that needed doing. I doubt I'd ever been to a shiva before that, but I knew what it was in concept. The lady on the phone promised that the other woman would instruct me.

I have never figured out why I was the one called upon that day. It all remains a bit of a mystery to me.

I was in tenth grade at the time, and I was navigating a significant transition—from the small private school I had attended previously to one of the large local public high schools. This new school was in a behemoth of a building, run by social rules I had yet to learn, and included fifteen hundred new faces. Recreational sport was no longer about intramural fun. The large pool of players allowed the true cream to rise, and athletic as I was, I was suddenly out of my league. This was a place where the door I chose to enter through in the morning was a statement: South doors were reserved for the "preppies," blue doors on the north side for the "techies," front doors for the goths and the misfits. None reflected who I felt I really was, but I didn't know of any other doors.

My parents divorced before I was ten, and their split was not one I would describe as amicable. It was a time when my father was struggling to keep his first restaurant, and there was some suspicion of betrayal. With the benefit of hindsight, I might be kind and suggest my father had some sort of breakdown and my mother ended up heartbroken, but for me as a nine-year-old, it was just confusing and lonely. My mother went back to school, found a job, remarried three years after the divorce, and all at once, my older brother and I had four stepsiblings in our lives.

When I switched high schools, I was two years into my mother's new marriage. My brother had gone off to university, and two of my stepsiblings were now living in my home, one an older girl who was recovering from a terrible car accident, the other a boy who was one year younger than I was. None of us got along especially well, and there were frequent arguments. Between a clash in parenting styles—one hands on, the other hands way off—the antiquated value system of my stepfather, who was eighteen years older than my mother; and the complicated personalities of my stepsiblings roaming the hallway outside my bedroom, my household felt chaotic. My biological parents remained at loggerheads, and I was stuck in the middle. I knew how I was expected to act but felt utterly at the mercy of my circumstances, both at home and at school. When my new English teacher announced that the day's assignment was to introduce ourselves in a short paragraph, I honestly had no idea what to say or even where to start.

When the strange but familiar-sounding woman called, asking me to help at the shiva, I agreed. I walked the fifteen minutes to the address she gave me and wondered what I'd gotten myself into. I was not especially scared, more curious than anything, feeling useful, in fact, and rather grown up. I knocked at the door of the modest brick home, and as promised, another woman greeted me. She instructed me on what was needed to prepare the house for the mourners who would soon be returning from the funeral. I covered the mirrors with cloth, as was custom. I laid out a bowl of water by the entranceway for the people coming back from the cemetery to wash their hands. I left the front door unlocked and plated some food for the expected guests. I didn't notice I was alone in the house until the telephone rang. In my mind, I debated whether I should answer it or not. Those were the days before everyone had an answering machine, so on the eighth ring, after no one else answered, I picked it up.

"May I speak with Mr. Morris, please?" asked the woman's voice on the other end of the line.

"Ummm, he's not here right now . . . who's calling?"

"It's Dr. Beck's office, I'm calling to confirm his appointment with us on Tuesday at two p.m."

"Oh . . . ummm . . . well . . . I don't think he's going to be at that appointment," I said. "I'm sorry to tell you, but . . . Mr. Morris died yesterday."

"Oh! I see . . . Well, yes, I understand. I'm sorry," the receptionist stumbled along. "I'm very sorry to bother you. Well, that is a surprise. Hmmm. Okay, well, thank you. And again, I'm very sorry for your loss."

I didn't have time before she hung up or even the words to begin to explain who I was or why I was the one standing in Mr. Morris's kitchen, answering his telephone on the day of his funeral. Although I remember feeling nervous when I picked up the phone, by the time I replaced the receiver in the cradle, I felt different, almost powerful.

I finished the preparations as instructed, and when the first mourners began to arrive, I slipped out the side door and walked home. I must have told my mother about my day, but I don't remember sharing it with anyone else. It was one of those moments when you look up and wonder how you got to be in this place, at this time, in a situation that seems so incongruous with anything routine, as if you're playing a role in someone else's life. It wasn't frightening, just odd. And my awareness of the peculiarity as it was unfolding only made it even more so. I had been asked to do something out of the norm, and I was interested. In an awkward position, I found the willingness to proceed and, in doing so, discovered a sense of control that, until then, seemed outside of my reach. Looking back, I wonder if this inspired me to consider walking into other spaces that felt unusual.

Of course, that one incident did not lead me straight to my current path of working as a provider of medically assisted deaths. I left home at seventeen, ready to get away. Following my academic interests, I found myself pursuing an undergraduate degree in physiology at the University of Toronto and almost completely surrounded by students dreaming of medical school. This particular goal had never occurred to me, but it was surprisingly appealing when I considered it. At first I was drawn to medicine because I was fascinated with the material—people and their physiology—and it tapped into a genuine desire to help. But looking back, the field also fulfilled a need I had for order, a structured way to approach a problem, and the possibility of an understanding. The practice of medicine promised, whether it was true or not, that if I worked hard and applied my knowledge properly, I would be rewarded with a sense of accomplishment, the general respect of society, and that long-sought sense of control and stability in my life.

With a world of science and discovery in front of me, I started questioning what I believed and why or why not. It wasn't that I set out to reject religion, it was that I felt more comfortable with scientific explanation. I still valued traditions and community and what those elements continued to provide me, but I left behind anything requiring blind faith. Above all, I discovered I wanted to help others, and knowing I would one day be able to do so was profoundly motivating. In medicine, I found my place in the world.

CHAPTER 3

IT IS THE MORNING OF Harvey's death. For five minutes I have been standing here in my bedroom, staring into the abyss that is my closet, considering choices and then discarding them immediately. I am at a complete loss as to how to move forward. What does one wear to a scheduled death? Wearing all black seems morbid. Harvey is certainly not morose. Bright color seems inappropriate, too festive for the family. I want to look professional but not cold, casual but no jeans. How can this be the hardest part of my day?

At the end of the upstairs hallway, there's a palpable silence. My son, Sam, is graduating from high school in just four days; he's blissfully asleep now that classes are over and exams complete. I expect he is dreaming of the life that awaits him on the other side of that ceremony. Meanwhile, my daughter, Sara, who just finished grade ten, has already walked to the local pharmacy to gather a few things she needs for summer camp: sunscreen, After Bite, Band-Aids.

Normal life is happening all around me, but nothing about today will be normal. It's June 16, 2016, the day Harvey has chosen to die. This event is all about Harvey, but it's momentous for everyone involved.

For now, I am stuck standing in my closet, feeling anxious, or could it be . . . excited? I am aware I'm about to make history. Wrapped in a towel, hair still wet, momentarily stymied by the prospect of the day's events. I'll be picking up the medication at ten a.m., I'm expected at Harvey's home by eleven, and I suspect he'll be dead before noon.

Harvey's MAiD application is complete, the documentation is done, every step in the provincial guidelines has been triple-checked. I meet with Dan again on the morning of the procedure, and we reassure ourselves that all the paperwork has been filled out and filed correctly. The forms we sent to the "special authority" desk at PharmaCare—the provincial drug plan that helps eligible residents with the cost of prescription drugs and medical supplies—were so newly created, they'd become available for use only the afternoon before. I speak to PharmaCare personally that morning and confirm the medication costs are fully covered. Dan and I sign the six-page prescription form in all the proper places. He copies all the pages so we can each keep a complete set of records. Only after all of this is done do I accept the medications and head to Harvey's home.

In the end, I had opted for gray jeans, a black sweater, and glasses in my hair. Casual but intelligent seemed the right look to go for, and with the medications in hand, I finally feel ready to proceed.

The bag is so much lighter than I expected. Dan has provided me with an extra set of medications in case of an unexpected emergency. There are two large clear plastic boxes—one blue lid and one green—cleverly labeled box one and box two, stacked one on top of the other, filling the bag to capacity. The irony of this lightweight, innocuous-looking bag conferring such a weighty responsibility is not lost on me. Wary of who might know what I'm carrying, I put on my best poker face and stow the lethal medications securely in the trunk of my car.

During the thirty-minute drive to Harvey's house, I daydream ridiculous scenarios. What if I am stopped by police for a broken taillight, or for speeding, or for a random check of some sort? "What's the hurry, ma'am?" I imagine. "Please open your trunk. What's in your bag there?"

Exactly how would I answer such questions? With the truth, of course, but I doubted many on the police force would even be aware this was now legal.

I drive slowly, but the trip to Harvey's home passes quickly. I pull up along the curb next to Harvey's house, close enough to have arrived, far enough that no one from inside can tell I'm here yet. I notice an older gentleman wearing a golf cap quietly walking his little Jack Russell around the neighborhood. I take a deep breath. In medical school, the saying was "see one, do one, teach one." But in this case, there has been no way for me to "see one." The law changed only a few days ago. I am about to take a big, blind step.

I look in the rearview mirror and give myself a silent pep talk. It's something I do, something I've always done. Before a big exam or a crucial encounter, I look squarely into the mirror for three or four seconds, not to adjust my collar or fix my hair but to remind myself that I've got this. I hoped my usual routine might do the trick, but this morning, it seems I need more. My heart is racing. Am I truly ready?

I take a moment to acknowledge my hesitation. Then I remember this event is not about me. I remind myself that despite whatever thoughts might pass through my mind, I am supposed to be the calmest, most confident person in the room. At the same time, no matter how many eyes might be trained on me, I should not be at the center of attention. There is an art to finding this balance, and I have to trust that all my years of providing maternity care, of laboring with hundreds of women, have prepared me for the role.

I leave the car and stride to the front door of Harvey's house without looking back. I let myself in and kick off my shoes when I see the disorderly array of footwear just inside the door, then I head up the carpeted steps to the open living and dining room space. I catch Norma's eye from across the room, but before I can get over to greet her, I meet Jessica, the nurse practitioner who will assist me, standing at the top of the stairs in her scrubs and stocking feet. We smile at each other and silently shake hands. She will be responsible for starting the IV we use today, but at this particular moment, all I can think of is that I do not want the family to suspect we have never actually met. I don't want to do anything that might remind them I have never done this before. I can tell by how Jessica greets me, with a slightly forced familiarity, that she intuitively feels the same way. I know immediately we will get along.

S
TEFANIE GREEN

There are eight close family members in the house this morning, and Norma introduces me to each one. I say hello to everyone politely, aware that I represent an uncomfortable unknown and that I'm probably provoking anxiety. I ask to speak privately with Harvey for a few minutes, and I'm told he is in his bedroom at the end of the short hallway on the right, so I head there. I put down the pharmacy bag just inside the bedroom doorway, sit down in the chair next to the bed, and begin. "How was your night?" I ask.

"It was what it was," he replies. "I'm ready to go. I need this to be over today."

Harvey does not hold back. He says what he means: No need to soften any blows. This time I'm the one who appreciates the direct speech.

The official purpose of this talk is for me to verify that Harvey is still capable of making this decision—that Harvey is clear of mind, that he still wishes to proceed—and, if so, to obtain his final consent.

"Are you having any second thoughts?"

"No, none at all."

"Okay, then let's go over what's going to happen."

I review the order of events. Harvey reassures me that his affairs are all in order; his funeral plans are made and already paid for, the names of his lawyer and his accountant are written out for the family to contact. He expresses some concern about those he is leaving behind. I try to reassure him that I will provide them some resources, but I match his no-nonsense attitude. I don't lie. I agree it will be difficult for everyone. We're both speaking with an appropriate frankness.

"Thank you for making this possible."

I don't recall who reached out first or when we began holding hands, but once again, he is holding mine a little longer and a little tighter than expected. He doesn't let go when I think our conversation is over. He clearly has something on his mind. I wait, stay seated, say nothing, knowing it will come when he is ready.

"You know, I'm a little scared."

"Of course you are . . . that's okay."

I catch myself. I want to answer him with the same degree of honesty he has offered me, but I'm not entirely certain what he is referring to. Does he mean he's scared of what he's about to do, of some unexpected discomfort or indignity? Or is he asking for more time? Has he changed his mind about proceeding? I quickly calculate my options and choose to give him a way out. "There is no rush, you know, we can wait a few more days if you prefer. Longer, even, if you want."

"No, no, I want to go ahead today, I'm just . . . a little scared," he says again. He smiles, shrugs, almost apologetically.

And there I am, in an unexpected moment. I recognize that this is not a casual remark or an ordinary conversation, that it would not be acceptable to simply pat his hand or placate. No. He wants to address this, needs me to hear him, needs . . . something. I feel a wave of self-doubt. What if I say the wrong thing? I am knowledgeable but still learning. He deserves more, someone who knows what they're doing, someone who can guide him to a more settled place. Why aren't my colleagues in palliative care here—isn't this part of what they do best? Who am I to be the one? This hesitation flies through my mind in under a second. And then I understand; I am all that he has. He has many people in his life, of course, but in this confession he has trusted only me. So I try to rise to the occasion, try to be human, stay curious. "Tell me, what scares you most?"

We talk, take the time we need. No one is in a rush.

"What do you think comes next, Dr. Green?"

"I really don't know, Harvey. What do you think?"

"I'm not a religious man, not even very spiritual or whatever. But I do not believe this is the end. It just can't be."

"Okay. But what if it were, Harvey?" I ask. "What would you change, do differently, or wish you'd done differently in your past?"

Our dialogue continues. I realize that expressing the question is as important as finding any answers. I listen, try to discover what he needs to explore. He continues to hold my hand. I hear his regrets—there are few—and of what he is most proud. I learn so much from Harvey. I am already grateful he is my first MAiD patient. His willingness to share his innermost feelings schools me in the profundity of this work.

At some point we both fall silent. I explain that I will go speak with his family to prepare them for what to expect. I promise to return in five minutes with his loved ones, and he nods his approval, looks away. The connection has passed. I hope it has been enough.

By now I've reassured myself that Harvey is still eligible and capable of making this choice. I hand him the required provincial form and watch as he scratches out an unsteady version of his signature. I tuck the form away for safekeeping.

I invite Jessica in to start Harvey's IV, then head back out to the living room. I join the family, and we sit in a makeshift circle on the couch, the love seat, and a few of the dining room chairs. I settle in and look around. There are two men with Scotch in their hands, one woman with what I think is gin. Norma is fussing with a balled-up Kleenex in her hand. Their grown children are staring blankly. Everyone is quiet, hesitant, and looking at me for answers.

"I want to go over exactly what will happen this morning, so there are no surprises," I begin. "And we're doing this here in the living room so you can feel free to ask me anything. Harvey has heard all of these details before, and he knows that we are talking."

I explain the order of events, the number of syringes, and the time for last words. We review who will stand or sit where. I ask if there is any ritual or ceremony they'd like to incorporate, and then I get down to the details.

"The first medication is an anti-anxiety medication called midazolam, and it will make Harvey relax, feel pretty good, pretty sleepy. He's already quite weak, so I expect he'll fall quickly into a nice light sleep. We might hear him snore; that's one way you'll know he's truly comfortable."

I have their full attention. I am trying to be as transparent and informative as I can.

"The second medication is a local anesthetic you've probably heard of called lidocaine. I use it to numb the vein. It may not be entirely necessary if Harvey is sleeping already, but I want to be a hundred percent certain he is comfortable. Some of the other medications can sting a bit, so I'll use this local anesthetic to numb his vein to be sure he won't feel any discomfort as we proceed."

I notice involuntary nodding from his brother, his son. I recognize relief on Norma's face and see blank stares on the others' . . . the reality is starting to sink in.

"The third medication is the stuff we would normally give someone to go to sleep for an operation, except it's a much larger dose. With this dose of propofol, Harvey will go from his nice light sleep down into a much deeper sleep, down into a coma, and into a deep unconscious state over the course of a couple minutes. You won't see much except that he is still sleeping. But if you're looking carefully, you might notice his breathing begins to space out with this medication . . ." I am using my hands now, widening them to gesture and explain what is going to happen. "His breathing will also become more shallow at this time and will most likely stop."

I am looking around at different faces, trying to judge reactions and ensure that all are okay while they are hearing this.

"Even though I expect this all to happen and I expect Harvey will die with this third medication, I will go ahead and use the fourth medication in our protocol, to make sure this is truly final. The fourth medication is called rocuronium, and it ensures there is no muscular movement in the body. I will let you know when his heart has stopped. This whole process, from the first medication to the end of his heart beating, is likely to last between eight and ten minutes."

I lower my voice a little. "I will of course stay with Harvey the entire time, making sure things go smoothly and comfortably, as I have promised him. And a couple of other things I should mention: I do not expect you will see any gasping or twitching or anything unsettling. My goal is to make this as comfortable and as dignified as possible. But there is a real possibility his breathing will stop before his heart does. And if that's the case, you will likely see some color changes, a paling of his face, maybe a bit of yellowing.

His mouth might drop open slightly. His lips may turn a bit blue. If you find yourself uncomfortable at any time, please feel free to step back, sit down, or step out. There is no medal for staying in the room. I will be focused on what I am doing, so I'll need you to take care of yourselves in those few moments, if necessary. Okay?"

Muted nods. A few people breathe out as if they hadn't realized they were holding their breath.

"That's the nuts and bolts of it. I expect it's all feeling a bit real right now. Any questions about the procedure itself or what you can expect?"

No one says anything or dares to move. Everyone still has eyes on me. There's a pregnant pause, and then a previously quiet man in his mid-seventies asks: "You got any extra of that anti-anxiety stuff, Doc? I could use a dose myself right about now."

As I head back into Harvey's room, I'm followed only by his wife and children. Harvey's bloated, bruised, and failing body is belied by his vivid green eyes. Opening wide when I walk back into the room, watching me carefully as I line up my syringes, his eyes are full of expression, still sparkling with life, and as I pull my chair in close to his bedside, they lock tightly on my own. I wonder what he sees reflecting back from my face. I hope it reassures him that I know what I am doing, even though we are both aware I have never done this before—never even seen this done before—and so I cannot truly know.

Harvey is calm, he is smiling, and he appears certain. His love for family has been evident from the start, and they are all here with him now. Norma is sitting on a chair tucked in tightly on his right side, leaning in, her face close to his; she is smiling and crying at the same time. Harvey's children are reaching out to touch him—his feet, his legs, his hands. We are all huddled in closely around his bed, all faces toward Harvey, everyone present, just as he asked. The support they give him in these final moments, putting his needs above their own, feels brave to me and very loving. I ask if anyone has anything left unsaid. Harvey's son reaches out from beside me and places his open palm directly onto Harvey's chest. He repeats that he loves Harvey and thanks him for being such a great dad. Harvey reminds them all that this is what he wants and asks them not to be sad.

I take hold of Harvey's left arm. Only after he looks me in the eye and thanks me one last time do I think to begin. When I announce I will start, I sense Jessica reach out from behind me. I didn't realize how tense I was until she put her hand on my back. When I feel the warmth of her palm, I realize the circle is complete, we are all connected physically, and none of us is alone. I feel myself relax as I push the first medication through the syringe.

"Maybe now is a good time to think of a great memory," I begin, "when you were doing something you loved, maybe with someone you loved doing it with . . . Go to that place now, be there, and feel that moment again . . . If you feel sleepy, go ahead and close your eyes, you've earned it. We're all here with you now. We're going to stay here with you."

Then Harvey dies exactly as he wished: being held by his children and gazing into the eyes of his wife as he begins to feel sleepy. His wife of fifty-two years. They connect here, forehead to forehead, whispering to each other as I continue. She holds his face in her hands, strokes his head, and tells him it's okay. She tells him she loves him, that she will miss him, but that she is all right. She whispers inaudible words, evoking private memories, and he smiles. The intimacy of this moment is so absorbing that I struggle to focus on what I'm doing. She tells him to let go, that she is here with him, and as on most nights of his life, hers are the last words he hears as he falls asleep.

Harvey musters a light snore. Norma recognizes the sound and dabs at her moist eyes. I continue with my protocol, and Harvey soon stops breathing; no one says anything when it becomes apparent, but I am certain we all take notice. I understand in that moment that I am witnessing this event as much as I am orchestrating it. I feel a certain relief with events unfolding as I had expected, but I remain vigilant for complications and alert to the unknown. I continue on to the final medication and immediately notice it doesn't flow as smoothly as the others did. I have an instant of panic, wondering if my IV line has become blocked, but it takes only a moment for me to understand it's because his blood is no longer circulating. I am certain Harvey's heart has stopped, but I continue nonetheless. Only after the last medication is delivered do I cap and lock the IV. Only after the empty syringes are resealed within the plastic container do I reach for my stethoscope. And only after I listen for a complete sixty seconds do I announce:

"He's gone."

Only then do his family members allow themselves to be overcome by the loss they've all been suffering. There are vocal sobs, tight-clenched hugs, and flowing tears. This man will be sorely missed. To my utter astonishment, there is also an immediate outpouring of gratitude for what I have just done, and for this, I'll admit, I was unprepared.

CHAPTER 4

I REMEMBER THE NIGHT I learned this work might become legal. It was October 15, 2014, almost two years before I helped Harvey to die. I had just returned from a twenty-four-hour shift at the hospital and was due to go to dinner with my husband and six of our friends.

I'd been working as a maternity doctor for over twenty years, and at the age of forty-six, I was beginning to wonder if it was time for a change. I adored the work, the interactions with my patients, the chance to support a woman through her pregnancy and birth, and to nurture her as she faced the challenges of feeding and caring for a newborn. It was such an honor to be present for the first few moments when a baby was delivered into the world, to share in the joy and relief of everyone involved. But there were drawbacks, and those were becoming more obvious as I aged. The time required to physically recover from a twenty-four-hour shift—during which I might deliver two or three babies, admit and investigate women with complications, and discharge new families home—was becoming longer and more difficult, and the toll wasn't lost on my husband. Jean-Marc had been asking me to cut back for everybody's sake. I kept brushing off his concern as unwarranted, and most times I was able to manage. Part of the reason I didn't contemplate a career shift was I couldn't imagine how anything else would compete with my love of being a maternity doctor. All other jobs seemed to pale in comparison. But that October night, I remember feeling exhausted and wondering how much longer I could keep it up.

I thought about the times I walked into the house when the kids were younger and they would come running to greet me. 'Round the corner they'd spin, slamming into my legs and grabbing hold like we hadn't seen each other in decades. I'd wobble happily as we embraced, backpack still on my back, no way to move my legs for balance. That delicious, tight squeeze of my younger children was a fleeting welcome I was aware would not last forever. Gradually there was a little less interest, a little less contact, and eventually just words from behind a laptop.

I heard Jean-Marc bustling around the kitchen, humming and occasionally singing along to the old pop songs he was streaming.

"Hello, daaahhh-ling!" He greeted me with a smile and his very best attempt at a British accent. "We're expected for dinner club at seven tonight. Mitch and Mona are hosting," he reminded me as he planted a little peck, "cutting it a little close, no?"

"Yes, yes . . . I just need to change."

After I was showered and prepped, I gave myself a minute to flip through the news on my phone, scrolling through the highlighted headlines. ISIS was in Syria, stock markets were slumping, most of this would be too depressing to discuss over dinner, but the last story caught my attention. The Supreme Court of Canada had heard an appeal seeking to overturn the legal ban on assisted dying. I recognized the name of the case, *Carter v. Canada*. It had been a while since I'd heard anything about it, but I remembered the details well.

It was not the first time this important issue had been in the news in our nation. In fact, Canadians had been debating and contemplating assisted dying for over twenty years.

The story of Canada's long journey to legalized assisted dying really begins in 1992, when a young mother named Sue Rodriguez first challenged the law that prohibited it. Rodriguez lived, coincidentally, in Victoria, BC.

I was twenty-three years old at the time, in my third year of medical school in Montreal, and I was taking a course in biomedical ethics. In our class, we discussed precedent-setting legal decisions and explored layered clinical scenarios, but thanks to the *Rodriguez* case, there was a riveting and equally relevant story unfolding in the national headlines. While I was being taught the definitions of ethical principles in the classroom—"beneficence: doing what is in the best interest of the patient" and "non-maleficence: the duty to not cause harm"—I needed only to look to *Rodriguez* for a real-life example of how these principles could come directly into conflict.

Sue Rodriguez was forty-one years old when she was diagnosed with amyotrophic lateral sclerosis (ALS), commonly known as Lou Gehrig's disease. ALS is a rapidly progressive neurologic disease with an average life expectancy of three to five years after diagnosis. Someone living with ALS will lose the ability to walk, talk, eat, swallow, and, eventually, to breathe. Help exists to alleviate symptoms as they begin to appear, but there continues to be no treatment for the disease itself, which is certainly fatal.

Rodriguez was diagnosed in 1991. After learning what lay ahead for her, Rodriguez wanted to have a say in how she died. She wanted a physician to be able to give her medication to end her life when the time came, so that her death could be quick and certain.

Sue Rodriguez captured the attention of the world when she presented a video statement to the Canadian Parliament and asked a simple but powerful question: "If I cannot give consent to my own death, whose body is this? Who owns my life?"

Those opposed to assisted dying, while sympathetic to her fate, clung to the sanctity of life. They warned of slippery slopes and the impossibility of building a system with adequate safeguards. Those in favor of assisted dying respected her ability to decide the time and nature of her death and argued that she had a right to choose for herself. The one thing everyone could agree upon was her bravery.

Like millions of other viewers, I was captivated by Rodriguez's video, and I sympathized with her circumstances. I had never considered the idea of assisted dying. The more we discussed her case in class, the more certain I became that Rodriguez "owned" her life. How could she not? Did that mean she could do with it what she wished, even if that meant decisions that led to harm, like drinking, smoking, or taking drugs? Most of my classmates thought so. Did that extend to taking her own life? Attempting suicide was decriminalized in 1972: So yes, society reluctantly agreed. So, what about helping her end her life? If she had the right to end her own life but was physically unable to do so, did the state have the right to prohibit someone from assisting her? Was that prudent and in the best interests of all, or did the prohibition infringe upon her rights and freedoms? I was beginning to form my own views.

In September 1993, soon after I graduated from medical school, in a five-to-four split decision, the Supreme Court of Canada denied Sue Rodriguez the right to have a physician assist her to die. Naively, I was shocked and felt she was robbed of a just decision. I eventually understood society wasn't ready for this change, but that didn't sway my newfound opinions. When Rodriguez defied the law less than five months after the Court's decision and ended her own life on her own terms with the help of an anonymous doctor, I'll admit, I felt relieved that she'd found her escape hatch.

Of course it wasn't just in Canada that this topic was being discussed.

By the early 1990s, there was a growing interest in the right-to-die movement globally. Public opinion surveys showed that over half of the American public were in favor of physician-assisted death, but the topic remained contentious. Dr. Jack Kevorkian, an American pathologist and assisted dying proponent, publicly facilitated his first of dozens of assisted suicides in 1990. His controversial approach and the media circus it created might not have done the right-to-die movement any favors, but his actions encouraged further debate on the topic in the United States as well as throughout Canada. In 1994, Oregon's Death with Dignity Act was passed through a voter ballot initiative, becoming the first law in U.S. history permitting physician-assisted dying (although, due to delays, it did not go into effect until October 1997).

By the turn of the millennium, there was a noticeable shift in perceptions around death and dying. At the beginning of the twentieth century, most patients in North America died at home, but by the 1990s, 80 percent of patients were dying in institutions. Death had become a challenge to be overcome by modern medicine rather than an inevitable part of life. Patients routinely received treatment after invasive treatment despite knowing that death was imminent. But after a global AIDS epidemic, or perhaps due to a generation of aging baby boomers, there was a rise in the effort to improve the quality of life remaining instead of focusing on extending life at any cost—there was a growing interest in reclaiming death and dying through good palliative care and, in a number of jurisdictions around the world, through assisted dying.

In 2011, the *Carter* case appeared in the news for the very first time and revealed just how much things had changed. By that point I was married with two tweens. I had been practicing family medicine for sixteen years and had a career I loved, a family I adored, and a group of maternity colleagues who kept my schedule (and therefore my life) well balanced. I was busy but happy, and my kids often teased that I couldn't walk through a shopping mall without running into an old maternity patient or two. I hadn't thought much about assisted dying since the *Rodriguez* case had ended, but the *Carter* suit brought the issue firmly back to mind.

Kay Carter was an eighty-nine-year-old woman in North Vancouver who had spinal stenosis, a progressive, painful, nonterminal condition that caused her intolerable suffering. Describing herself as "fiercely independent," she was determined to have some control over the end of her life. As it was still illegal in Canada to seek assistance to die, Carter traveled with her daughter and son-in-law to Switzerland, a country that allows foreigners to receive end-of-life care, and had an assisted death on January 15, 2010.

Around the same time, Gloria Taylor, a sixty-one-year-old mother of two and an avid motorcyclist, was diagnosed with ALS, the same disease that had afflicted Sue Rodriguez. Taylor also expressed a strong desire for control at the end of her life, but she didn't want to travel to another country in order to obtain it.

In 2011, the *Carter* lawsuit was filed arguing that the prohibition of assisted dying violated the right to life, liberty, and security of person of grievously and irremediably ill patients. When Gloria Taylor joined the lawsuit a few months later, a novel argument was added: that without the possibility of a physician's assistance, someone like Taylor might be forced to consider ending her life, while she was still physically capable of doing so on her own, at a time earlier than she might otherwise prefer, thereby robbing herself of her constitutional right to life. It was a bold argument, and it worked.

In June 2012, Madam Justice Lynn Smith penned her decision. She concluded that a blanket prohibition against physician-assisted death (the term used at the time) breached a person's constitutional rights. The 395-page decision stunned the nation and was met with jubilation by right-to-die advocates—and great concern by its opponents. But, of course, it didn't end there. The ramifications were far too significant. The government was expected to appeal, which it soon did. The BC Court of Appeals overturned the original decision in October 2013, but the legal team that represented Taylor and the original plaintiffs wasn't satisfied with the setback, so the case headed to the Supreme Court.

It was all very reminiscent of the *Rodriguez* story twenty-two years earlier, but with one significant difference. Since *Rodriguez*, public sentiment had shifted, and a new openness was in the air. A national poll had recently found that 84 percent of Canadians supported assisted dying. Even among those who self-described as Catholic, 83 percent agreed with the idea.

———

The night when the *Carter* case reappeared in the headlines following the Supreme Court hearing, Jean-Marc and I had dinner with six friends, as planned. The food, conversation, and wine were plentiful. Among other topics, we discussed the details of the *Carter* case, and I suspect the responses at our table were representative of other tables across the nation. When our friend Mitch brought up the subject and declared that he firmly supported a change in the law to allow assisted dying, no one was surprised. But we could always depend on Jackie to play devil's advocate.

"I agree with you in principle," Jackie began, "but in actuality, I see a problem. I have little faith in mankind. We could easily get this wrong. Nuclear power is also a great idea, but look how that turned out. I recognize we need to balance society's responsibility to protect the truly vulnerable with the rights of individuals, but how do we make sure no one is forced to make this decision because someone else thinks it's the best course of action? I think it's too risky, to be honest."

"All I know is that two years ago I had my dog put down," Mitch replied. "She was only eight, and I was upset for weeks, but it was absolutely the best decision. I mean, Maggie was really suffering. And she died so peacefully in my arms." He shook his head a little and scanned the faces around the table, then focused in on Jackie. "Is it okay that we're more compassionate toward our pets than to our human family of loved ones?"

I couldn't have articulated it better myself, and I wondered if this time, the decision would lead to an actual change in the law.

———

Four months later, at 6:28 a.m. on a gray Saturday morning in February, I was hustling out the door to walk our family dog, Benji, before an early breakfast meeting with my maternity group. I was listening to the radio via headphones and took in the fresh, crisp air as the six-thirty news headlines began.

"Yesterday, on February sixth, 2015, the Supreme Court of Canada ruled in favor of the BC Civil Liberties Association [BCCLA], Gloria Taylor, and the family of Kay Carter, and struck down the prohibition of assisted dying in Canada. This means a competent adult who is suffering intolerably from a grievous and irremediable condition can now ask a clinician to assist them to die, and that a clinician can help them to do so without being criminally charged."

The decision had been unanimous, and it was signed by "the Court": a gesture seldom used in Canada and meant to impose its greater authority by having the entire court speak as a single voice.

Despite knowing this outcome was possible, I was amazed when it was finally announced. As the news sank in, I couldn't help thinking of Sue Rodriguez. While Benji tugged on the leash, eager to get on with his walk, I stood and marveled at the strength of the three courageous women who challenged and then changed the law in this country.

In the days following the decision, opponents of assisted dying claimed it was the end of judicial restraint. Disability rights groups feared their members were especially vulnerable to abuse and would be coerced into ending their lives. Many groups suggested we must not lose sight of the need to improve palliative care, and the Canadian Medical Association reminded us that not all doctors would be willing to participate. That was a good point. Who, exactly, would step forward to provide this care? But the vocal minority was clearly overshadowed by the masses. The BCCLA was "overjoyed." The Canadian public roared their approval, and people everywhere seemed satisfied by, even proud of, the outcome.

I saw the decision as more than a legal one. It also seemed a compassionate ruling, perhaps a mark of our humanity. Even so, nothing would be happening immediately. The Court had suspended its ruling for twelve months in order to give the government some time to legislate the practice.

That was the same year Prince William, England's heir to the throne, had a baby girl, and eight hundred thousand refugees sought asylum in Germany. It was the year the U.S. Supreme Court struck down the ban on same-sex marriage, and Donald Trump announced his candidacy for president. Change was happening all around me, and I'd soon long for some in my own life too.

I remember one night I was at the hospital. I had just helped deliver a baby boy and was ducking into an on-call sleep room to catch what I hoped would be a few hours of slumber before the next bit of work might arise. I checked my email before turning out the light and found a short video clip sent from Jean-Marc. It was a welcome surprise, and I almost laughed out loud when I saw the kooky antics my family had gotten up to earlier that evening. They'd had a pajama party, and I knew the video was sent to make me feel included, but in truth, it only emphasized my distance. I became acutely aware of what I was missing. Their evening of innocent fun reminded me that time was flying by, that my children would get older and soon leave our nest. Sam was entering his last year of high school, and Sara was growing up faster than anyone's youngest child should.

To add force to the winds of change, after twelve years of successful practice, my on-call maternity group was quietly coming to an end—one member was due to retire, another was going on sabbatical, and others hoped to cut back to part-time within a year or two, leaving us with serious personnel problems. It was not the first time I'd wondered if I was ready for a new direction. Jean-Marc had been encouraging me to consider other possibilities for months, if not years. For the first time I gave myself permission to start thinking about it. What else could I do, in medicine or otherwise? What else would I *want* to do?

That fall, even our government was in transition, and our new prime minister realized his team was meant to have legislated assisted dying by February 2016—an impossible deadline. He asked the Court for a six-month extension and was granted only four. Law or no law, on June 6, 2016, assisted dying would become legal in Canada. Assisted dying was back in the news, and I paid even more attention.

As I began to think more seriously about a career change, I considered what had brought me to maternity care in the first place. Maternity and newborn care were challenging but mostly joyful medicine, an opportunity to be part of something extremely special. I was proud to share my particular knowledge to help guide women and their families through the experience of having a baby, and I'd grown to be very good at it. But I was also attracted to the intensity. In fact, the more demanding the situation, the more I seemed to want to be involved—the pregnant teen who was considering adoption; the pregnancy that was medically complex due to a previously unrecognized condition. I found caregiving in challenging circumstances gratifying, and I was used to a certain degree of controversy in my work. For the past four years, in addition to maternity care, I had also been providing infant male circumcision.

Circumcision is a highly divisive issue where I live, and unlike my experience in maternity care, I was professionally isolated in the work (though I was accompanied by a small band of protesters who gathered outside my office when I first started advertising my services). My rationale for providing this care was based as much on my belief in the importance of patient autonomy as on my own skill set. Both the American Academy of Pediatrics and the Canadian Paediatric Society have position statements suggesting that families should be given the most up-to-date, objective medical information on neonatal circumcision and encouraged to filter that information through the context of their family traditions, their core values, and their cultural or religious beliefs. As the American Medical Association writes: "The ultimate decision regarding circumcision of a baby boy is the parents'. Parents should feel both informed and supported in this decision." It may not be for everyone, but if parents choose this procedure for their son, I believe it should be readily accessible and done with expert care.

Assisted dying was certainly unusual—no doubt I was intrigued by the unknown, but it was much more that drew me in. I didn't see assisted dying as ending someone's life; the underlying illness and suffering were doing that. I understood it more as facilitating someone's wishes. And it seemed to me that a health care provider might be the right person to do this work. Certainly, as clinicians, we were familiar with the medications. We knew the health care system, and we understood the illnesses that came before the end stages of disease. But it was a monumental shift in philosophy for many within the medical community. We were always taught to "first, do no harm," and helping end a life was always assumed to be a harm. But to me, and now in law, in certain specific circumstances, it wasn't harm as much as help.

The simple truth is that most people enter medicine with a desire to help others, and for me, assisted dying was an extension of that instinct. I didn't see this work as differing significantly from the work I did as a physician. I help people diagnose problems. When possible, I help fight illness. If given the opportunity, I help prevent illness and promote wellness. And just as often, when there is nothing more to "do," I sit with my patients and try to journey with them, stay present, provide a listening ear, and answer their questions as best I can. This is what a doctor does. "To cure sometimes, to relieve often, to comfort always."

———

All of this was swimming in my head that winter, late January 2016, when I went to visit my mother in Nova Scotia. On the longest leg of my return trip, I sat down in my seat next to a middle-aged woman with short gray hair. We exchanged pleasantries and started chatting, and I learned she was visiting from the U.S. and heading to see her son in the interior of BC. Her name was Enid.

Enid told me she was a retired midwife, and when I probed for more details, she revealed that she'd had an injury, she couldn't return to work, and she missed her career dearly. I understood what she had lost. I mentioned I was a maternity doc and was contemplating a change in my focus. She looked at me inquisitively, and after realizing I'd likely never see her again, I decided to explain.

For the first time ever, I was able to articulate all the factors swirling inside my head—pressure from my husband to cut back at work, a desire to be more present with my children before they left home, and at the heart of my schedule, a maternity group that was imminently collapsing. I had developed a growing willingness to consider what my options might truly be, and I had the interest and opportunity to contemplate work in a newly emerging field, yet I felt a nagging insistence that nothing else could ever engage me the way maternity care had for the past twenty years.

It all came pouring out of me. There was something about speaking to a person entirely outside my own bubble that allowed me to speak freely. I suppose many bartenders have been on the receiving end of a similar exchange. I wanted to clarify my thoughts in my own mind before broaching the topic more fully with Jean-Marc, and in Enid I found someone who had stood roughly where I had stood, done what I had done, and although not voluntarily, left it all behind.

I went on to tell her about my growing interest in assisted dying. I explained what was happening with Canadian law and what I had learned about the subject. I explained that it was about empowering the person (not the disease) to decide when, where, how, and with whom they would be when they died, and to hopefully afford a sense of dignity and some peace.

As I spoke to Enid, it became more clear to me that I was seriously considering entering the field, and I found myself getting more animated as we explored the topic together.

"You should only give up maternity care if you decide it's truly time," Enid told me. "Don't let anyone or anything else dictate this decision for you, or you'll always regret it." She was adamant on this point. "It may be time to walk away from maternity care, but if at all possible, it needs to be your decision."

Although I never saw her again, Enid was fundamental in helping me make my choice. Talking to her, I felt as though I had received permission not, to my great surprise, to remain in maternity care but to move on from it.

I realized that if I was serious about the idea, I would need to dig a little deeper into how the process of assisted dying would work. Who would be doing the work: The family doctors? The palliative care docs? The internists? No one was talking about it; it seemed no one knew anything at all. I decided to look for answers.

A quick phone call to the CPSBC, the organization responsible for my medical licensing, reminded me that although any eventual law on assisted dying would be federal, health care was administered provincially, and I learned that every health authority within our province (British Columbia has six) was developing its own regional MAiD program. The person on the other end of the line suggested I speak directly to the people at Island Health—the local health authority that financed and administered health care on Vancouver Island—but he couldn't give me a name. He did, however, offer me the names of two clinicians who had been asking questions as well. One of them I recognized, Dr. Konia Trouton, the owner of a large local women's health clinic. The other was a young internist I didn't know, Dr. Jesse Pewarchuk. I called Jesse, and he reiterated that the physicians with the most experience in assisted dying were in Europe.

"If you want to learn more about the practice itself, you should consider attending the upcoming conference in Amsterdam in May," he told me. He was definitely going.

Next I called Konia, who had already spoken to Jesse and was planning to attend the conference too. She encouraged me to join them both in Europe.

The conference was called Euthanasia 2016, and it was due to be held May 11 to 14, in Amsterdam. It was the World Federation of Right to Die Societies' biennial convention to discuss medical, legal, and political matters around the topic of assisted dying. When Jesse had first mentioned it, I couldn't quite imagine a conference dedicated to dying, and I was wary of the potential for controversy that might attract a less than legitimate crowd. In fact, as I soon learned, the conference was absolutely reputable, and it was taking place in central Amsterdam at one of the largest conference centers in Europe. The organizers were expecting hundreds of international delegates: clinicians, researchers, scholars, lawyers, advocates, ethicists, and administrators. It seemed almost odd that everything was so open: I was struck by the absence of secrecy or shame.

The idea of going to the conference began to take shape in my mind, but I knew it would be a real commitment—of both time and finances.

One night after dinner, I was sitting with Jean-Marc on our favorite old couch in our living room. I decided it was a good time to have a discussion. I wanted to know what he thought. Was it crazy to consider working in the field of assisted dying? Should I go to Amsterdam? He'd made significant career changes over the years—he'd left academia, started a business, worked with NASA, and was now creating a graphic novel. I knew he'd listen carefully and with an open mind, but I also knew I could trust him to speak frankly if he thought there was a problem.

Jean-Marc listened attentively. He made no comments or judgments, he just let me speak. Then he asked why I was so interested, and as I answered him, I could tell he intuitively understood the appeal and the imperative right away.

But Jean-Marc was also a realist. "Ideology aside, I have to tell you what you're talking about makes me squeamish. I find it all a bit . . . morbid, to be honest. Do you really believe you could do this work? And do you actually want to? Won't it depress you?"

I was pretty sure I could do it. The intensity didn't scare me. And I didn't find it morbid—I saw it as a service, the facilitation of a person's considered choice. What was more, I wouldn't have any more call shifts. No more twenty-four hours away followed by twenty-four more to recover. But, I confessed, I didn't know everything about the practice, so I was still hesitant. "That's why I think Amsterdam's a good idea."

Seven days away was a commitment, but he agreed it made sense to go.

The next morning, I booked my flight, excited to embark on what felt like a substantial adventure, the outcome of which remained uncertain.

CHAPTER 5

WHEN I ARRIVED AT THE RAI Center in Amsterdam for a welcome reception on the night of May 11, 2016, I was first struck by the size of the complex. It was more like a campus of conference and exhibition halls. Even so, I had no trouble choosing which entrance to use. Above one doorway hung an enormous banner reading "Euthanasia 2016." I looked around before approaching the doorway. There were no protesters, no extra security, and no hiding what this meeting was about. I knew there was public support for assisted dying in the Netherlands, but I still felt self-conscious as I walked under that banner and into the spacious entrance hall.

There were probably a hundred people at the reception, several hundred more were expected the next day, and it was much like any other conference but with better wine. Around the edges of the room, advocacy groups were hawking political pamphlets, and do-it-yourselfers were selling books on various methods of self-deliverance. But the real action was in the center, where there was a great mingling of professionals, projects, and languages. Everyone seemed to already know somebody else in the room.

I was relieved to spot Konia within the first few minutes and made my way over to say hello. She introduced me to Dr. Ellen Wiebe, an outspoken activist, well-known abortionist, and early supporter of assisted dying who had just arrived from Vancouver. Soon we were joined by Jesse and then Darren Kopetsky and Dr. Grace Park, also from Vancouver. We were six Canadians—five physicians and an administrator—all from BC. We shared our bewilderment at finding ourselves in Amsterdam. Where were all the other Canadians? Because our law was due to change in less than a month, we had expected to meet lots of others from across our country. But outside of our group, there were only two ethicists from Ontario.

That evening, I reviewed the next day's program. There would be several sessions running simultaneously, so I circled the names of the presentations I most wanted to sit in on—"The Dutch Review Board: How Oversight Works and Last Year's Data"; "Euthanasia in Europe: Is There Evidence of a Slippery Slope?"; "Ethical Dilemmas: How Our Opponents Are Actually Our Friends."

The next morning, I started off by seeking out some foundational information and attended a presentation on Dutch data. The chairs in the room were mostly occupied by delegates from countries where assisted dying was not yet legalized—Japan, France, Mexico, the UK, and several U.S. states. The speaker was a woman who had a strong Dutch accent but remarkably fluent English. She seemed calm and well prepared, and I liked how she contextualized the information for those of us from other countries.

She told us that researchers had been compiling statistics on what had been happening in the Netherlands with respect to assisted dying since 2002, and as a result, she was able to compare her numbers to those from other European countries. I was eager to hear who asked for the care, who provided it, how it was perceived, and how oversight occurred.

"Before we begin to dive deeply into the published Dutch data, please remember the Netherlands has a strong primary care health system," she continued, "and almost everyone in our country has a general practitioner. The most recent data suggests ninety-three percent of general practitioners have been asked for euthanasia at some point during their career, seventy-nine percent have granted a request, and only seven percent have stated they would never do so."

She went on to display a great many bar graphs and pie charts. There were breakdowns by gender, geography, average ages, and underlying illnesses. "Of all cases of assisted dying in the Netherlands," she informed us, "seventy-three percent have an underlying diagnosis of cancer."

That was not surprising, but some of the data was. I had assumed that people requested assistance in dying because they were suffering from physical pain, but I was informed that the most commonly mentioned end-of-life concerns were a loss of autonomy, the loss of ability to engage in activities that brought meaning or joy to life, and the loss of a sense of dignity. It seemed that for many patients, psychological suffering was as bad as or even worse than any physical symptoms, which were less commonly cited and, I suspected, could be sufficiently managed with good palliative care.

I was riveted. By the end of that first morning, I had an idea how assisted dying worked in a number of jurisdictions. I understood how often euthanasia was performed across Europe, who was asking for it, their reasons for requesting care, and the most common underlying diagnoses. I found the subject even more intellectually fascinating and ethically complex than I had imagined, and it was clear there was so much more to learn.

Over lunch, our small group of Canadians expanded to include new colleagues that each of us had met, so we cross-pollinated and introduced ourselves as we ate our prepared soup and sandwiches. We were curious about the information each of us had learned, and we quickly realized the value in sharing notes.

"Why don't we divide up and make sure at least one of us attends each lecture, every day," someone suggested. "We can choose each morning who will attend what, and we can share notes with each other by email at night."

We all agreed, exchanged email addresses, and chose our preferences for the rest of the day. Looking back now, I see that camaraderie as the seed of what was to become a much larger project. I could already sense how having a group of supportive colleagues would prove vital as we stepped forward into this challenging new work together.

Every day of that conference was a long one, and every minute of those days I was busy. I learned about drug protocols, which medications to use, and how to administer them. I would use the Dutch protocol, borrowed by British Columbia and which I first saw in Amsterdam, that first time with Harvey and with all other cases going forward. I met people who had been in the newspapers, who had testified in previous court cases or were bringing new and powerful stories to the headlines. I spoke with physicians who practiced this kind of clinical work and the researchers who studied the outcomes. The physicians cautioned me to practice self-care when doing such work, advising that it could prove draining if I didn't set aside time to rest and renew. I was meeting, listening, learning, making contacts, and discovering different elements—the roles of the regulators, clinicians, lawyers, advocates, spiritual guides, ethicists, and family members. There was a buzz about the place, and the week flew by.

The most captivating hour of the entire conference was the closed-door session with experienced providers of medically assisted dying. It took place on the last day, and I couldn't wait to hear from the front lines, from the practitioners themselves. In my experience, medicine was an apprenticeship: I had learned to deliver babies by sitting with hundreds of laboring women and observing the experienced hands of nurses and physicians. I wouldn't be able to witness anyone administering an assisted death at home in Canada, so I hoped to mine the speakers for information about how it felt to administer the medication, to shoulder the responsibility of ending a person's life.

At the front of the room stood one woman, an elegantly dressed, hospital-based medical specialist, and four men, all community-based general practitioners. All of them were Dutch, and each had at least fifteen years of experience providing assisted dying. The doors were closed, the cameras were off, and for a change there were no microphones or recording devices. I was sitting in the fourth row, absorbing everything they offered about their earliest experiences with assisted dying. When the floor was opened to questions, I decided to ask what I really wanted to know.

"I have been a physician for over twenty years in the field of maternity care, and although learning all the time, I am finally comfortable with my skill set. We in Canada are about to embark on something completely new.

I must tell you, I feel like a medical student again, like I have no idea exactly what I need to do or exactly how to go about doing it. Can you each give me a few pearls of wisdom—the things you wish you had known when you first began doing this work?"

"You want to choreograph the event," the elegant specialist began, "even down to the little details."

That made immediate sense. The concept of "choreographing" a medical event, a birth, for example, was familiar to me—who would be invited, what role would each person play. With end of life, there were some other questions to address: Would pets be allowed to attend, and what about last words?

"Think beforehand what you will say at the end." This came from one of the family physicians. "You can't say 'see you later' or 'take care.' I suggest you already have in mind what you will say when you know they will be the last words you speak to your patient."

A birth plan, a death plan. It struck a deep chord. This was the first time I made the connection between my skills in maternity care and the skills required to provide a good death. Both situations involved intense emotional experiences and carried a strong sense of the event's significance. Both called up complex family dynamics and required a patient-centered approach to care. Perhaps my expertise would be transferable after all. Perhaps I was not as inexperienced as I felt.

"Take a spare set of medications with you, just in case there is some problem."

I was writing down every idea.

"And don't go on your own. Have a colleague with you, at least the first few times."

I left the closed-door session committed to starting work in this new field, with tremendous gratitude for the practical advice and intending to use every piece of it going forward.

Landing back in Canada, I no longer worried about the work feeling sinister, as opponents might have had me believe, or depressing, as Jean-Marc had feared. It felt important, challenging, and novel. There were colleagues with experience who were willing to share their expertise, and colleagues who, like me, were just beginning to get involved. I felt supported by both and welcomed into a community.

When I returned from the trip, I walked into my house and couldn't stop talking. It was impossible to impart everything I had learned to Jean-Marc, but I did my best to explain why I was so determined to pivot toward this work. He was supportive, but I could tell he was still nervous. One evening, we were back on our favorite couch in front of the fireplace.

"Okay, this all sounds pretty reasonable," he said, "but have you considered the possible consequences?" He reminded me of the protests outside my office building over the circumcision practice. "I can only assume MAiD would be even more controversial."

"I think if there is any pushback to assisted dying, it may well be minimal," I insisted. "Public support for the law is running high, and we have such progressive politics here in BC."

"I suppose so," he acknowledged, slightly shaking his head. "But it only takes one committed opponent to really mess up your world. Don't you have *any* concerns about doing this work, Stef?"

I'll admit, his question did give me pause. As eager as I was to get started, there was one thing I feared: If I worked outside the established limits, if I helped a patient who wasn't strictly eligible, I could be liable for prison time. I knew I wouldn't do so intentionally, but what if I made a mistake?

"I promise you, I will always work within the law," I reassured Jean-Marc, and myself. "I will not risk going to jail over the issue."

Only three weeks remained before MAiD would be legal. I told my kids that I had decided to make a change in my work, that I was planning on assisting people who were very sick and were asking for help to die, and that if they had any questions, I would be happy to answer them. Both kids were old enough to understand the issues around the topic, and I was grateful for their support . . .

"It sounds like important work, Mom, very cool," said Sam. "Gotta run, though. I'm out!" he added as he brushed by and went to meet his friends.

. . . even if their attention was fleeting.

There was little time and a lot to prepare. I reached out to the local Dying With Dignity chapter and informed them of my plan to offer assisted deaths. They wanted to meet and asked if they could send me referrals. I called the CPSBC—the medical licensing body—and explained to the deputy registrar all that I'd learned in Europe. He agreed I met the criteria to be licensed and would be able to provide the care, and he released the newly created provincial prescription for MAiD for my professional use. In concert with Jesse and Konia, I connected with the health authority executives in charge of the MAiD program on Vancouver Island, and they agreed to complete the paperwork granting the three of us the credentials to provide MAiD in the hospital.

Next I had to deal with my office. I called my office manager, Karen, explained my plans, and invited her to continue working with me as I moved from maternity to assisted dying. Since my on-call group had disbanded, I hadn't taken on any new pregnant patients, so she must have wondered about my career plans. I was grateful when she agreed to stay on, and she didn't miss a beat, immediately drawing up a to-do list and suggesting we meet the next morning to tackle some of the new logistics.

We were sitting together in her workstation the last week in May as I looked around the office and tried to see it with fresh eyes. The space wasn't large or modern, but it was perfectly comfortable for all my professional necessities, and people loved the fact that the walls were plastered with photos of the babies I'd delivered. What might I have to change? How should we adapt our procedures, even the space, to serve our new needs?

"How will people find you?" Karen asked, getting down to business right away.

"I'll have a website with our contact information, and I'll send a notice to the family docs in town letting them know they can refer patients. Some folks will find me through word of mouth, I imagine. Island Health has my name and number in case people call and inquire, and Dying With Dignity is aware of my plans; they may also send people to us." I was trying to make myself accessible but didn't know which avenues would be most effective.

"So, patients can self-refer by telephone"—Karen was making notes—"or what . . . have their doctors consult us by fax?"

Faxes were the most secure in terms of privacy, and many doctors' offices still used them for this reason. "Yes," I confirmed. "Like before, with the maternity patients."

I looked around, remembering the day I'd moved into this space and all the decisions we'd made back then. I would miss the familiarity of prenatal visits and the confidence that came from experience, but I was determined to make this change and felt strongly that assisted dying should be available. I caught sight of the baby scale draped with a blanket set up in the back room. I decided it could go.

"What about the office answering machine?" Karen continued, "Exactly how explicit do you want the message to be?"

I didn't yet have that answer. What should our recorded greeting say?

"And what information do you want me to gather when I call people back? Am I calling people back, by the way, or are you?"

I looked at Karen, sitting at her desk, pen in hand, spiral notebook at the ready, and it occurred to me, not for the first time, that it wasn't always obvious who ran this place.

Thanks to Karen's diligence, we were ready to receive the fax about Harvey when it arrived on June 6. Ten days after I received it, I was sitting at his bedside, surrounded by his wife and children, as Harvey became my first.

Part 2

SUMMER

CHAPTER 6

THE DAY OF HARVEY'S DEATH, I took the afternoon off to allow myself to feel whatever I might be feeling. I did the puzzles from the weekend paper. I took the dog on a long walk to the beach and watched him dig in the sand and chew sticks. I monitored myself for any adverse reactions. Was I feeling distressed in any way? Unsettled? As far as I could tell, I was fine, although I did wonder how long it had taken the funeral home to arrive after I left. I decided I would call Norma in a week to check in. I felt unsure of my role now that the event was over. I could tell Jean-Marc was watching me too, protectively and with a hint of concern.

I emailed my colleagues in the group that had started in Amsterdam to share my experience helping Harvey and his family. Our numbers had grown since the conference. Konia, Ellen, Jesse, Grace, and I had been joined by Dr. Jonathan Reggler, a British-born-and-trained family physician in Comox Valley, BC, whose name I'd seen in the local paper when he gave an interview about his intention to provide MAiD in the near future. He'd brought along his colleague Dr. Tanja Daws, a South African family physician who'd emigrated with her young family a number of years before. Ellen brought in Dr. Roey Malleson, a colleague from Vancouver with whom she had already provided an assisted death under an earlier court exemption, and suddenly we were eight—eight clinicians in the province with the intention to provide MAiD. In my email to them, I described my preparations, the event itself, and how I had felt throughout.

"Things went pretty smoothly, but I'm still unclear about the aftercare. Are you guys planning to provide follow-up counseling when they're not patients from your own practice?"

By the end of the afternoon, everyone had responded to my message. They were relieved to know it had gone so well. Tanja and Jonathan were envious of my access to a nurse for IV support, and they mentioned that they'd arranged some refresher sessions for themselves at their hospital to become more comfortable with starting IVs.

"Thanks for sharing your experience, Stefanie, I'm certain I will learn from it. Not sure I can say 'congratulations' or 'job well done,' but it seems the right sentiment to me."

That grassroots, collegial support from my new group of colleagues felt tremendously valuable. Jean-Marc could be supportive, but there were few who could truly understand exactly what I was doing.

Harvey was my first patient, but he wasn't my last that month. The second person I helped came to me through my pharmacist, Dan. This elderly man was one of Dan's long-standing patrons, and he was nearing the end of his battle with cancer. When the law changed, his wife mentioned to Dan that they were interested in learning more about assisted dying. She said she didn't want to lose her husband, but she hoped he would be eligible for care because he was suffering so terribly. Dan put us in touch. I found him eligible, and my second procedure went ahead.

That first month, I saw another three people in consultation. Not everyone qualified for an assisted death, and some were just looking for information, but as there were so few clinicians, I was soon fielding numerous inquiries each week. In Victoria, we were three MAiD providers in a city of just over three hundred and fifty thousand. On Vancouver Island, there were five of us serving a population of eight hundred thousand, and we were considered lucky. In Toronto, I knew of only two clinicians providing MAiD outside of the hospital setting to a population of nearly six million. Meanwhile, there were vast regions of our country with no providers at all. While there had been an initial sense of relief among the public that this care was now available, my colleagues began reporting they were hearing from desperate families in communities that didn't offer it.

As June turned into July, I received one such call from a woman named Louise who lived in a small town in BC's Interior region about eight hundred kilometers away.

Louise was a sixty-nine-year-old with diffusely metastatic breast cancer who was being cared for by her family physician. She'd watched her mother die of ovarian cancer at the age of sixty-eight, and she'd lost two sisters to breast cancer three and five years earlier. She was unfortunately aware of the decline that awaited her in the last weeks of life. Although she felt well cared for, she wanted the possibility of an assisted death so she might control the timing and the final circumstances of her passing. While her family doctor was willing to support her application and serve as one of the assessors of eligibility, no one in her region was yet willing to offer the procedure. After searching online, she'd found my website and contacted my office to explore her options.

When I first spoke with Louise, the idea was that she would travel to me. "Dr. Green, if you'd be willing to help me, my husband, Greg, and I would fly to Victoria," she told me. "We have family we can stay with, and they've already said we're welcome."

I suspected that in her condition travel would be exhausting, as she was several hours away and would need to change planes in Vancouver.

"I'd be immensely grateful if you'd consider taking me on as a patient," she continued. "I hoped you could do your initial assessment remotely, by telehealth, and I could just come to Victoria once, at the end, for my death."

Though it seemed an unusual arrangement, I couldn't see why I shouldn't accept her into my practice.

Louise's case was the first time I had the opportunity to assess a patient by telehealth. From the beginning, in recognition of the significant amount of rural area in our province, British Columbia permitted one of the two required assessments for eligibility for MAiD to be provided through a secure, hospital-based telemedicine system. My office was conveniently located across the street from the Royal Jubilee Hospital. I looked in the hospital directory and discovered a telemedicine department, which I promptly called to book a room and a computer for my interview with Louise.

On the morning of our appointment, I sat in front of a large screen while Louise sat with Greg in an equivalent space within her local hospital. With his dark-rimmed glasses and layered outerwear, Greg looked every bit the engineer he was. Louise was frail-looking but smiling, sitting in a wheelchair, and bundled into a turtleneck sweater despite the summer temperatures. I hoped it hadn't been too difficult to get her out and readied for this meeting. There was a home care nurse with them as well, because provincial guidelines demanded a witness be present for any virtual assessments. It was an odd setup for a conversation about fears and final wishes, but it would have to do.

"Why are we talking now, Louise?" I asked. "What, if anything, has changed? You didn't reach out to me last week, and you didn't want to wait another month . . . what made you decide to call now?"

Louise lamented her inability to eat, her loss of sense of taste, her overall lack of appetite. She told me she could manage to get out of bed and into an easy chair on her own, and she could still get herself to the bathroom when necessary, but she couldn't go outside without help.

"I'm much too wobbly on my feet," she said. "I spend most of my day watching TV or napping. I don't even really want visitors. I can't read for more than a few minutes, I can't do my crossword puzzles anymore, I'm really just existing more than living."

She explained that her disease had been progressing despite treatment, so she'd stopped her chemotherapy about a month ago. Since then, her pain had been increasing weekly.

"I know what's coming next," she said, "and I'd rather skip it. There's no need for my family to go through that, nor me, if I can avoid it."

"Well, how about your family—you've said they know you're sick, but what do they think of this idea? Have you told them you're considering an assisted death?"

"My close friends and family all know. Everyone is supportive, they remember how it went with my sisters, but my son, Pete"—she looked at Greg before continuing—"he's struggling a little bit." She smiled. "He wants every last minute he can squeeze out of me."

We spoke for ninety minutes. I reviewed her medical records, spoke to her oncologist, and approximately one week after our original phone call, I found Louise eligible for MAiD. She was clearly in decline, resting much of the time, but still managing at home with support. Her family doctor agreed that she was eligible, so we started making plans to carry out the procedure in Victoria in two weeks' time, as she'd requested.

Unfortunately, within days, Louise developed a painful partial bowel obstruction, became completely bedbound, and required significant amounts of analgesics. Greg called to ask if I'd be willing to come to them instead.

"I know it sounds a bit crazy, Dr. Green, but I promised Louise I would do my best to give her some control at the end. I'll care for her at home regardless, but I want to try to fulfill her wishes. Will you consider it, please?"

Those were the days when I was in the habit of saying yes to everything. I wanted to prove this work could be done, done well, and made available to all. I knew I could probably travel there and back in one day. The kids were both away at summer camp, and Jean-Marc would likely be supportive. Greg and I agreed it should happen in two days' time, but there were other practicalities I hadn't yet considered.

The first issue was the flight itself. In the Canadian health system, a physician bills the provincial government for every health service rendered through an itemized, indexed fee code. I hadn't been reimbursed for any of my MAiD work to date because no fee codes existed yet for MAiD. So there was little chance I could expect any health authority to pay for my flight to administer an assisted death. Greg was gracious enough to suggest that the family would cover my expenses, but for a medical practitioner in a universal health care system, the notion that a patient would have to pay for anything, let alone such a significant expense for a covered, legal medical act, was anathema. I wondered if it was even permissible for me to accept his offer. I was so uncomfortable with the whole idea that I called the CPSBC and once again spoke to the deputy registrar.

"There's no professional conflict here," he reassured me, "the family can pay for your flight. But obviously, this is not something that can become routine. The public shouldn't have to bear such expenses. The province will need to address the issue of the insufficient number of providers. I appreciate your checking with us first. Good luck."

So I agreed to accept Greg's offer and continued to make plans.

The second practical issue was one I hadn't foreseen: I was so accustomed to having a supportive pharmacist that I had forgotten not all pharmacies would be as willing to help me obtain medications for an assisted death.

I first called the local pharmacist who had been serving Louise for decades. He was a pleasant fellow who was obviously uncomfortable with my prescription. When I encouraged him to at least consider becoming involved, he quickly decided he would have nothing to do with "this stuff" and hung up. My second call was to his only competitor in town. She told me she might be willing to get involved but didn't believe she could source the medications within two days. She suggested I call a pharmacy in a larger town, approximately an hour's drive away. This time I spoke with a pharmacist who wasn't completely unwilling to help but who also wasn't convinced that MAiD was a legal procedure. He requested time to speak with his head office about official company policy. By the time he got back to me late the next day to say they would not yet be taking part in such work, I was already determined to bring the medications with me from Victoria.

The problem was how.

The medications, once drawn up, would be good for twenty-four hours. I had to sign for them at my pharmacy in Victoria and was personally responsible for them, of course, so there was no way I would consider checking them with the airline. I would need to carry them on the flight. Fair enough. But what would I say to airport security when asked what I was carrying and why? This was not a vial of insulin, it was two complete sets of lethal medications drawn up in multiple syringes. I asked Karen to find out what she could about what was and wasn't allowed, but we had so little time, there was really only one way to find out.

The afternoon before Louise's scheduled death, I confirmed the plan with Louise and Greg. She was declining but still alert enough to speak with me on the phone—a promising sign that she would be able to provide the necessary consent immediately before I began the procedure. I picked up the prescription and kept the containers sealed and in my fridge overnight. (Yes, it was unsettling when I reached in to grab an orange and saw the lethal prescription sitting next to our dinner leftovers.) At five a.m., I left my house to drive to the airport. I took only a backpack holding a stethoscope and Louise's chart, and a cooler bag I'd carefully packed with the syringes.

I checked in for my flight at a self-serve machine and headed straight to airport security, where, despite the early hour, the line snaked around the entire waiting area. That long wait gave me ample opportunity to play out several scenarios in my mind. What if I was pulled to the side? What if they decided to involve the police? What if I missed my flight?

In the end, it all went smoothly. As it turned out, prescription medications can be taken on board no matter the amount; the security agent didn't even ask me what the medications were for. I confess, after all the buildup, I was a little disappointed.

After two flights, a layover, and a ninety-minute drive, I arrived at Louise's home, which was set back off a quiet road by a small forest of spruce trees. From where I parked, I could see a lake just beyond the back of the house and a large screened-in porch at the front where I noticed several people had gathered.

As I climbed out of the car, a man I recognized as Greg stepped forward to greet me. He introduced me to his guests: Louise's brother and sister-in-law, her niece and nephew, and two close friends of the family. The mood was somber but welcoming.

"It's good we're doing this today," Greg said as he led me inside the house. "She's going downhill quickly. But don't worry, she's expecting you. She sleeps a lot of the time, but she knows what's going on. She's been asking me all morning what time you're coming."

We walked through the open-plan kitchen and on into Louise's bedroom. She was dozing in bed, her sparse hair partially covered with a dark blue toque. A man who looked to be in his late thirties sat quietly on the edge of the bed next to her. Greg introduced him as their son, Pete. Despite his shaggy dark hair, he had an unexpected red beard. I remembered that Louise had said he was ambivalent about her decision to end her life, and I wondered if he was still feeling that way. Pete watched me take off my jacket and unpack my few things, and then he and Greg left the room to give Louise and me a bit of privacy.

"I'm so glad to finally meet you, Dr. Green." Louise spoke softly, sounding exhausted. The difference from even a few days ago was stark. The thought flashed through my mind: Did it make sense for me to come all this way? I suspected that even without my assistance, Louise would likely die within the week. I briefly wondered, after all this was over, would the family feel that it had been worth the money and effort to bring me here? Would Pete feel as if I had taken the last week of his mother's life away from him?

I pushed the thoughts aside and focused on Louise.

"I love my family dearly," she told me, "but I am so very, very ready."

I was coming to cherish this time alone with the patient, technically affirming their capacity and seeking their consent before we formally began. First with Harvey, then with my second patient, and now with Louise, I was struck by the honesty of our conversations. There was a raw reality to these bedside chats: Patients said exactly what they meant. When I sat down and asked people how they were doing, no one answered, "Just fine." All three were eager to proceed, stating: "I'm ready," or "I need this to be over." No bullshit, as Harvey might say. This private time also helped ensure there was no element of coercion, that my patient wasn't being coaxed into an assisted death in any way. As much as these conversations might have been reassuring for the patient, they were reassuring for me too.

After our talk but before we got started, I checked Louise's IV site for unimpeded flow. Her family doctor had started the IV earlier that morning. He'd been so involved that I had expected him to stay behind and witness the event himself, but when I'd called him the day before to go over the details, he'd informed me that he wouldn't be attending.

"I think I can't be present because . . . I'm pretty sure that I will cry."

He caught me off guard with his candor.

"I totally support this decision," he went on, "and I really care for this family. I've known them all for a very long time, but I don't think it's helpful if they see my tears."

I started to disagree with his thinking but then stopped myself. He was just being honest, and it was his choice to make. It seemed every person I met, from the pharmacist to the family doc, was trying to find their footing in this very new field of care. The knee-jerk reaction was to back away and not get involved. I had to hope that, over time, as the work became more familiar, this might shift.

After confirming that everything was in order with Louise and her IV, I invited Greg and Pete back in to begin the formal process, exactly as she'd requested. Louise was especially drowsy. She expressed her love for her family, but soon she just closed her eyes and asked me to start. It was quiet as I began.

As I was administering the third of eight syringes, Pete suddenly broke away and left the room. I heard him head out of the house, and I thought he'd probably keep on walking, but it sounded more like he went straight into the arms of a loved one on the porch. His sobbing remained audible in the background.

"Don't worry," explained Greg, "he'll be fine. They were close. I think it's because he's an only child, and this has been really hard on him. They had a really good talk last night. They said all their goodbyes . . . His uncle's out there. He'll be okay."

I wasn't sure which one of us he was reassuring. Greg then turned his attention back to Louise, holding her hand in both of his.

Louise fell deeper into unconsciousness, and a few minutes later, her breathing stopped and the color went from her face. Greg remained fixed by her side, her hand still enfolded in his, unable to take his eyes from her, a pillar of support to the very end.

I waited for a moment, then used my stethoscope to check Louise's chest for any trace of heartbeat. There was none. I gave my condolences to Greg and silently noted the time of death. He briefly looked at me, nodded, and returned his gaze to Louise. I gathered up my things as quietly as possible, instinctively trying to leave no trace of my presence. I decided there might be plenty of memories of Louise triggered by the contents of this house, but evidence of used syringes or any medical procedures need not be among them.

Then I excused myself to the dining room, where I planned to sit down to complete the necessary paperwork, leaving Greg alone with his wife. First I had to pass an area with large windows and a door that led directly onto the porch, where the guests were still sitting and waiting. All eyes were on me as I exited the bedroom and entered the larger living space. Louise's family and friends must have known the truth of the situation by then, but they seemed to be waiting for me to say it out loud before they could believe it. I went over, opened the door, and stood in the doorway with the bag of medications in my hand, the stethoscope around my neck, and Louise's chart tucked under my arm.

"She's gone," I announced. "It was very peaceful. Greg is having a few moments alone with her now."

I felt awkward standing there like that, so I turned back inside as their chatter restarted, and I went over to the dining room table and sat down. I filled out the medical certificate of death. I wrote down the details of the procedure, the time each medication was administered, and filled out the paperwork for an expected death at home. I checked the box on a different form confirming I'd obtained consent from Louise immediately prior to beginning. There were lots of forms to complete, seventeen pages in total, and I carefully made my way through each and every one. I also made a mental note to prefill anything and everything possible when preparing for future cases.

Greg walked in and offered me a Scotch. He looked pale, shaken, yet somehow resigned. I settled for a glass of water and joined him in the kitchen area. We were quickly joined by two others from the porch— Louise's brother and a close family friend—who were seeking a taste of that Scotch, and they stayed, soon to be joined by the others.

I was wondering how they might respond to what had just happened. Was it a terrible day in their lives, or was there some sense that they'd helped provide the ending Louise had asked for? She had been so close to the end. Where was Pete and how was he feeling? Everyone's reactions, in that moment, seemed more important than any of my own impressions.

"We called the golf course," the friend announced, "and they'll be flying the flag at half-mast today in her honor." Greg nodded his approval as he leaned against the counter.

By now we were eight people gathered in that space, and I talked about how impressed I was with all their support, with the love Louise had around her. I recognized out loud that today was probably harder for them than it had been for Louise, and that their presence and support had been a real gift to her. I hoped they saw it that way.

This seemed to trigger an emotional release. There was silent nodding, general agreement, and suddenly, a lot more tears. I noted to myself that articulating some of the underlying feelings seemed to be helping people process the moment. I would keep this in mind going forward.

In these early months of providing MAiD, I was constantly adding to my mental checklist of what worked well and what didn't, what I wanted to try to say and when, as well as what was and wasn't appropriate. When I told Louise's family and friends they had "given their loved one a gift" by putting her needs and wishes above their own for the day, I was drawing on what I had just witnessed at her bedside but also from my experience with Harvey's family.

We all continued to sip our drinks in a huddle in the kitchen. It struck me that I had met most of these people only today and under these circumstances, and that very soon, I would disappear again from their lives. Outside the window, I could see the taller shadows of the afternoon beginning to appear. My flight was at four p.m., so I still had a little bit of time, but it was hard to know how long to stay. What was my role here, now that the procedure was over? It was not well defined, but certainly it was finite—I knew I would likely never see Greg or his family and friends ever again. Although my work was finished, I wanted to be available if any questions arose; I made sure Greg had all my contact information. I also knew I wasn't going to leave without acknowledging that everyone in the house had just lost someone very dear to them. How best to convey this?

That afternoon in Louise's home, I realized I had checked in with everyone except Pete. I could see him through the window, smoking a cigarette on the porch by himself.

I began to sense it was time for me to leave. I didn't want to be rude, but I did have a long trip ahead of me. So I gathered my bags, said goodbye to Greg, and walked out the door. I headed toward my car still wondering, despite the kitchen conversation, if the expense and trouble of my trip had been worth it to this family.

"Dr. Green!" Pete called out.

I turned back around. He stepped off the porch and came toward me. It crossed my mind that he might be upset with me and was going to give me a piece of his mind.

"Can I hug you?" he asked, his voice cracking.

"Of course," I said as I took a step toward him. "I'm a big believer in hugs."

"Thank you so much for coming," he whispered as he wrapped me in his arms. "You gave her the one thing none of us could."

CHAPTER 7

"**HE HAS CANCER OF THE** pancreas . . . he's very sick now, very weak . . ." A woman named Carol was leaving a message on my office answering machine about her husband, Charlie. I heard the crack in her voice, but she managed to compose herself and continued a bit more quietly: "I think he's not too far from the end now . . . I hope you can see him soon. He's pleading for your help."

She went on to explain that Charlie was currently admitted to the hospital across the street from my office, and she trusted I could come and see him there.

As I listened to her leaving her cell number, I looked back over at Karen and saw she was so affected by the emotion in Carol's voice that tears were welling up in her eyes. It was so different from a message announcing a new patient was pregnant. I was reminded that these unguarded, somber revelations were still new to us and that sorrow could be contagious.

"I hope I can help them both," I told her.

I decided to conduct an initial visit with Charlie at the hospital. If he was eligible, I'd figure out the logistics of providing an assisted death within an institutional setting. This was the first time I would be working "out in public" rather than in someone's home, and I'd be surrounded by nurses, orderlies, medical colleagues, cleaning staff, and receptionists. I had no way of knowing how the individuals within the system would react to my role or to me. A hospital is an entire institution devoted to helping patients survive, but I was a doctor whose mission was, well, something of the opposite. I hoped the hospital staff would view MAiD as I did, as patient-centered care that tried to restore some control and dignity when a person could no longer tolerate living. Yet I knew that some in the medical community remained opposed to assisted dying based on their own moral grounds. So far, the pushback from the Canadian public had been minimal, with limited protests, but I was wise enough to understand that not everyone was going to be supportive.

On the day of Charlie's consultation, twenty-four hours later, I entered the hospital with the unsettled feeling that I didn't know where I was going.

There are three hospitals serving Victoria, and I have admitting privileges in all of them. One is a small community hospital run by family doctors, about a forty-minute drive from my home. The Victoria General Hospital (VGH) is thirty minutes away in a different direction, and is the only hospital offering obstetric and pediatric care. It's a place I am familiar with from my maternity days (I even know which day the cafeteria serves its famous butter chicken). The Royal Jubilee Hospital, where Charlie had been admitted and where I had conducted my telemedicine call with Louise, is a larger, older campus. Though it's located across the street from my office, it's the facility with which I am least familiar.

I hitched my backpack a little tighter and made sure my hospital ID badge was hanging around my neck as I set off to find the elevators and room 436. The feeling was distinctly different than the last time I'd entered a hospital to meet with a patient in person. For twenty years, I'd arrived at hospitals in anticipation of delivering a baby, with all the excitement of what was to come. Entering as a MAiD practitioner was another experience entirely. While maternity and MAiD had their similarities—both were significant transitions—there was one difference that I hadn't fully appreciated until now: other people's reactions.

The emotional response to the outcome of a birth was pretty consistent: Families were overjoyed, nurses were satisfied, everyone was thrilled when it was over, and most people were happy to see me when I walked in the room. It was the unfolding of the process of childbirth that could be highly variable—and often outside my control—with some women remaining in labor for twenty-four hours and others only three, some delivering in an operating room and others in the back-seat of a car. Assisted dying, on the other hand, was shaping up to be the reverse. The procedure itself was very predictable: I administered the medication in a specific, prescribed order, and the expected results occurred without much variation. The emotional reactions of the people involved, however, were proving more difficult to foresee: The family might embrace the experience, as Harvey's had done, or flee the room, like Louise's son, Pete. Now I had to take into account the possible reactions of a full roster of hospital staff. Would the medical team know I was coming? And if they did, would they understand my role? Would they think I was offering help or harm?

I walked over to a busy unit clerk on the fourth floor, a young woman who appeared to be in constant motion at the large workstation in the center of the hallway. I was thankful to have my ID badge on its royal blue lanyard, a golden ticket within the hospital.

"Hello, I'm Dr. Green. I'm looking for the room of Mr. Winslow."

"Mr. Winslow . . . let me see . . . yes, 436. He's on the other side, on 4 North." She flashed a quick smile, and then she looked down again, filling in a form while simultaneously speaking into her headset.

I spun around and walked back out the doors, past the bank of elevators, and entered 4 North. I wanted to read Charlie's chart before I went in to see him, but I wasn't sure where the patient charts were kept. Part of good medical practice is projecting confidence even when you're not feeling it. The other part is knowing your own limits. This time I chose false confidence and strode directly past the unit clerk into a back room.

Inside, five or six clinicians were sitting and reading or writing in patient charts. A few looked up when I entered. Most ignored me. A woman in purple scrubs watched as I went through the motions of checking names on all the abandoned binders strewn along the desktops. "Who are you looking for?" she finally asked in a surprisingly pleasant voice.

"Mr. Winslow, room 436."

"It's probably down at the nursing station near his room at the end of the hallway. They like to keep their own down there. Which service are you from?"

"I'm Dr. Green. I'm here to do a MAiD assessment." As the words left my mouth, I suddenly worried about my patient's confidentiality, but how else could I explain who I was?

"MAiD . . . what's that?" she asked, genuinely unsure.

"Mr. Winslow has requested an assisted death, so I'm here to help assess if that's going to be possible. I'm from the MAiD team." In truth, there was no MAiD team: It was a fictitious club that I made up on the spot to try to sound more official. "MAiD is 'medical assistance in dying.'"

"Oh! Right, is that legal now?"

"Yes, it is, but not everyone qualifies. Which service are you from?" I was a bit wary of continuing this conversation without knowing this woman, especially with so many ears potentially listening.

"I'm one of the physios."

"Great. Nice to meet you." We shook hands.

It occurred to me that there was a lot more work to be done to educate people, both the public and the health care community, about this change in law. But that would have to wait. I quickly turned my attention to the task at hand and headed to Charlie's room.

I had to steady myself when I walked in. Charlie was shockingly emaciated, likely unrecognizable to his friends and family. According to the chart, he was sixty-seven years old. He still had a thin tuft of dark hair, and from his chiseled jawline, I could see that he might have been quite handsome once. But on this day, he resembled a living skeleton. He was lying in bed on his side, pillows between his knobby knees and ankles, pillows propping him up from behind. His skin was jaundiced, and his hospital gown hung off him like a sheet. He looked like he was resting. He looked like he was dying. He opened his eyes when I walked in: two beacons of light in his darkened, sunken face, but a frightening amount of yellow where there should have been some white.

His wife, Carol, offered me her chair next to Charlie's bedside. Dressed in stylish activewear, Carol looked fit and capable, but her face was worn with worry. She took a seat behind me as I introduced myself.

Charlie spoke in short, quiet sentences. He was remarkably clear in thought, considering how obviously weak he was. He told his story—the history of his symptoms, testing, biopsy, diagnosis of pancreatic cancer, and trajectory of rapid decline—without moving, as if conserving all his energy for speech.

"I came in this time because of a bowel obstruction. I was vomiting nonstop . . . It was very painful . . . They put a tube through my nose . . . They said I couldn't have surgery . . . I thought I might die, but it resolved on its own . . . Pain's better, but I'm very weak . . . I never, ever want to experience that again."

Charlie explained that he was too weak to return home and was awaiting a bed in the hospice unit. He was grateful for all the care, but he told me he dearly hoped to die, preferably before the bed even became available.

"This is not who Charlie is," Carol interjected. I turned around to look at her. "He's someone who used to be so fit, always outside, cycling and hiking, being in nature." She looked down, shook her head. "Nothing could stop him."

Charlie had recently committed to stop eating and drinking in order to hasten his own death, but he admitted he was struggling with his thirst. "I haven't had the guts to pull out my IV yet."

Charlie's was not a complicated medical assessment. He clearly met all the criteria. I tried to focus our meeting on his reasoning, his wishes, what was bothering him the most, but he was so ill, there was a limit to how much we could connect.

"Keeping me alive isn't doing me any favors," he insisted.

"Please, Dr. Green," interjected Carol, "there's only more suffering in front of him. Please help him to go . . . now, before he suffers more." Her voice cracked on the last word, and she closed her eyes tightly, silently crying at this thought.

I understood the request. I promised I would try to help them, then summed up next steps: I would need a written request form. I would arrange for a second assessment, hopefully from Charlie's primary care doctor, and then get back to them as soon as I could. I stood up and put my notes back in my bag, gathered my coat, and went to shake Charlie's emaciated hand. He took my hand in both of his, quiet at first, just holding it. He looked up into my face. "Thank you, Dr. Green . . . thank you."

I told Charlie I was sorry we had to meet under these circumstances, but that it was my honor to do so, and I would be in touch soon. Then I left and headed back to my office across the street. I settled in behind my desk and started typing my consultation notes.

When I was done, I called Charlie's family physician to see if he'd be willing to provide an assessment. When I told the receptionist why I was calling, she put me through right away.

"Hi, Burt, this is Stefanie Green," I explained. "I'm one of the MAiD physicians in town, and I wanted to talk with you about your patient Charlie Winslow. I saw him today in the hospital, at the Jubilee."

"Sorry . . . what kind of physician?"

"I'm one of the physicians who help people with assisted dying. Charlie is applying for an assisted death . . . I thought you knew, I'm sorry. I saw him today at the hospital to give him some information about the process."

"Oh, yes, his wife asked me about that a while back. I told her I don't know anything about it."

"Well, no worries—luckily, I do!" It just came out. I hadn't meant to sound cheeky. I paused. No response. I checked my tone and went on to explain that Charlie was serious about his application, and that he was going to need another clinician to determine if he was eligible. "Seeing as you've known Charlie for several years, I was wondering if you might feel comfortable being that other clinician. I'm happy to help explain how the process works and all. I just thought it would make sense to ask you instead of bringing someone new on board. Would probably make it easier for Charlie."

There was another pause, longer this time, then I jumped back in, sensing where this might be going. "I know you've not likely done this before . . . It's all very new, but it doesn't require any skill you don't already possess. I don't mean to put you on the spot, though . . . Perhaps this is not something you are comfortable discussing?"

A clearing of the throat.

I realized then that, just as people might need a little time to get used to MAiD, I would need a minute to get used to their reticence. When I called previously, as a maternity doctor, colleagues had generally been happy to chat with me.

"Umm . . . I understand Charlie's wishes, and I wish him only the best," Burt began. "I've known Charlie for seven or eight years now. But this isn't something I feel comfortable getting involved with, you know? It's legal now in BC, is it?"

"Yes, legal across the entire country," I answered. "Okay, I understand. I can ask a colleague to do the second assessment, if you prefer. I just thought it would make sense to ask you first. But no worries."

"No, not something I want to get mixed up in." His tone changed to routine, more professional: "Yes. Thanks. Appreciate the call," and he hung up.

Fair enough, this was not for everyone. But it seemed to me that a lack of knowledge or even a familiarity with the topic was at least as much of an obstacle as any question of morality.

I called the office of my colleague Konia and arranged for a second assessment to be done in two days. Next I called Rosanne Beuthin, the regional health authority's new clinical nurse specialist in charge of implementing and coordinating the new MAiD program. She promised to contact the clinical nurse leader (CNL) on Charlie's floor to help me coordinate his care, to make sure the hospital staff knew what to expect on the day of Charlie's MAiD procedure, and to ensure that they were comfortable being involved. She mentioned that there had already been one other in-hospital procedure, which I was glad to hear, and that the staff had appreciated a debriefing.

"Certainly . . . happy to do it," I responded. "I'll need someone to start the IV for me; otherwise, I can work independently."

I hung up, grateful for Rosanne and her willingness to help pave the way forward. Until now, MAiD was work I had done on my own with the help of Jessica and a pharmacist, but in a hospital, I couldn't do my job without the cooperation of nursing staff, hospital administration, and a whole host of medical colleagues.

Charlie's assisted death happened five days after our first meeting, in his hospital room, with his brother, his wife, and two close friends in attendance. His favorite jazz music was playing in the background when I walked in—a nice personal touch in an otherwise standard hospital room. Charlie's primary nurse, a woman named Balvinder, was present to record the exact times I administered the medications, as required for the records. Within someone's home, we would have been surrounded by photos, meaningful trinkets, and any number of loved ones. But Charlie didn't seem to care where he was; he just wanted to proceed.

"Is there anything left unsaid by anyone here today?" I asked before I began.

"It's all been said," answered Carol without looking away from Charlie. "He knows how much we love him and that we'll miss him dearly." She kissed his hand.

"Thank you all for being here and for supporting me," said Charlie, his eyes remaining closed. "Now let's do this."

Reassured by his certainty, I nodded and began. Charlie fell asleep with the first medication. He was so weak, I suspected he died before the second one was in, but I continued without pause through each medication of the protocol. When I was finished, Charlie's brother turned around and silently opened the window.

"He asked to be set free," Carol explained, "to return to the outdoors he loved so much."

I told them how sorry I was for their loss and left the room to give them all some time alone together. When they were ready, we met again in the sunroom down the hall.

It was uncomfortably quiet at first. Charlie's loved ones looked stunned by what had just taken place. I was reminded that even when we know to expect the exact date and time of a death, it doesn't necessarily increase the brain's ability to cope with the reality of loss. I waited until everyone was present, but still no one broke the silence. It was as if none of us knew how to move forward. I took it as my responsibility to begin. I suggested that, from a technical point of view, all had gone smoothly.

"Yes," began his brother, "it was so calm."

"So peaceful," added Carol.

Once again, I cared deeply about how these events would be perceived. I was aware that they were singular moments in the lives of everyone involved, and the feelings would linger long after the details would fade away.

The family listened as I explained that I thought it was a great gift they had given Charlie, the gift of their support. As with Louise's family, that was when they broke. They allowed themselves to cry, reach for Kleenex, nod quietly.

"Thank you for saying that, Stefanie," Carol said. "It's been really hard on all of us, but I am certain it's what he wanted. And he was so grateful for your care, for this possibility."

I was pleased that she had used my first name. It wasn't something my maternity patients commonly did unless they came back for second and third babies, by which time we had been through the challenges of childbirth and newborn care together. Carol calling me Stefanie rather than Dr. Green made me feel that we'd achieved a connection in an overwhelming but short period of time. I decided I would allow (or maybe encourage?) all my MAiD patients and families to call me by my first name if they wished.

I made sure Charlie's family members were aware of the hospital bereavement program, and I once again left my email address and phone number with Carol. This was something else that was new in my role as a MAiD provider—I'd never considered offering my direct contact information to any of my maternity clients; they always had to find me via my office or an answering service. With MAiD, I wanted family members to reach out to me directly if any questions arose. There were fewer people who could answer their questions, and I wanted to ease the process as much as possible. It might have been because it was still so new and I had attended only a handful of deaths, but I felt more instrumental in the outcome of the encounter than I ever had at a birth. There was a sudden shared intimacy among those who were present that was hard to ignore.

When my paperwork was finished, I notified the CNL that I was ready to meet with the hospital staff, happy to follow through on my promise to Rosanne of a debriefing.

We convened in the teaching room, down a different hallway. The CNL let me know that her entire nursing staff had asked to attend, as well as an orderly, a lab technician, and a member of the cleaning staff. It seemed everyone was interested, and several people wanted to ask questions. "Dr. Green, can you tell us who exactly is eligible for an assisted death, what medications you use, and in what dose?" I answered as succinctly and transparently as possible.

While I was talking, a young nurse from the unit shook her head as if trying to clear her thoughts, then stood up abruptly after only a few minutes and started to leave.

"Cindy"—the CNL was trying to smooth things over—"you can leave if you're feeling uncomfortable, but before you go, is there anything you want to ask Dr. Green that might help you right now?"

"I just don't think this is right," Cindy answered. "I don't believe in this. I don't want anything to do with it." Her voice was rising. "You can't make me do this." She seemed distressed more than angry.

"I totally understand," I said. "You have every right not to be involved." Cindy had stopped at the door and was looking at me, hearing me out. "Everyone is entitled to their own opinions and values, and if you are uncomfortable with anything happening on the floor or the unit, please speak to the CNL. I understand she can help change your shifts around if needed. I fully respect your opinion and your level of involvement or noninvolvement, whatever you decide it should be. I would only ask that you equally respect the decisions of your colleagues and, most important, those of the patient."

"Thank you," Cindy answered sincerely as she stood by the door. "I appreciate that, and I can do that. I don't understand this assisted dying, and I would never do it myself, but I can let Mr. Winslow do what he wishes." Then she paused and looked me directly in the eye. "But tell me, Doctor, don't you feel badly when you do this?"

I hadn't expected to answer this kind of question today, so it caught me a little off guard. There was a slightly elongated silence as everyone turned back to look at me.

"To tell you the truth, it's all still very new. But so far, I don't feel bad, no. I feel like I'm helping. There is a law, a rigorous process, and several safeguards in place. I follow those rules, and if someone is eligible, I tell them so. Then it's up to them. If they wish to proceed, I help them. I don't have to. If I wasn't comfortable, I could also say no. Just as nothing compels you to be involved, nothing obligates me. But I'm willing to do this work when people follow the rules. And so far, patients and their families have been grateful."

"I was in the room with Dr. Green and Mr. Winslow"—it was Balvinder, Charlie's nurse—"and I have to tell you that it was one of the most peaceful deaths I have ever seen. It was actually kind of beautiful."

The tone of the meeting shifted. People began sharing their own experiences of witnessing death. Some spoke of loved ones they had nursed in their own homes, some to a peaceful natural death, others who were not quite so lucky. Most spoke of watching their patients die at work, primarily negative stories of witnessing pain or terminal delusions, of patients needing to be restrained at the end of life, of family members pleading for help.

Cindy stayed by the door for another few moments, then slipped out, back to the ward. I spent another forty minutes with the team before gathering up my things, leaving the floor, and exiting through the lobby where I had entered, out into the bright July afternoon.

My first time providing MAiD in a hospital had been unlike anything I'd experienced as a maternity doctor, where the territory was familiar and the support of everyone around me was assured. I hoped that, thanks to our conversation, the next MAiD provision on this hospital unit would be slightly easier for everyone involved. I was grateful that, for Charlie and his family, there had been no hint of judgment or awkwardness, and that by our working together, his final wish had been fulfilled. I suspected it was a curious experience for all of us, finding our way into this new field of care, a bit like searching for a light switch in the dark after entering an unfamiliar room.

CHAPTER 8

AS AUGUST APPROACHED, I GOT a call at my office from a local radio station wanting to schedule an interview. It wasn't the first time the press had contacted me. I'd already been interviewed in the earliest weeks of MAiD, when the media was looking for comment on the changes in the law and how it might affect my medical practice. I was quite nervous about being scrutinized by interviewers, about making a terrible blunder, about not explaining myself clearly. But I came to appreciate that interviews presented opportunities to share accurate information about MAiD with the public.

This latest interview was scheduled for a Thursday morning, so I made sure to be at my desk in my office. In the minutes leading up to the interview, Karen and I ran through a short list of office-related issues she had for me. When we were done, she added one last point: "And I've confirmed with the family that Gary's umm . . . his, uh . . . his . . . MAiD, I guess, will be tomorrow. They're expecting you at one-thirty at the house." The phone rang before I could answer her, so I just nodded my confirmation and shut the door as she stepped out of my office.

The interviewer asked a number of questions, and we quickly established a comfortable banter, but I noted that, like the other journalists I had spoken with, he struggled to find the right words to use when asking about my work. For example: "So, Dr. Green, can you tell us the rules around this, uh . . . this stuff?" and, "When it comes to the actual . . . uh . . . event, let's say . . . what exactly happens? What should people expect?"

I answered as concisely as I could, filling in all the blanks. I referred to MAiD as a medical procedure, but I also tried out "scheduled death." Like Karen, who had stumbled over wording, the interviewer and I were still deciding what the proper terminology ought to be.

Toward the end of the interview, the radio host asked me a question that I hadn't been asked before, one that made me pause: "Who does this kind of work? And what kind of training do you get? . . . How do you learn what you need to know?"

I explained I had attended a conference in Amsterdam and alluded to the information I had learned there—the drug protocols, the tips from experienced providers, the data to inform my practice. But I admitted that my first experience had been a bit daunting, that it was one of the first cases of MAiD in the country, and that I was grateful to have a group of colleagues with whom I was developing best practices.

After the interview ended, I hung up the phone, but I wasn't satisfied with my response to his last question: "How do you learn what you need to know?" It warranted a more thoughtful answer, I thought, one I was still working out in my mind.

———

The first time I ever witnessed a death was twenty-two years ago, as a first-year family medicine resident in Montreal doing a monthlong rotation in the Cardiac Care Unit (CCU). The man's name was Mr. King, and he was a seventy-one-year-old with terrible heart disease. Every third night of that month I was on call overnight, meaning I was responsible for the care of the sickest cardiac patients in the hospital until eight the next morning. In truth, the nurses did most of the work. I was available if they had questions or if something really went sideways, but everyone knew the CCU nurses knew more cardiac medicine than most residents, me included.

Mr. King had already had several heart attacks and more than one cardiac surgery. Recently, he had begun going into arrhythmia, an abnormal heart rhythm that required invasive intervention to return his heartbeat to a normal pattern. He had a number of other serious medical conditions and was in poor health overall.

Mr. King's family had been in discussion all week about optimal care and only today had agreed, upon his continued insistence, to allow him to become DNR, the acronym clinicians use for "do not resuscitate," meaning no heroics would be used if he suffered further arrhythmia or cardiac arrest. In other words, we were no longer supposed to administer CPR (cardiopulmonary resuscitation) or use aggressive maneuvers to bring him back to life. No pumping on his chest in rhythm, no electric paddles to reset his heart's cadency, just oxygen and comfort measures. Mr. King had been consistent in this preference, but it had taken until today for his daughter to acquiesce. She finally understood there was a certain futility, even indignity, in treating him so aggressively at this end stage of his life.

As part of the CCU code team that week, I was the person responsible for running down hallways and up through the stairwells when the overhead system announced an emergency. I took my turn administering CPR and an algorithm of medications in an attempt to resuscitate those whose hearts had stopped. Most times we were unsuccessful, but at least we could say we tried.

And so it happened at one-thirty a.m., while sitting and chatting with some colleagues, that I received a call from Mr. King's nurse informing me that he looked to be having a rather large heart attack and could I please come quickly. I arrived in under a minute to find the situation exactly as described and with the unfamiliar, somewhat terrifying thought that I was supposed to do . . . nothing. This was contrary to what I had spent years training for. To my young mind, the practice of medicine was an act: You diagnosed, you gave medicine, you intervened.

I knew that by doing nothing, I was respecting Mr. King's wishes, and that "shocking" him back into normal rhythm, even if it could be done, would simply delay the inevitable and likely be very painful. I understood all of that completely, but the weight of responsibility was still overwhelming.

As I stood there contemplating my inaction, Mr. King's daughter burst through the doors. She had been called and had arrived in tears, somewhat frantic, and demanded we "do something" to help her father. I went over and began to explain what was happening. She would have none of it and got quite angry, demanding again that we help him, save him, something. We had other patients trying to sleep, so the nurse kindly but firmly escorted her out of the CCU into the family waiting area and stayed to speak with her while I remained with Mr. King and administered a dose of previously ordered pain medication.

He was dying. I could see on the monitor that his heart was failing. I made sure he was comfortable and stood by his bedside as I literally watched the life drain out of him. Witnessing this death was like watching two cars crashing in front of me. I felt completely helpless. It didn't take very long. Maybe fifteen minutes in total. When I sensed the end was near, I removed his oxygen mask and called his daughter in. She was calmer by then and had accepted the fact that her father was going to die tonight. She just wanted to be with him. She sat on the side of his bed and took his hand, laid her head on his chest, and said goodbye. She started crying quietly, and we turned down the volume on the monitors so she wouldn't be alerted to the flatline when it arrived. By the time his daughter looked up to see what was happening, we told her he was gone. She nodded and started to cry again, more softly this time. She patted her father on the chest and excused herself to go call family.

The nurse and I stood on either side of the bed, looking at each other. It made perfect sense and no sense at all.

Was this how it was supposed to happen? Had we done the right thing? I knew we had, but it was still unsettling. I was conflicted: I was there to learn what to do, but I was being asked to do nothing. Was that still doing something, just in a different way?

Perhaps speaking with the family was just as important as administering pain medication. This was the value of a clinical apprenticeship over a formal classroom: I could learn the *art* of practicing medicine. But I was haunted by the sense that I could have done something more, that in my inaction, I had failed to give Mr. King's daughter some vital element that would have made his death a little bit easier for her.

I had no idea, at the time, what that was.

———

Although I went on to choose family medicine with maternity care as my subspecialty and rarely had to deal with the death of my patients, that didn't mean I didn't sometimes encounter mortality. These are the kinds of stories you don't often hear about from doctors and nurses who deliver babies. We prefer to focus on the positive, on the joys and the wonder of birth. But my years in maternity care also forced me to face some of life's most anguishing moments.

I will always remember one couple in particular. I was on call at the hospital, covering for my colleagues, when the labor and delivery ward called me to the floor. A couple had arrived from home and were ready to begin their planned labor. Julia was twenty weeks pregnant and carrying a baby with a terminal genetic disease. The baby had recently died, and Julia was being admitted to the hospital to labor and deliver her stillborn daughter. I suspected it would be a difficult, emotional night.

We had a special area on the labor and delivery ward for these kinds of situations, away from the other actively laboring women, so it was quiet and private.

The way my call system was organized, I had not yet met Julia, or her husband, Doug, before that day. They were both in their early to mid-thirties, he a salesman, she an accountant. They had been eager to start their family, she explained, and were understandably devastated with the results of their genetic screening.

Doug was not especially talkative, and given the circumstances, I didn't expect otherwise. Though I often tried to meet people where they were, this was not an occasion when I believed silence would be helpful. We spoke about what would likely happen. It wasn't easy, but we discussed whether they wanted pictures of their baby, a footprint, perhaps, or to hold her.

Doug answered first and made it clear he did not want to hold his daughter. It wasn't that he didn't love her, he explained, but he was scared of what he might see. Julia, on the other hand, was certain she wanted to hold her daughter. She wondered if the baby would feel cold, and she seemed relieved when I said her daughter would feel warm. Doug and Julia had obviously talked about all of this beforehand, and they seemed certain of their choices.

The room was quiet as I placed the laminaria in Julia's cervix to stimulate her labor. I checked back infrequently at first. But as Julia's body kicked into labor later that night, things started happening quickly: Contractions that began sporadically were steadily arriving every three or four minutes. Doug was pacing by the window. As her contractions continued to mount, Julia had plenty of medication for the physical pain, but her tears became steadier. Julia delivered her daughter very quickly and, to her great surprise, with physical ease.

I took their tiny, lifeless baby, no bigger than a grown man's hand, off to the side and did a quick scan. She had many of the physical findings we expected of her condition, but at this early stage, not much would be glaringly obvious to her parents. I wrapped her in a blanket to present to Julia, first checking, as promised, to see if she was ready. She nodded that she was. Doug had retreated to a chair in the corner of the room and was crying quietly into his hands. I handed the tiny girl to Julia and watched with a lump in my throat as she held her daughter, tears rolling down her cheeks. I didn't move. I didn't speak. This simply had to unfold.

After two minutes of keeping her eyes closed and holding her baby away from her body, Julia opened her eyes, took a breath, and looked down at her daughter. She brought her closer to her own chest. She began inspecting her face. After some thought, she commented out loud that she had her grandfather's eyes. Doug got up and quietly came over to the side of the bed, but he didn't dare reach out. He looked at his wife, and he watched as she continued to examine their baby girl. He finally looked down, and after a moment, he agreed about the shape of her eyes. He looked back at Julia and they smiled at each other. And so began the complete inspection of their daughter. Julia slowly opened the blanket, revealing the shiny, translucent skin one bit at a time. She eventually opened the wrapping completely and fully explored the little body: her hands with five fingers each, and her feet, each with five perfectly distinct tiny toes. Julia was whispering her findings to herself, but at some point, she began talking to her daughter and telling her about the relatives she had taken after. She told her that she loved her.

After ten minutes, there was a noticeable change. Julia was still sitting in the hospital bed with her daughter nestled in close, but she was no longer talking. She closed her eyes once again and laid her head back on the pillow and began crying, harder than before. Julia looked exhausted, as if the sobs were being pulled out of her, painfully, every few seconds. Doug was close by, but neither spoke. When Julia next opened her eyes, she looked down at her daughter and began wrapping her slowly back up in the blanket. Ever so carefully, she tended to her task.

When she was done, as if it were the most natural thing he would do, Doug took the baby, sat back down in the corner chair, and cradled her. Tears rolled down his cheeks as he leaned in close and whispered something to her. He looked up at me for the first time and told me her name. It was unusual but lovely, meaning a little gem from the heavens. Julia explained where it came from, and then Doug confirmed with her that they had said their final goodbyes. He handed their daughter gently back to me, so small there was more blanket than baby.

I remembered I had work to do. I handed the baby carefully to the nurse outside the room who would care for the body, then returned to check on Julia. I began by acknowledging their loss. I checked that there were no signs of abnormal bleeding and that all was medically stable. Then I explained the next steps they could expect: the milk that would likely come in, the follow-up plans they'd need to arrange.

Before they left the hospital several hours later, I returned to tell them what I believed I had witnessed. Like any other new parents, they had met their daughter today. They had examined her, and recognized her, and loved her as their own. They'd also had the incredibly difficult task of saying goodbye, and they had done that too. I had been there for countless births, the joy, the physical release. But this was something else. That Julia and Doug could meet their daughter and say goodbye in such a short period of time showed incredible strength. No doubt, they would continue to mourn their loss for a long time to come. I told them they were extraordinary parents and that I would not soon forget them or their beautiful daughter. I never have.

It's true, there was no official training during those first few months in the "art" of providing an assisted death, but I often thought about Doug and Julia. They reminded me there was much more to the work than choosing which drug to administer; that maybe my role during such a great transition was more than just to guide, it was to respectfully witness; that sometimes my job was to reflect back what I was observing in the most compassionate way possible.

As for what to call the "events"—the radio interviewer's uncertainty had mirrored my own. What should I call these assisted deaths? After I took some time to think about it, the solution became clear to me. Among professional colleagues, I would call them "procedures," but within my family and with Karen at the office, I started calling each event a "delivery." It was a nod to my maternity background but also a fitting shorthand for how I saw my role. At one end, I was helping deliver a baby, usually into life. At the other end, I was helping deliver a person out of intolerable suffering and through to their death. I liked the symmetry the term evoked, the poetry of it. Turned out, my patients like it too.

CHAPTER 9

AS THE LONG DAYS OF August drew on, I was beginning to recognize how much had changed since I'd assisted Harvey's death in June. I no longer stood in front of my closet deliberating about what to wear: I wasn't as anxious about the prospect of my day, and I knew a simple pair of pants and a blouse did the trick. I was no longer daunted by trying to remember the eligibility criteria or filling out the reams of paperwork required for MAiD. I'd also become a lot more comfortable explaining the procedure to families and navigating the sometimes delicate conversations encouraging participation with my primary care colleagues. Throughout that summer, I received requests to provide MAiD in smaller cities farther north on Vancouver Island, as well as on the small Gulf Islands between here and the mainland. There were appeals from families to fly to the northern, interior, and coastal towns of BC. Travel to these regions could involve provincial ferries, private water taxis, solo driving, or flight. It also called for considerable amounts of time away from home and, I had to admit, a certain sense of adventure. In the first few months, I took those ferries, propeller planes, highways, and water taxis. And it wasn't just me. My new colleagues did the same. Until more clinicians stepped forward to provide the care, we felt obliged to do our very best for those who were suffering and asking for help.

In those earliest months, it didn't occur to me to put parameters around the work; I hadn't any idea how busy I was going to be or what the demand would be like. If a patient needed me, I did my best to be there. If they wanted to die in the early evening, I said yes. I was ready and willing to go wherever the work took me, and I felt compelled to make myself available for what was, after all, a life-and-death situation. I sometimes missed out on time with my own family as a result, but I was certain that my schedule would settle down soon and I'd be able to reclaim some balance. As one of only a few people involved in this new work, I was in uncharted territory, wading through both practical and personal challenges. In this respect, I felt immensely grateful to have a growing community of supportive colleagues waiting at the end of an email, eager to share stories, problems, and advice.

Although we were protective of the small group we had created after Amsterdam, we had also seen the potential benefit of cautiously expanding our ranks. Few clinicians in the country were speaking openly about providing MAiD, but we suspected there were others who might be working in isolation. We reached out to the few we had heard of in other regions, and some of them brought along a close colleague or two. Lianne and Tim joined in from Nova Scotia. Ed and Chantal signed up from Ontario, followed quickly by Gerry, Jean, and Bill. Two or three more clinicians from the prairies got involved. We soon included a lone doc from Alberta, and within the first two months, our numbers grew to twenty. We were a diverse bunch—family physicians like me, a number of nurse practitioners, a handful of anesthesiologists, a few palliative care clinicians, an ob-gyn, and at least one internist.

After my experiences with Louise and Charlie, I asked if others were encountering similar issues: Were people finding clinicians reluctant to get involved in the MAiD process? Was it challenging to source medications or willing pharmacists where they lived? What was happening with MAiD provision in their provinces, cities, and towns? The law regulating MAiD was federal, but health care was administered provincially, and we soon discovered significant discrepancies between the multiple regions.

"Here in Ontario, we have to report everything to the coroner," wrote Ed from Toronto. "In fact, we have to call the coroner's office from the home of the patient before we leave them after the death. We need to review the entire case, our determination of eligibility, everything. The coroner then speaks with the family, on the spot, over the phone, to verify the details. It's really cumbersome, it takes forever, and it's awkward for everyone."

A colleague from the prairie provinces in central-western Canada had a different conundrum: "What are you writing as cause of death on the death certificate? Do you write MAiD, or the underlying illness? Here in Saskatchewan we've been told it must say 'suicide,' but that just doesn't seem right to me. And it certainly doesn't sit well with many of the families."

If I posted a question in the morning, I could expect an answer or two within an hour, several by midday, and for some topics, an ongoing thread for another day or two. We were often able to help each other by sharing what we had already learned. Solutions that had worked in one region were offered to another and then adapted for local conditions. Jonathan and Tanja had spent the last two months setting up a MAiD practice in a rural community; they got to work creating a handbook for others who wanted to do the same, sharing it with colleagues across the country. When several people reported that their patients were having trouble finding witnesses for their MAiD request forms, another colleague suggested contacting Dying With Dignity Canada. In Ontario, she told us, DWDC had started sending volunteer witnesses to homes and health care facilities. There was talk of expanding the program to other regions. Perhaps they could help? Ed shared a comprehensive, templated assessment form he'd developed, several of us shared our slide decks for giving talks on the topic of MAiD, and everyone opened up about what had worked well and what had not when assisting their patients to die.

Of course, there were some issues no one had a solution for.

"I know this might seem awkward but . . . any of you getting paid for this work yet?"

Every province was different, but none of them had billing codes set up for MAiD. There was no legitimate way to bill the provincial health care plans for our work, so we were all looking for reasonable substitutes.

"I'm billing a geriatric assessment," said one colleague.

"I'm billing it as palliative care," said another.

"I'm not billing anything at all."

Some provinces, like BC, had instituted interim fee codes, but they paid shockingly little, so many of us didn't bother. We preferred to get together and propose an alternative fee guide based on comparable existing fee codes, but our request was languishing, wrapped in red tape, in some administrator's inbox.

Within our growing email group, we felt safe exploring the multitude of new issues we faced. Just as valuable as the practical advice was our willingness to share stories of anonymized patients. We spoke of the decisions they made for their final hours and our own reactions to what we had seen and heard.

In only two months, I'd met some people who were strong-willed and knew exactly what they wanted for their final moments and others who were simply desperate for help and pleading for an end to their suffering. For some people, planning for death was only as complicated as deciding between two dates. For others, it was a more elaborate affair. Patients' choices for how they wanted to die, whether alone or in a quiet setting with classical music playing, or out on the back deck with gathered guests, rock music, and champagne, often reflected who they were.

"Today I listened as two sons read 'Ode to a Nightingale,'" someone posted. "Well, really performed it for their mother just before we began. Although we were all sitting on the side of her bed, it was like being in the theater . . . they were amazing. I'm sure at least one must work professionally onstage. She'd requested this reading as a last gift, and although physically exhausted, she whispered several lines along with them. It was clearly very meaningful to her."

"At this afternoon's event I heard the most stirring piece of bagpipe music," another colleague wrote. "Not normally my instrument of choice, but it was really very moving. And it was a refreshing change from Sinatra's 'My Way.'"

These were the little slivers of beauty, humor, and tragedy that we were all witnessing.

Jonathan piped in from the Comox Valley: "I was mortified recently when I realized I hadn't turned off my cell phone, and it rang as my patient was passing into a coma." I cringed as I read his email, and I made a mental note to add "make sure all cell phones are turned off" to my growing pre-event checklist. "But then there was a pause, I'm happy to report, as the gathered guests and I smiled in recognition of the familiar, befitting ringtone . . . it's the opening riff from 'Stairway to Heaven.'"

I chuckled when I read the end of that post, and I couldn't resist adding my own recent experience with a patient's playlist. "My favorite so far was the gentleman who'd queued up a song on his stereo and insisted someone hit play just as I began injecting. He had a huge grin on his face as he fell asleep to AC/DC's 'Highway to Hell.'"

I was intrigued to know what others did beforehand to feel grounded and ready for a delivery, and afterward, when they came home from a death.

"Where I work," Jyothi began, "I must draw up all my own medications. I purposely do that in another room, on my own, and in the patient's home. It doesn't take too long, and I use that time to reflect on the patient, what I know about them and their life. It's my own way of clearing my mind and staying focused on the person I am caring for. I find it very centering."

"In my community," Shelley offered, "we always have at least two members of our team involved in provisions, and afterward, we always have a debriefing for everyone involved. I personally try to take the afternoon off after a provision, and I journal about each patient that I care for."

A newer member of the group chimed in: "I had trouble sleeping the night before the procedure, and I asked my partner to come drive me home afterward. I was completely emotionally drained."

"I like to take a couple hours to myself after it's over, but it's not because of emotional drain," said Tim. "Rather, everything in life seems that much easier for me to appreciate—my kids, my hobbies, even the fresh air."

Although there was a range of reactions and suggestions, I was relieved that everyone seemed to be coping—or learning how to.

Our colleagues in Amsterdam had emphasized the importance of self-care, and we continued to share ways in which we tried to strike the right balance, staying committed to our patients while also remaining aware of our own needs and those of our families. Everyone understood this was important.

Sometimes, though, the toughest lessons came not from one another but from the patients themselves.

———

Katie had been a vigorous, active woman who was happily married for sixty-nine years, but she'd remained staunchly independent. She and her husband, Ken, had lived on the same acreage for seven decades, and they had built, cultivated, and reaped its bounty with their own hands. Ken came from a family of eleven children, Katie from a family of fifteen. They'd raised six children of their own, and she'd helped to care for the entire family, their children, grandchildren, and great-grandchildren, keeping everyone close by.

At the age of ninety, Katie's heart had had enough. Due to a combination of valvular disease and erratic rhythms, it was not proving responsive to any medical treatment, and Katie declined quickly over a few months. At her request, her family doctor called my office and asked me to provide a consultation.

I don't know how many acres they had on their homestead, but it's a beautiful property; set high up on the side of a small mountain, overlooking wild greenery and rugged landscapes. While the land felt vast, the house was a modest structure with an open-plan kitchen, dining and living space, and smaller bedrooms decorated with Shaker-style wooden furniture.

When we first met, Katie was lying on her side in the bedroom with a quilted blanket covering her up to the chest. I'd guess she weighed no more than seventy-five pounds. Her mouth was open, she was breathing rapidly, and her lips were parched. It was difficult for me to imagine Katie in any other state, but even so, I tried to picture her as the bustling, busy farmer she surely must have been.

"I'm so tired . . . I can't do anything," she explained. "I can't even sit up."

Her eligibility was not in dispute, and we moved forward somewhat swiftly, with Katie's cardiologist providing the second assessment. On the morning of the procedure, I arrived with Jessica, the wonderful nurse who helped me with IVs when I was out in the local community. MAiD was never routine, and no two procedures were the same, but by now Jessica and I had begun to establish a rhythm to our work. We found we could often anticipate people's needs, whether the family's or each other's, so after introductions, Jessica went into Katie's room to get herself set up while I called everyone together for a meeting in the living room.

A group of twelve or so was gathered—Katie's husband, several of her children (men and women in their sixties), some with partners, and a handful of in-laws. I reviewed with them what was about to take place. Katie had originally wanted to die in the living room so there would be space for everyone who wanted to attend. We considered transporting her from the bedroom, but her son Jim spoke against the idea, noting that moving her at this point would be physically cruel. Katie willingly conceded, so we set ourselves up at her bedside. The room's size limited the bystanders to seven or eight; the rest remained behind in the living room. We packed ourselves in tightly around her bed. Ken was sitting on a small wooden chair to Katie's left, holding her hand but saying little.

Katie was exhausted and ready to proceed. I went through the steps of asking if anyone had anything left to say. They had already said all their goodbyes. Naturally, I offered Katie the last word.

"I love you all . . . Don't be sad . . . Take good care of each other."

I started the medication. There was silence as she fell asleep with the first injection. Thirty seconds passed.

"Strawberry jam."

I believe it was Katie's youngest daughter, behind me on my right, who had spoken. I tried not to react, but it was an odd statement at a time like this. There was utter silence. Then all of a sudden, I heard a humming of agreement from someone across the room.

"Christmas cake," from another corner. That prompted a quiet "Oh yeah" from someone on the left.

"Knitted wool socks for everyone."

A slight chuckle. The idea was settling in.

"Taking the grandchildren without any notice."

"Canning tomatoes."

Every few seconds, another memory. Every few seconds for the entire length of the procedure, another tribute to something she was known for.

It was stunning, this spontaneous outpouring, and strangely powerful in its simplicity. Outside the window, a large oak tree cast dappled light into the room and across Katie's quilted blanket. I looked on at this beautiful moment unfolding before me.

After I left Katie's house that day, I drove to the waterfront, taking the long way back to my office. I couldn't help reflecting on what I had been privileged to witness. I had learned a lot about Katie during those eight minutes. I'd learned the ways she had touched the lives of her children and her grandchildren, the infinite little things for which she was known, loved, and appreciated. Katie had lived her life with generous intention, and her family had celebrated her with a profound and fitting tribute. She was clearly the matriarch, the special force behind the shaping of her family. I was almost fifty years old and hoped for many more decades of life, but when my time came, I wondered, what would be said about me? What would I hope to be remembered for? I pulled over and parked the car in a small lookout directly across from the Olympic Mountains, the sunlight chasing shadows of clouds across their peaks.

I thought of that scene in the farmhouse bedroom, and I asked myself: Whose hand would I want holding mine? Jean-Marc's, I was certain. After twenty years of marriage, it felt good to be sure this was true. With my children nearby? Yes, I'd hope so. But who else was important in my life, and why? Had I even spoken with them recently? Would there be a crowd to pack in tightly around me or only a significant one or two? Who would stand by my side when death was near?

Katie's family had shared the meaningful gestures that they instinctively associated with her. Would this be true for me? I had given up twenty-four-hour on-call maternity work to be more present for my husband and children, but I questioned whether I was any more present than I had been before. Was it possible I had become so consumed by my new work that I had overlooked my commitment to family? Only last week I had missed a family dinner because I'd stayed to reminisce with relatives of a man whose life I had helped to end. I loved learning about people and their lives; it was part of what inspired me in this work. I had a tendency to bring these stories home and to get lost in the detail of my cases. There was nothing inherently wrong with this—I wanted to model for my son and daughter the importance of finding a vocation in life—but I once again wondered if it left me less attuned to the happenings within my own home. Was I paying enough attention?

Ultimately, what was more important, being constantly available for my work or being more consistently available to my family?

I restarted my engine, turned away from the water, but carried on reflecting. How different this felt from my maternity patients, where my own life experience helped inform my practice and was hopefully of value to new parents. Now I was faced with a patient's life experience helping to inform me. Katie inspired me to do better, to be more present for the people of my life, and to live with the generous intention that I knew I wanted.

I wondered what else I might learn from my MAiD patients.

Not long after I assisted at Katie's death, I made a vow to myself that from now on, as much as I was committed to my work, there would be no MAiD on weekends or after five p.m. I'd build my schedule around those limits, shielding some time for myself and my family. I wondered if I would be able to stick to it. I hoped, if ever I was tempted to break the rule, I might pause and remember Katie.

CHAPTER 10

HELEN WAS IN HER SEVENTIES by the time I met her. Fifty-six years of chain-smoking had taken their toll, and lung disease had left her haggard and frail. Despite maximum medical therapy and close follow-up by a respirologist, by the time I assessed her, she couldn't walk to the bathroom without her oxygen tank, and she would become short of breath just from talking. But, she confided, she had loved to smoke. Helen had given up her beloved cigarettes only when the need for home oxygen became absolute. She missed smoking dearly, and she dreamed of one last cigarette before she died.

Helen's grandson, Tim, had come to live with her in a small town outside of Victoria at the age of seven while his mother was in rehab, and he stayed his entire adolescence while his mother struggled with addiction issues. Now thirty-one and between jobs, Tim still shared Helen's two-bedroom apartment, but whenever I asked about him, she rolled her eyes and waved me away. When I pushed for more information, she told me Tim was "not a good person," suggesting he was self-centered and irresponsible. She accused him of stealing from her for over a decade, of lying to her consistently, and of fueling his gambling habit by selling her possessions. Helen seemed to alternate between being angry at Tim and scared of him, but mostly, she didn't want to discuss him. She hadn't allowed him to be involved in any of my visits.

When I arrived on the morning of her scheduled death, I found Helen flanked by her three close girlfriends. At least one of these women had been present at each of our prior meetings, and together they were caring for Helen with groceries, housecleaning, and companionship. These women had been friends for nearly fifty years and had regaled me with stories about their youthful escapades. I could picture them as if in a movie reel: dressed for a night out, walking arm in arm, laughing and turning heads. They were all in their early seventies now, and their lifetime of sisterhood and loyalty was enviable. They had shared every milestone, and now they were going to be here for Helen's death.

To my surprise, on the day of Helen's delivery, Tim was present too.

He was wearing an oversize hoodie and was repetitively twirling some sort of vaping device in his hand. He appeared restless, even irritated, and he stayed mostly in another room while I prepared for the procedure. Helen, like many I'd seen in her position, seemed calm, determined, and ready. But at the end of our private chat, when I asked her to sign the paper to provide her final consent, she hesitated. "Wait a moment," she said, "I'm not quite ready."

This was a first in my experience with MAiD. I had never sensed even a hint of hesitancy in her.

"Okay. Do you have more questions about what will happen?" I asked. "Or do you mean you need more time?"

She paused, picked up the pen, then stopped again. "No, I'm just not ready yet."

"No problem, really. I understand. Why don't I head out and call you in a few days to see how you're feeling about things? Would that be okay?"

"What? No, you stay right here! I just need to talk to Tim. Go get Tim for me, will you? And get the girls. I need them by my side."

I asked the others to come into the living room. They were expecting us to proceed, so I mentioned that we weren't quite ready. The ladies looked as mystified as I was at the news, but when I told Tim that his grandmother wanted to speak to him first, a smug expression crossed his face. He sat down in a chair across from Helen and, taking her hand in his, asked what she wanted to say.

Generally, once a patient had decided on a day, they intuitively understood that they had a window of opportunity to tie up loose ends. Some patients were able to speak to friends in distant parts of the country to say goodbye. Other patients wanted to settle business or other practical matters, such as transferring passwords and important information. They often told me how much they appreciated the chance to deal with their affairs before it was too late. And then there were the patients who had expressions of love, or pain, or gratitude, or forgiveness that they wanted to share with certain family and friends in their final hours together. Frequently, I was in the room for those conversations. More often than not, the words spoken were tender and the scenes almost unbearably poignant. But in Helen's case, this last exchange took an unexpected turn.

For a woman who became short of breath when speaking, Helen did not hold back.

"What kind of a man steals from his own grandmother?" she began. "I raised you to be better than this. You've squandered all your opportunities. You drink, and you smoke, and you take all those drugs . . . you think that I don't know?"

Tim was too shocked to say anything at first. When he started to protest, Helen cut him off. "With my dying words, I warn you to smarten up," she told him, her tone acidic. "No one will love you like I did. No one else will put up with your lies. You were mean, and you took advantage of me, and now that's over. You're getting nothing from me when I go. No money, no furniture, nothing but my advice to clean up your crap!"

Helen's words seemed to nudge Tim from shock into anger. He stormed out of the room, fists clenched, and left the apartment. I could hear him pacing and muttering to himself in the hallway through the partly open door. Helen asked us to wait. No one said a word. Everyone was dumbfounded. I wandered into the apartment's kitchen and exchanged whispered contingency plans with Jessica, who was providing IV support for me that day.

"Not sure where this is going . . . ," I said.

"Yeah, this is a first," she answered. She was smiling but serious. "I suggest you keep those extra medications close to you at all times."

Tim eventually came back in and sat down across from Helen. Once again, he reached for her hand. He took a deep breath, looked slightly to the side, and began to speak. "Look, Nana, I'm sorry things got so out of hand—"

But Helen wasn't ready to listen. She cut him off and resumed dressing down her grandson. I remained close to the kitchen, trying not to intrude. I worried she was creating a risk for us all; there was no way of knowing whether Tim would capitulate or explode. I held my breath. He remained motionless and silent. Then, finally, I heard his sobs.

"Jesus, Nan . . . I've been such an ass," he began.

Tim begged his grandmother for forgiveness, admitted he had been cruel, told her he was going to miss her. She listened, nodded, patted his hand, and told him to leave the room. He was stunned and didn't move.

"I'm ready now, Dr. Green," she said, beckoning me, "and I don't want Tim anywhere near me." She turned back to her grandson for the final blow. "Get out now, ya hear? And smarten up when I'm gone!"

She withdrew her hand and looked away. Tim stood up, bewildered. Red-faced, confused, he bent down and placed an awkward kiss on her right cheek, then left the room.

Helen turned to me and said: "I needed to get that out of my system. I'm ready now, let's do this."

Driving home after Helen's death, I was struck by her resolve. Decades of unspoken emotions had come to the surface, and I was somewhat delighted for her that she'd taken the opportunity to get things off her chest. She seemed wholly satisfied with herself.

The interim between leaving a patient's side and arriving back at my office or home was proving to be a fertile time for thought and reflection. I had subconsciously started to project myself and my own family dynamics into whatever scenario I had just encountered. As a result, I imagined myself in a variety of roles—sometimes as the grieving daughter or wife, sometimes as the dying mother. The reality was that at some point in my life, I would have to assume at least one of those roles. It was excruciating at times, but if I allowed the various scenarios to play out in my mind, it could also prove insightful.

With Helen, I could clearly see unresolved emotion, and with that, I thought of my father.

———

My dad had died almost exactly ten years before, in October 2006, the same week I happened to be home in Halifax for Canadian Thanksgiving. Although Thanksgiving does not have the importance in Canada that it does in the U.S., it was a good excuse to spend a long weekend together. This was during the time when I had young children and was busy building my maternity practice in Victoria. Traveling to Halifax on the East Coast meant a minimum of two flights and an entire day's journey. The night before I left, my father called to say he was in the emergency room. He'd been in and out of the hospital many times over the past few years. Although only sixty-five, he was diabetic, morbidly obese, had undergone open-heart surgery, and had an amputated leg. He informed me that he wouldn't be home over the weekend, I'd have to visit him in the hospital, and he hoped that would be all right.

My relationship with my father was strained at the best of times. It was limited since his divorce from my mother, superficial by nature, often centered around his health, and not particularly nourishing to me personally. This was a man who I felt had never really been there for me during my childhood. I had begun to come to terms with him when I was in university, and after I became a parent myself, I'd started the slow process of acknowledging his strengths alongside his deficiencies. But it often felt to me like our relationship was a duty of sorts and one I couldn't seem to break away from. I knew he loved me, I knew he cared, but I'd learned over the years that you cannot ask of someone what they're not capable of providing. He had divorced and remarried three more times since my mother, so there were often new personalities to contend with on my visits, which probably didn't help. I kept my expectations low, tried my best to fulfill what I thought were my obligations, and hoped my children would know their grandfather. Perhaps their relationship could flourish in ways only a grandparent-grandchild relationship could. Though my father and I lived five thousand kilometers (over three thousand miles) apart, saw each other twice a year at most, and rarely spoke on the phone, I felt bound to keep trying.

Those were the days when I stayed with my mother whenever I visited Halifax. Since the late 1990s, Mom had been battling a chronic, progressive neurologic condition that was slowly gnawing away at her every physical function, stealing her pride and independence, while leaving her mind intact. It was always tough to see her diminished, but her resilience was impressive—she hadn't let her illness stop her from divorcing her second husband.

I called to give her the heads-up that my father was in the hospital. My parents had never resolved their animosity, and I often found myself caught between them. As soon as I was in a room with either of my parents, I unconsciously reverted to my childhood role. In my everyday life, I was a mother, a doctor, and an adult. But in Halifax, I went back to being stuck in the middle, seeking to appease both parents. I spent years navigating that dynamic: making time to see them separately, finding ways to juggle graduations, holidays, and weddings. Managing those relationships was a challenge, often on a practical level and always on an emotional one—I felt guilty if I spent too much time with one or if I made time or special allowances for the other.

It seemed this trip would be no different.

"Well . . . I'm sorry to hear he's in the hospital again," my mother responded. "Will you be going over to see him?"

Did she actually expect I might be in Halifax at a time when my father was in the hospital and *not* plan to see him?

With a certain amount of trepidation, I took my children, then aged six and eight, to see their zayde—the Yiddish word for grandfather—in the hospital. My father's face lit up when we walked in the room. He was delighted to see them. The kids were too shy to get close at first, but they eventually followed my somewhat forced lead, and by the end, we were all glad we had come. The next day, I received a call from my father's wife, Linda, whom he had married four years before. My father was doing much worse, and she suggested I come by without the kids. I visited that afternoon, and he was indeed in bad shape, barely awake and short of breath. I promised to come back the next day, and when I did, things had not improved.

I was scheduled to fly home with my children the following morning, but I couldn't shake the feeling that leaving was unwise. I didn't want to get on a plane for the West Coast if my father was at risk of dying. But my kids didn't need to be here. Of course, they also couldn't travel alone. I called Jean-Marc and we discussed the situation. He agreed it would be best if I stayed a few more days and the children returned home. We decided they would fly unaccompanied to Calgary, and Jean-Marc would fly there to meet them. I got Sam and Sara on the plane, and I stayed until it took off (as was required), then promptly returned to the hospital.

All day, my father's condition worsened. Linda loved him dearly, and she was understandably upset and looking for guidance. By afternoon, we were in discussions with the intensive care unit (ICU) about whether he ought to be transferred to their care. Linda eagerly deferred to me as the one with medical knowledge.

Suddenly, I found myself in a position I had not sought out. I was being asked if my father would want to be intubated and admitted to the ICU; if he would want to be resuscitated. I was being asked to make these decisions on behalf of a man I felt I barely knew. I'd never discussed these matters with him. I had only recently come to a modus vivendi with our strained relationship. As far as I was concerned, he was being cared for by his wife, someone who knew him far better than I did. The last thing I wanted was to make his end-of-life decisions, but what else could I do? I found myself feeling angry, resentful, and above all, helpless.

I called my brother in Vancouver. He was upset. He was closer to my father than I, and I secretly would have been pleased if our roles had been reversed. We agreed our father would not want to be intubated; we agreed he would likely never be extubated. There was little choice. Linda confirmed she was on board with the plan, and we spoke to the ICU physician together. No ICU, thank you, he would remain on this floor and be kept comfortable. The doctor warned us he might die overnight. And he did.

I was standing at the foot of the bed when it happened. Linda was draped over his chest, weeping. I watched my father take his last few breaths.

I was utterly uncomfortable. I would have preferred to be just about anywhere else on earth. There was no resolution of our unfinished business, only the reality of what was happening and my inescapable role within it. So I was the one who told Linda he had finally stopped breathing. I was the one who called for the doctor when I knew it was time to pronounce him dead. I was the one who held Linda when she finally separated herself from his body. I was the one who called the rabbi, and I was the one who called my brother. Thankfully, he was the one who called our uncles and aunt.

When I told my mother that he had died, she was astonished. I spoke with the chevra kadisha, the volunteer group within the Jewish community who organize and perform the final rites for the deceased and ensure the body is never left alone. I went to bed but didn't sleep. My confusion about my relationship with my father and my ambivalence about my role as he died had left me reeling. In the morning, I met with the rabbi and planned the details of the funeral. I made decisions about the shiva, where it would be held and who would arrange the food. I went to the local Walmart and bought some appropriate black clothing. My brother met me at the funeral home after he got into town, and we attended the funeral the next day. We hosted the shiva gathering at the hotel. We sat with our father's siblings after everyone had left and ate one of his cheesecakes, for which he was famous. It was the last one in his freezer, and it was delicious.

I felt like an adult in Halifax for the first time, and I wasn't sure I liked it.

My father's death was my first personal experience of the turmoil that can surround the passing of a family member, of things left unsaid and the range of emotions—the confusion and especially the fear—that arise when plans have never been discussed or even considered. What child (or spouse or sibling) wants the responsibility of these decisions? How can we ease this burden? By making our wishes known and speaking to one another *before* we end up in a coma in a hospital. Easier said than done, I know. I hadn't done it myself. But it was more than just planning that was important. My experience with Helen and her grandson, Tim, reminded me that letting hard feelings fester was not helpful to anyone either.

One of the most memorable moments of that entire week was when I was walking out of my mother's condominium on the way to plan the funeral with the rabbi. I turned to see my mother standing in her doorway.

"You know," my mother said, "we had some pretty good times, your father and I."

Her words floored me. I had never heard her say anything like that before. The animosity during and after their divorce had weighed heavily on me and perhaps on her as well. I was relieved by her statement in a way I never would have expected. What would it have felt like, for all of us, for her to have admitted that a little earlier?

As I began to settle into my work as a MAiD provider, my experience with my father gave me some insight into the emotional turmoil that families can experience as they confront the death of a loved one—and a curiosity about how things might be concluded differently. At the same time, my new experiences tending to dying patients and their family members were prompting me to reflect more deeply on my own relationships, leading me to reconsider not only past events but how I hoped things might unfold in the future.

Part 3

FALL
BECOMES
WINTER

CHAPTER 11

FALL IN VICTORIA OFTEN CREEPS up unexpectedly—you can be forgiven for not noticing the change of seasons. Our midday warmth and sunshine can continue well into October, but the unmistakable signs of autumn are the quickly changing light, as five-thirty a.m. sunrises and the accompanying birdsong give way to progressively darker mornings, distinctly cooler air, and the familiar, soothing sounds of ships calling to one another from the Strait of Georgia or Juan de Fuca. I love the feel of autumn, it's by far my favorite season.

On days when I knew I was going to end someone's life, I developed a new routine. I first took my dog for a walk on the beach. I relished this morning ritual with Benji, out in the fresh air, mountains in full view, free from the responsibilities of the day. I'd trained myself not to look at my phone during that precious hour. In the mornings, the beach was filled with rambunctious dogs chasing birds and balls, greeting newcomers and old friends alike, facilitating introductions, and encouraging their owners to live more fully in the moment.

As the seasons shifted, I found I was focusing less on the minutiae of providing care—where to get IV tubing and when to fax forms and to whom—and becoming more attuned to other, more subtle aspects of the job that hadn't been obvious to me at an earlier stage. I noted that the process of determining if someone was eligible tended to be stressful for the patient, so I proceeded as quickly as I responsibly could through interviews and health records until we had a clear answer. There was terrible disappointment for patients who didn't meet all the requirements, but as soon as I said the words "You're eligible," a transformation occurred: a physical relaxing of the body—a slight drop of the shoulders, often a smile spreading across the face, an almost imperceptible nod. The sense of relief was palpable. Telling someone they were eligible for an assisted death was proving therapeutic in and of itself. Once my patients were no longer fearful of how they might die, they focused intently on living and allowed themselves to more fully embrace the life they had left. MAiD, in this way, was less about dying and more about how people wanted to live.

Every now and again, confirming a patient's eligibility led them to delay wanting to schedule their death, if only by an extra week or two. Just knowing they could take back some control at the end of life had the effect of (objectively) reducing suffering, at times giving a patient the will, the freedom, to try to live a little longer. As every physician knows, sometimes just prescribing an anti-anxiety medication is enough to reduce a patient's stress levels, even if the pills remain untouched inside the bathroom cabinet.

In the early months of providing MAiD, we all made mistakes: little things like missed signatures or improper dating on witnessing forms. More crucially, we were trying to strike a balance between too restrictive or too liberal in our interpretations of eligibility. The law was new and much of it untested. By this time, I had the requirements memorized—I no longer had to review them before an initial meeting—but the precise understanding of what constituted "a grievous and irremediable condition" remained obscure. Some parts of the definition were very specific, other parts a little vague, but one thing was abundantly clear: If I broke the law, if I assisted someone when those criteria were not fulfilled, I was open to criminal prosecution and liable for up to fourteen years in prison. I was not interested in testing that threshold. The fear of getting things wrong was always in the back of my mind, and I suspect similar concerns kept the number of practitioners low.

By the fall of that year, my confidence was increasing, but I also had a new support system. If a clinical matter seemed unclear to me, I discussed it with my growing community of medical and nursing colleagues. For process questions, I had access to a number of trusted administrators, and being an academic, I could call upon a variety of scholars (legal and ethics, for example). The organization upon which I would call to defend me against a claim of medical malpractice, the Canadian Medical Protective Association (CMPA), is the same organization I would turn to in case of a criminal charge resulting from my work in assisted dying. First with Harvey, then with Louise, as with all the other patients I had helped, I called the CMPA. They had me explain the details of every MAiD request to counsel, send over my clinical notes with the medical records, answer any lingering questions, and leave the dossier with the lawyer to consider. Then they'd advise me on whether they believed the case was at high or low legal risk. During those early months, the situations all seemed straightforward and it felt reasonable to proceed.

Then came Nevin.

Nevin was a seventy-nine-year-old man living in a small Northern community several hours by plane from Victoria. We first spoke on the telephone. His voice on the line had a particular warmth but also a familiar cadence: The words were fired in short spaced bursts. He was trying to sound casual but he was holding his breath between salvos; the sound of a person in pain. Nevin told me he lived with Robert, eleven years his junior and his primary caregiver. As I got to know Nevin better, he let me know that they had been partners for the last thirty-seven years. On that first call, Nevin explained that he had been suffering with a number of strange and debilitating health issues for some time, but that recently they had become overwhelming.

It had all started four years earlier with blurred vision and a tingling on his cheek. Later came a headache at the base of his skull, and then facial pain that was intense, frequent, and crippling. Since then, he had lost his sense of taste, the hearing in his right ear, and, eventually, his sense of smell. More recently, his symptoms included the spread of a numbness so profound that he no longer required anesthesia in parts of his mouth for dental work. Where he wasn't numb, he was experiencing tremendous pain, and the pain pattern now included most of his head. He felt dizzy all the time and had fallen twice in the past two months, once breaking his wrist and spraining his elbow. He'd become extremely weak and increasingly frail. Although no one in his region was willing to provide an assisted death, his family doctor was supportive and amenable to being one of the assessors.

Nevin didn't think he could get to a hospital for a formal telemedicine session, so we agreed to meet via videoconference on Robert's iPad. I told Nevin that if he qualified, I would be willing to travel to assist him.

"The pain is constant, Dr. Green, always there, always present," he told me during our first meeting. "If I take my medications, it's a six out of ten, as you doctors like to say. Too many pills and I feel woozy in my head. Too few and the pain is even more unbearable. I keep it at a six or a seven so I can think straight. But it's always there, and it's terrible. The only time I don't feel it is when I am asleep, and I need different pills for that."

Nevin could no longer put anything solid in his mouth. Even drinking was becoming difficult. He'd lost twenty-seven pounds off his 145-pound frame in the last six weeks. He was dying. He knew it, his doctors knew it, his partner knew it, and now I knew it.

Nevin had visited six different specialists, in four different fields of medicine, including several pain specialists across two different cities. Between them, they had painted a confusing picture. Originally, he was diagnosed with late-onset multiple sclerosis, later with trigeminal neuralgia, and eventually a "connective tissue disorder of unknown origin." Recently, the possibility of a different diagnosis, amyloidosis, had arisen. This is a rare disease that occurs when an abnormal protein, called amyloid, builds up in the organs and interferes with normal function. It is not always easy to diagnose. The specialists were unable to be definitive, and the cornucopia of medications they prescribed didn't seem to control Nevin's deterioration. Meanwhile, he had decided to stop investigating the cause of his troubles;

the effort of going to specialized appointments had become unbearable. He was determined to die at home with Robert by his side and was resistant to any hospitalization. Nevin told me that if he didn't qualify for an assisted death, he would find a way to do it on his own. "There's a cliff edge I could probably find enough strength to topple over." But the idea of the cliff terrified Nevin. What if he didn't succeed?

When I asked about the support around him, he reiterated Robert was his rock and that he'd pledged to try to help him stay at home and arrange for an assisted death. At the same time, Nevin was aware that his increasing physical needs were becoming a challenge for Robert. He also mentioned a younger brother, Albie, with whom he was close but who was explicitly opposed to MAiD and was encouraging Nevin to get proper nursing support or go into a palliative care bed at the hospital: completely reasonable options. His brother's opposition made me nervous about proceeding. Until now, I'd always had the support of a patient's friends and family members prior to a scheduled death. I knew what would happen if I broke the law. But what if I legally proceeded with MAiD against the wishes of a loved one?

In fact, the law was quite clear that the decision was up to the patient. If he or she had the clinical capacity to make such a request—as long as that request wasn't coerced and eligibility criteria were met—I could legally assist that person no matter who objected. It could put me in an awkward position, but family and friends ultimately had no standing, and there would be no legal ramifications.

Of course, there were other avenues of complaint. An unhappy sibling, spouse, friend, or child could go to the medical regulatory body, the CPSBC, with a charge of professional misconduct and make a formal complaint. They might believe I had acted unprofessionally or was rude or dismissive. They might believe I hadn't followed the law or provincial guidelines in some way. They might be so overcome with grief that they wouldn't know who else to blame. The College's mandate is to protect the public, so it would take the complaint seriously, launch an investigation, gather and review the facts, obtain written statements, and, if required, interview those involved. They would set up a small panel authorized to consider the information and render a binding decision. The process would typically take six to twelve months. If professional misconduct was determined, the required course of action might include financial penalty, additional coursework, possible probation or restrictions on practice, even suspension or the revoking of a medical license. The CPSBC, like similar regulating bodies in other territories, had issued a professional practice standard on MAiD. It was different from the federal legislation in that it outlined what ought to be included in practitioners' interactions with patients: "Physicians must inform the patient requesting MAiD of the following . . ." I knew the language well, followed their suggestions, and felt safe from sanction as long as I adhered to the guideline as if it were law.

Angry family members were one thing; hungry prosecutors were another. Federal MAiD law involved the criminal code, so nonadherence, intentional or otherwise, carried significant potential ramifications. As a small community of providers in the early days of MAiD, my fellow practitioners and I were cautiously looking for signs of prosecutorial intention. Were the judiciary content to turn a blind eye to any good-faith early mistakes, or were they watching and waiting, ready to pounce, to make an example of a reckless colleague? No one I knew wanted to get this wrong. No one wanted to be made an example of, and no one wanted to go to jail. So far, no one I knew of had, and we wanted to keep it that way. All of this was in the back of my mind as I helped my early patients, but for the first time, as I contemplated assisting Nevin, the idea I might suffer a penalty if I agreed to proceed felt a little too real.

I could see that Nevin was adamant in his wish to move forward with MAiD, and in my opinion, he was eligible. But I felt a need to be cautious, so assuring his anonymity, I outlined a description of the case and sought various opinions.

One regulator I spoke with suggested the case was not so simple. He was not convinced such a patient met the criteria of having a grievous and irremediable condition. "I'm concerned about the lack of clarity around diagnosis," he said.

It was true: The specialists had not been clear on his diagnosis, but Nevin was unable to tolerate further investigation. What exactly was the definition of a grievous and irremediable condition?

The first requirement was that you must have a serious illness, disease, or disability. I knew Nevin had a serious illness, it's just that no one knew precisely what it was. But how accurate did a diagnosis have to be in order to qualify as serious? If a patient were riddled with metastatic cancer, for example, how important was it to know from which organ it started?

"Accurate diagnosis for Nevin is an academic pursuit at this point," I insisted. "An interesting but irrelevant question. He is acutely, actively dying."

The second requirement was that the patient be in an advanced state of decline in capability. What exactly did that mean, and who decided such matters? This was not especially clear to anyone and was frequently discussed in our email group.

"I think it means that you are no longer able to function in the way that you used to, because of your illness. And not just in a small way, but in an advanced way," a colleague suggested.

This might involve what clinicians call your activities of daily living— whether you can mobilize, dress yourself, feed yourself, or care for your own needs in the washroom. But it could mean other things as well.

"I think it's meant to be individualized to each person," someone else added. "If you used to work construction, an advanced state of decline might look very different than if you used to be a linguist."

We arrived at a reasonable consensus. This was a clinical criterion, we decided, to be determined by the clinician. It certainly seemed like a clinical judgment to me, and I judged Nevin to be in an advanced state of decline.

The third requirement was that the advanced state of decline be considered irreversible. Was Nevin's decline irreversible? Some suggested that if I wasn't certain of his diagnosis, there was no way to know for sure. But others noted the law suggested that the advanced decline must be irreversible *by any means acceptable to the patient.* Nevin had been clear that he was done with more investigations or treatment trials, so I suggested the criteria were met.

Intolerable suffering, either physical or emotional, was the fourth required element of a grievous and irremediable condition, and was primarily accepted as subjective. This could be determined only by Nevin, who had explained to me how he was suffering, and I had no reason to doubt him.

The final requirement was that the patient must have a natural death that was deemed to be reasonably foreseeable. For Nevin, that unfortunately appeared to be true, but for many, it was much less clear.

Lawyers across the country had their opinions on what this bit of law meant, and I learned from my colleagues that those opinions varied. Clinicians too had their own opinions on what "reasonably foreseeable" meant, and they were sometimes significantly different from what we were hearing from some lawyers. Patients had opinions about what was "reasonably foreseeable," but their opinions weren't always consistent with those of their families. The health authorities admittedly had no idea what the phrase signified but several made policy based on their own interpretation. This raised really interesting questions. What did "reasonably foreseeable" mean? And who should decide?

There was an interplay going on here between the realms of clinical decision-making and legal interpretation. There was no doubt that legislation established a fence, a limit to what a person could or could not do in our society based on a set of written, legislated criteria. But there was some ambiguity; what was meant by the words that were chosen (how did one define a serious illness, for example?). While I didn't have the expertise to interpret a clause of the Criminal Code of Canada, I questioned if anyone other than a health care practitioner could determine if a person had a serious illness, was in an advanced state of decline, or if their natural death was reasonably foreseeable.

Debates about what the law required were ongoing that year—online, in newspaper articles, in legal and academic circles, and in hospitals across the country. Meanwhile, suffering people were asking for help, so it was left to my colleagues and me to try to make some new and difficult decisions. I wasn't rushing to any conclusions, but I felt more and more certain that the decision about eligibility was meant to be between a patient and his or her doctor, not debated around a table in a boardroom.

Meanwhile, Nevin was declining. He was having trouble swallowing his own saliva, and he was fearful that he might choke. This was especially true at night, so he was scared to sleep. He was weak and unsteady on his feet, he was at high risk for falling, and he was begging for help to die.

I believed Nevin was eligible for MAiD but without clarity or consensus, I didn't think I could move forward. Nevin's support team also continued to disagree about his best course of action, whether he should stay home and have MAiD or go to the hospital for palliative care. While we all continued to discuss and debate, Nevin lost another three pounds and asked if I would fly out and help him in two to three days' time.

It was during this ongoing turmoil that I was introduced to Suzanne. Suzanne's diagnosis was clear; she had an aggressive form of breast cancer and, at the age of sixty-two, had been told she had less than two years left to live. This would have been devastating to anyone, and it was all the more maddening to the once-active triathlete who no longer had the energy to walk to the end of her block. Confined to her home with fatigue and constant pain, limited to puttering around only when necessary, she had tried chemotherapy and radiation but had discontinued both due to intolerable side effects. She knew if she could withstand these treatments, she might extend her life by several years, but she was unwilling to accept the trade-off.

Suzanne referred herself for MAiD and hoped to proceed within a few short weeks in order to avoid living through dying. Her oncologist outlined the aggressive nature of her diagnosis and wrote a letter explaining her limited prognosis. The palliative care physician was frustrated at Suzanne's unwillingness to use certain medications for pain control but accepted that Suzanne had the right to do so and live with the uncomfortable consequences. No one expressed concern about Suzanne's capacity to make her own health care decisions, and I found no evidence of any mental health disorder. I felt that Suzanne likely met the criteria. I was preparing to offer her an assisted death but I wasn't 100 percent clear on the acceptable boundaries of "reasonably foreseeable," so I sought out other opinions.

"Oh, I think her death is reasonably foreseeable," said one academic, "and I believe that she is suffering. I'm just not clear that she is yet in an advanced state of decline."

"What?" I was stumped.

"Well, it's not well defined in the law, and you said she's still puttering around the house," he continued. "I think it's the intention of the law to help people who are dying, not reduce suffering in those who are living."

I needed a moment to understand the implications of this statement. It was the exact opposite of what I thought the Supreme Court had intended.

"Well, an advanced state of decline in function cannot generally be defined," I began, "because it's so very individual, and isn't it a clinical decision? Are you suggesting I might need to wait until she is in a worse state of decline, until she is functioning less, suffering more, essentially 'dying more'? She's already unable to leave her home. Isn't the point of this law to allow people to decide for themselves when enough is enough? Are you suggesting the law might require me to wait until she is bedbound or in more pain? That seems a bit cruel to me."

Nevin was dying, but I wasn't certain from what. Suzanne was dying but perhaps not quickly enough, and she wasn't yet in as bad a shape as some thought she ought to be in to satisfy the rules and regulations. My role was to provide the best clinical care. The role of lawyers in giving clinicians advice, I believed, was to reduce the likelihood of any (successful) prosecution. Administrators were meant to ensure adherence to process while simultaneously facilitating access within a regional structure, and scholars, it seemed, had fodder for endless debate. Everyone had an opinion, none of us had the exclusive right to determine how to move forward, but I would be the one held responsible for any action taken.

One beautiful sunny morning in the midst of all this stress I decided to let off steam. I cleared a few hours in my schedule and took my kayak for a paddle near the beach close to our house. As soon as I pushed off from the shore, I was in a different world. There were birds everywhere, flocks of seagulls, flocks of geese, eagles overhead, and herons on the boulders. Despite the stunning surroundings, I could not stop thinking of Nevin's case. Out on the water, I realized that ultimately it was about boundaries: who determined them, who defined them, and who, if anyone, could test them.

Pop culture and the media have reinforced several stereotypical clinicians: the nerdy generalist who knows and does a bit of everything and often goes above and beyond (think Marcus Welby, MD); the machismo "cowboy" outlier (often a surgeon) who takes risks and wins big or goes home (think of characters from *ER* or *Grey's Anatomy*); the passionate mission-driven activist who will challenge or even break the law to help a patient and to prove a point (think Dr. Jack Kevorkian or Dr. Henry Morgentaler). I wasn't any of these. I didn't want, didn't like, and didn't need to break any laws. We could argue about whether the fence posts were hammered into the right place or not, but boundaries had been drawn. Follow the rules and MAiD was legal, get it wrong and it was not. Throughout my career I'd always wanted to offer compassionate, patient-centered, high-quality care, but always within the law, be it in women's health, newborn care, or an end-of-life environment. My conundrum was bigger than Nevin, or Suzanne, or me. MAiD was new, there were legitimate questions, and I may have thought I had the answers, but there were others whom I respected who held important, differing opinions.

When I reached a protected bay, I paddled to shore, grounded my kayak on a rocky beach, and dug my cell phone out from the dry bag. I couldn't go any farther until I emailed some thoughts to several of my trusted sounding boards. We had a vigorous back-and-forth but no new clarity emerged. I called and commiserated with Nevin's family physician, then tried to explain the lack of consensus to Robert before paddling, hard, back home.

That morning, I discovered that in the face of ongoing uncertainty, I did not have the courage to risk providing Nevin an assisted death. Getting these decisions right meant being able to provide help to people who were "suffering intolerably," as the criteria clearly required. Getting them wrong looked very different. My practice, my family life, and my personal freedom would be at risk.

Meanwhile, Nevin's closest supporters remained locked in disagreement. Robert continued to try to help him stay home; Albie begged him to go to the hospital. Nevin remained fearful that the palliative care team would block his access to an assisted death, but in the end, he became even more frightened that he might choke to death in the middle of the night, so he reluctantly agreed to be admitted to the hospital.

I initially believed this was for the best, but Nevin's fears were realized. When he arrived, the doctor increased Nevin's pain medications, and Nevin became so sleepy that he lost the ability to make his own decisions. The physician declared him incapable of consenting to MAiD and assumed Nevin's end-of-life care. While I am certain this decision was carried out with the best of intentions, Robert called me several times in tears, reminding me that this was exactly what Nevin had feared. Robert begged the doctor to reduce the pain medications so Nevin could direct his own care, but the physician categorically declined, citing it would be cruel to do so. When I suggested the family physician consider stepping in, his response was understandable but heartbreaking. "There is only one palliative specialist in town," he told me. "I cannot break with his recommendations. I have to work with this specialist going forward, and this sort of disagreement could be catastrophic for any future patients' care."

Politics, unclear law, and fear were all playing a role.

That same week, I returned to visit Suzanne. I tried to explain that it wasn't that she was ineligible, only that she wasn't quite eligible *yet*. She was kind in her understanding but told me she would find a way to take care of it herself. I urged her to stay in touch, to let me know when things were worsening. She thanked me for my time and my work in general. She said it was important and told me I was brave to do it.

I wasn't feeling brave. I felt selfish for putting my own worries ahead of hers and Nevin's. But the reality is that not everyone is eligible for an assisted death, and safeguards are in place for a reason. Just because I *want* to help doesn't mean I *should*, and just because I *can* help someone doesn't mean I *must*. There is law, there are practice standards, there are clinical opinions, and there are personal limits. I had to be respectful of all these boundaries and both clear about and comfortable with my own level of involvement.

Not long after, I heard that Suzanne sought a second opinion. Another MAiD provider believed Suzanne *was* eligible. A third clinician agreed. In the end, Suzanne got her wish and had an assisted death. No one complained, and no one was prosecuted.

Suzanne's sister, Nancy, called to tell me when it was over. She didn't know if the other clinicians had spoken with any administrators or called upon lawyers, and she didn't care. She just wanted to tell me how relieved she was that Suzanne hadn't needed to resort to killing herself. She felt strongly that she would have tried to do so.

A few days later, I received word that Nevin had died in the hospital, sedated and under palliative care. I was glad he wasn't suffering anymore.

I'll never know if I made the proper legal choice by not moving forward in these two circumstances, but I wish I'd had the courage to proceed with Suzanne. I wish I'd had the courage to get on that plane and assist Nevin in his home. That was how he'd hoped to die. That was what he considered dignified. That was what he had requested when he was still completely capable. In the end, I know he was scared: scared of a disease we couldn't understand, let alone treat; scared enough to relent and go to the hospital, to give up on his end-of-life goals. Overwhelmed by the inevitable, he had reached out to me for help, and to this day, I cannot shake the feeling that I let him down.

CHAPTER 12

"PLEASE CALL THE MINISTER AT the United Church, he has a request."

At the end of September, when I received the text from Karen along with a phone number, it caught me by surprise. I was out in the community seeing patients in their homes. I wondered what this request could possibly be about. A patient from their community in need? A congregant they rather hoped I would not assist?

I doubted he was calling to tell me he disapproved of my work. Across the province, and in Canada more broadly, public support for MAiD was running high, although occasionally, colleagues from other regions would share negative stories on our online forum. They reported hurtful or snide comments whispered by nurses walking through hospital wards, attempts at shaming in professional settings by long-standing colleagues who felt the need to express their anti–assisted dying views, and a few anecdotes about aggressive heckling from members of the audience at public speaking events. A team in another region had received credible death threats from a psychiatric patient who was told he was ineligible, and a colleague closer by had the word "killer" spray-painted on the exterior of his office. Interestingly, the majority of negative sentiment had come from within the health care community itself. Of course there were vocal disagreements from the Church, opinion pieces in the papers, a few protests outside government buildings, but the response from the religious community as a whole had been more muted than expected. If this minister felt angry, it would be more effective to write a letter to the local paper than to call and risk my hanging up on him.

After I received his message, I reminded myself that I had promised to discuss assisted dying with anyone who took the time to ask, so I picked up the telephone and dialed his number.

To my surprise, a woman answered the phone. She was filling in for the minister and had been calling with an invitation.

"We're hoping you can join us for a seminar on end-of-life issues," she explained. "We're holding an eight-week series: one topic per week, one night for each topic, and we thought one evening could be devoted to assisted dying. A lot of congregants are interested in the subject, and we all want to know more. Would you be willing to come talk to us later this fall? We usually meet for ninety minutes on a Wednesday night. There are already forty-five people signed up for the series."

I was impressed. This church was making a proactive effort toward greater understanding, which I wished other community leaders would adopt. "I would be honored," I quickly replied.

I knew how uncomfortable discussions around death could be and was pleased to have a chance to break through some of the stigma in a public setting. In the same way that avoiding the topic of sex education only serves to confuse and disempower young people, I was convinced that sidestepping conversations about death was doing the same for those who were dying. What we need are open discussions and information around end-of-life options. That way, people could form educated opinions and then, hopefully, make the most appropriate decisions for themselves.

Days were busy and evenings I was tired, so I used my weekend to consider what I wanted to present, what the audience was asking to hear, and start developing some slides. I planned to quickly review how MAiD came about in our country, explain how the process and procedure worked, and go over the eligibility criteria. I knew that in order to summarize the story succinctly, I'd need to understand it in greater detail. That way, I could emphasize the crucial pieces. I went back to my early notes on the legal challenges and reread the background, the court cases, and the decisions. I could probably summarize the *Rodriguez* and *Carter* cases in two slides, but before moving on to our legislation, I needed to explain the significant difference between what the Supreme Court concluded in the *Carter* decision and what eventually became our law.

After the Supreme Court struck down the prohibition against assisted dying in Canada, the judges left it to the government to make a law to regulate the practice. In doing so, the government tried to further define what was meant by a "grievous and irremediable condition" and establish procedural safeguards. Many claimed the government went too far. Bill C14, which eventually became law, was arguably not representative of the Court's groundbreaking decision but significantly more restrictive. Specifically, Bill C14 introduced the notion that assisted dying would be limited to people whose death was reasonably foreseeable (without any particular time frame imposed within its definition—neither six months nor two years) and that he or she must already be in an advanced state of decline in function. This element of, or requirement for, a reasonably foreseeable death (which many *incorrectly* interpreted as meaning a person needed to be at the end of their life) had not been part of the *Carter* decision, which was centered instead around the presence of a serious and incurable illness and intolerable suffering. Regardless, C14 became the law, and while some continued to fight through the courts for its revision, it was this law and its eligibility criteria for MAiD that I worked within and wanted to explain to my audience.

As I continued to prepare for my talk, I received another phone call, this time from a resident of Washington State. He was a sixty-eight-year-old man suffering from advanced-stage multiple sclerosis, and he wanted to know if he could access MAiD in Canada. It was uncommon that someone from the U.S. called north of the border seeking medical care, so it caught me by surprise.

"I've had MS for over sixteen years," he explained, "but now I'm in a whole new stage. I need almost full-time care. I use an electric wheelchair to get around, but I'm becoming more and more bedbound with fatigue. My speech and swallowing are getting much worse, but I don't think I'll ever accept a feeding tube. When it's over, it's over. I'm not sure how much longer I've got. My specialist thinks maybe a year or two, depending on if I get more infections—mostly urinary, but I also had a bad pneumonia recently."

For now, he was coping at home with help from family and friends and with regular home care nursing supports, but he knew it was becoming too much. Very soon, he would need to consider a move to a more institutionalized environment. He very much did not want that or to be living away from family for his final months or years. He preferred to die sooner, surrounded by his loved ones, and most importantly, on his own terms. Could I help?

The answer was, unfortunately, easy. I could not. I told him that in order to qualify for MAiD, he had to be eligible for Canadian health care. That didn't mean he needed to be a citizen—permanent residents and refugees also qualify—but foreign visitors with private payments were not legally allowed to be assisted.

It was only after I hung up that I began to wonder why he had even felt the need to ask. Washington State had passed a law legalizing assisted dying back in November 2008, and it had been in effect since March 2009. Why would he need to seek care here? In an effort to better understand his motives, and as background preparation for my talk, I decided to seek more detail about assisted dying in the U.S.

I learned that an assisted death looks very different across the border. In 2016, there were only five American states that legally allowed for assisted dying, and there was variability among them regarding eligibility criteria and procedural safeguards. The two most common elements were modeled on the Oregon Death with Dignity Act of 1994, which has served as the template for all subsequent MAiD statutes within the United States.

In the U.S., in order to find a patient eligible for an assisted death, a doctor must first determine that he or she is terminally ill, which is specifically defined in the statutes as someone who is expected to die within six months, never mind that clinicians are, by their own admission, terrible at prognosticating. I recognized that the requirement that the patient be at the very end of life was (at the time) unique among global jurisdictions that permit some form of assisted death. The Dutch emphasize the eligibility requirement of unbearable suffering, the Belgians focus on the presence of a medically hopeless situation, the Swiss require only that the medication be self-administered and that there is an absence of selfish motivation in the one who is assisting, and we Canadians have our "grievous and irremediable" criteria. None of these assisted dying programs is designed to be used exclusively at end of life; they are focused on autonomy, patient suffering, and irremediability as the key factors in determining eligibility.

More strikingly, in the few American states that allow assisted dying, the patient is required to self-administer the medication, and this commonly occurs without a doctor present. Although a doctor in the U.S. is required to evaluate the patient for any number of eligibility requirements and is responsible for writing the prescription for the medication, it is the patient or family who fills the prescription and the patient who is required to take the medication—usually a bitter-tasting liquid mixture of barbiturates— without any assistance. Therefore, in order to have an assisted death in the U.S., a patient usually has to be able to sit upright, hold a glass or at least be able to sip from a straw, swallow liquid, and digest it—things that many people at the very end of life cannot do. This emphasis on the patient as the sole actor in the death is presumably meant to guarantee that the death is self-determined. The problem is, without a clinician present, there have been reports of complications—regurgitation, significant delay in time until death—and attempts that were unsuccessful.

Americans don't know what they don't know. In Canada, we offer a legal choice between a self-administered drink or a clinician-administered intravenous. By the time I was prepping for my talk, I had used only the IV protocol—there wasn't a single patient who had requested the drink. And as I looked further into the details, I learned that in locations where this alternative was available—Belgium, Luxembourg, and the Netherlands—the overwhelming majority of patients choose doctor-administered care over the self-administered drink. One report from the Netherlands showed that in 2015, 96 percent of all reported cases of assisted dying were with an IV and a physician present. Complication rates are much lower when an IV route is used, and a wider range of patients with a broader variety of symptoms can be served.

It was no longer hard to see why the man from Washington State had reached out to me. His prognosis was unclear, he had a declining ability to swallow, and he didn't want to live away from family as he became increasingly sick. In fact, he didn't want to slip into greater decline at all. He wanted to be free to end his life on his own terms. Unfortunately, that wasn't going to be possible in the U.S. or Canada. He could fly to Switzerland, where citizens of other countries are allowed to die with assistance, but I suspected that might be too expensive or far for him to go.

My research had been enlightening, so during my talk, I decided to mention a few of the facts I'd learned in order to highlight the benefits of the Canadian model. As I was preparing my slides summarizing the *Carter* and *Rodriguez* stories, it occurred to me that something unique had happened here in Canada. Change had come through a constitutional challenge in the courts, meaning the subject of assisted dying was a *rights-based* issue. This was not a voter-initiated idea, not a political party's preference— both of which were more likely to shift again in the future—but a patient right; a human rights issue.

Thanks to my trip to Amsterdam, the other jurisdiction I was most familiar with was the Netherlands. Even though the country hadn't legalized assisted dying until 2002, Dutch physicians had been challenging their laws against assisted dying since the early 1970s, and the practice had been tolerated since the early 1980s. The AIDS crisis brought the subject of assisted dying into the public eye in Holland when doctors, who were caring for patients suffering horrible deaths and begging for assistance, found themselves faced with an ethical dilemma: They had a duty to sustain and preserve health, but they had also sworn to relieve patient suffering. Dutch law was amended in 2002. Assisted dying remained illegal in the Netherlands, but if a physician followed what are known as the "due care criteria" of action, he or she could not be prosecuted. I had to read those due care criteria several times before the key difference dawned on me.

The requirements state: *1) the doctor must be convinced that the patient had made a voluntary and well considered request; 2) the doctor must be convinced that the patient's suffering is hopeless and unbearable; 3) the doctor must . . .*

It went on. But what was all this talk about "the doctor"? That's when it hit me. True to its origins, the Dutch framework was physician-centric. By contrast, in Canada, our eligibility criteria read "a *patient* must" be an adult, "*a patient* must" have a grievous and irremediable condition, "a *patient* must" make a voluntary request. Considering our law was the result of a rights-based constitutional challenge, this made perfect sense.

This might seem like a minor technicality, but to me, it served to emphasize that the Canadian law was grounded in a patient's rights, so it created legal language that was wholly patient-centric. This in turn fostered a model of care, including infrastructure and supports, that revolved fundamentally—and, in my view, appropriately—around the patient.

And what about the U.S.? In the U.S., laws around assisted dying changed not as a recognition of constitutionally granted rights or a physician-centric philosophy, but thanks to voter ballot initiatives or legislative process. As a result, voters' concerns remained at the center of the model, not the patient. When a patient who is terminally ill has to hold a drink and swallow it, this isn't because it's best for the patient but because it was deemed safer by the voter or politician in his or her stead.

"Compromise was the order of the day," says the American legal scholar and end-of-life expert Thaddeus Pope of the way in which the U.S. law was drafted. "To garner enough votes for change, drafters reluctantly included onerous eligibility requirements and safeguards."

By the time it was my night to speak, the lecture series at the church had already covered the topics of advanced-care planning, wills and powers of attorney, palliative care, and what the gospel says about the end of life. As promised, there were easily fifty people in the large modern chapel when I arrived.

When I looked around, I saw the audience was primarily elderly, which seemed in keeping with the topic. My patient data would soon show that the average age of my patients was seventy-five, equally split between male and female; 65 percent with cancer, 15 percent with neurological diagnoses, and a similar number with end-stage organ failure of some sort (heart, lung, or liver). Everyone fell quiet the moment I stepped in front of them. I took a deep breath and dove straight in, clicking my first slide into view.

I felt a responsibility to be transparent and as clear as possible, especially with this group, who I thought might hold religious beliefs that made them wary of MAiD. I had come prepared for some pushback, but for the most part, people were keen to know more about the nuances of the eligibility criteria, whether someone with dementia could ever qualify, and whether life insurance was adversely affected. Near the end, when the questions from the audience were slowing down, someone asked how I felt when I did this work, whether it was as intensely emotional as they might expect, and how I coped personally. I decided to answer with a quick story about an event that was still fresh in my mind.

I didn't go into a lot of detail because I needed to protect my patient's privacy. I mentioned that she was a musician—a composer, performer, and lover of music who was humming a famous aria on the day that I met her.

"This woman had arranged to check into a hotel with a spectacular view of the waterfront three days before her scheduled death. Her husband arranged for a large-screen TV to be set up and perpetually scrolling through hundreds of family photos. She then held court on the king-size bed for two days as friends and neighbors paraded in and out during designated hours to visit and say their goodbyes." I paused. People seemed to be listening more keenly than they had been at any other time during my presentation.

"On the day of her death," I continued, "by the time I arrived, there were fourteen close friends and family members gathered. As we moved closer to the final moments, she asked for 'one last family hug,' and without further ado, fourteen people encircled her bed. They were tightly woven, arm in arm, and were smiling, reminiscing, and offering words of love. At one point, she asked that I turn up the music. It was a playlist she herself had created for the day, and her favorite classical pieces filled the room in stereo through Bluetooth speakers. When the familiar strains of Pavarotti's 'Nessun Dorma' began to play, she looked at me and said, 'Now, please, Dr. Green.'

"She lifted her granddaughter's hand and kissed it, then laid her head back and fell asleep as the room was enveloped by the soaring tenor. I administered the remaining medications, and seven minutes later, she died—exactly as she wished, surrounded by the people she loved, at a time and a place of her choosing.

"How do I feel when I do this work? I find the people I meet to be extraordinary. I am amazed at the expressions of love and support that I see. I start to wonder how I would wish my own death to look, and then I go home and hold my own family a little tighter."

After the talk, several people approached me at the podium. Among them was a robust-looking elderly man sporting a well-groomed white mustache, a debonair jacket and tie, and carrying an elegant walking stick. He introduced himself as Richard.

"Thank you for the talk," he said, looking me in the eye. "May I have your business card?"

I dug one out of my backpack and gave it to him.

"I hope we meet again soon," he said.

Unlike some of the others who had wanted to share details of their medical history with me, Richard was discreet. I couldn't imagine he would need my services. But as I watched him leave, I realized that his walking stick was a cane, and his gait was slow and at times hesitant. You just never know, I thought.

CHAPTER 13

EARLY THAT FALL, I MADE one of my regular visits to see my mother in Nova Scotia. Normally, I would go to see her at the assisted living facility where she had been residing for the past five years. This time, I arrived the night before, checked into my hotel, and showed up at nine-thirty a.m. with plans for us to go to the mall (my mother in a wheelchair) and then afterward out for lunch.

When I walked into her apartment, she tried to stand up to greet me. My mother wanted so badly to get out of that chair. She had always been stubborn—and insistent on her independence. I remember how long it took me to convince her to give up driving. I knew being able to get up on her own was likely a point of pride, but I was annoyed that she wouldn't wait for me to help her. She braced herself with both hands on the arm-rests, took a breath, rocked once or twice, and then lifted, all to no avail. She got almost halfway up, paused, and fell back down into the seat. I came to her side and, without a word, offered the slightest bit of support under one arm. She easily rose to her feet. I heard a whispered "thank you" as she looked down, her speech slurred.

Ten years after my father's death, it felt like my mother was now the one nearing the end. She was in her seventies, and her chronic neurologic condition was only getting worse. It seemed as if she had shrunk since I'd visited last: She was slightly more hunched, the tremor in her leg more obvious, the bobbing of her head more severe. It was hard for her to walk, harder still to change directions, actually dangerous to try to step backward. She could no longer write or perform certain manual tasks, she had trouble communicating verbally, and she was wholly reliant on caregivers to take her outside. I was bracing myself for the next stage—a slight increase in symptoms might mean she wouldn't be able to safely swallow.

My relationship with my mother was nothing like the strained and distant one I'd had with my father, yet it had its own complexities. She was my primary caregiver throughout my childhood, the one who fed me, clothed me, took me to the doctor when I was sick, and tried to teach me the value of education. She provided a family for my brother and me, and I knew she loved us deeply. But between the divorce from my father, her remarriage to my stepfather, and the chaos that brought into our lives, I sometimes felt I had spent my formative years concerned for her happiness and well-being more than the other way around. I knew it wasn't intentional on her part, but it was probably why, as an adult, I often felt conflicted when we were together, wanting to help but still feeling a bit like the wounded child inside.

That day, it flashed through my mind that no matter how I felt about my mother, I did not have an infinite number of conversations left with her. In the years that had passed since my father's death, I still hadn't spoken with her about her end-of-life wishes, and the conversation was long overdue. What was important to her? If she became very sick with pneumonia, would she want to be intubated and cared for in the ICU? Would she want someone to start CPR if her heart stopped? Did she prefer to be buried or cremated? I decided I would not talk to her about whether she would ever consider an assisted death unless she explicitly brought it up. I wanted no sense of coercion, no judgment, no whiff of bias from my direction. But what about when it was my mother's turn to occupy that hospital bed? I thought about my father and how I had been called upon to make end-of-life decisions on behalf of a man whose wishes were a mystery to me. I definitely didn't want to repeat that experience.

That day, I took my mother to the mall, and we shopped and had lunch. We chatted about her grandchildren, local gossip, her friends, and her few remaining activities. It was more of a one-sided conversation due to her limited speech, and I did not broach the deeper questions roiling in my mind. She asked me about my work in assisted dying but didn't probe much after I answered in the most generic of terms. She wanted to know if I'd really given up the maternity work I had been so passionate about, and when I told her yes, she looked at me long and silently. "Don't give it up completely," she mumbled while pointing her index finger at me.

"There were reasons," I began to answer, "and careful thought . . . I assure you."

Instead of discussing this any further, my mother surprised me by asking if I was interested in a game of bridge.

We'd never played together, and I certainly hadn't expected her to ask, but as soon as she did, I was in. I'd been struggling to find ways to connect with my mother over something other than her illness. For the past few years, matters of her health had taken over everything. A game of cards felt like a natural activity for both of us. I couldn't count how many conversations we'd had in my childhood over a game of cribbage or a hand of gin. Most parents know the trick of having a serious conversation with their kids while driving in the car, without directly looking at each other. In my mother's household, card games and backgammon allowed us to pretend to be focused on strategy while we discussed some of the difficult things going on in our lives—my father moving out, new stepsiblings moving in.

I would have been eleven the year my mother learned to play bridge. We were living in my childhood home, my mother, brother, and I, in the early months after my parents' divorce. Mom had gone briefly back to school, taken in a boarder, and finally found work selling insurance to help support us. To my mother, her new life must have seemed . . . unexpected. But to me, she was still my mom—my guardian, my champion, my protector. She had yet to date my stepfather. For me, this was distinctly "before": before she remarried and a new family moved in, before the negativity and the brewing chaos. Before my home became less safe.

I remember sitting at our kitchen table, me at one corner, silent, my mother laying down the cards, faceup, according to her lesson plan. She'd just look at them for a while, then begin to play it through. I remember watching her, learning how the hand was played, impressed with what a trump card could do. I didn't understand the auction or what the final contract meant, but I followed along as she practiced her lessons, and I saw her as I like to remember her: smart, capable, and present.

My mother remarried the week I turned thirteen, and my stepfather and two of his children moved in. Sometime after that, I felt I lost my mother. In retrospect, I think it was around the period of the telephone call. I must have been fourteen by then. I had called her one afternoon at work. It was unusual for me to do so, but I needed some help.

"There's a problem," I told her.

My stepfather's son was pestering me insistently. He would plead for my help with something, beg me to help him with his homework, anything, until I said sure, just to make him go away. Once inside my room, he wouldn't leave, taunting and harassing me. Our verbal fights often deteriorated into physical ones. He was a full year younger than I was, and not yet grown, so I could usually restrain him and prevent him from besting me, but there was a lot of questionable contact during those physical fights that I absolutely did not invite.

That afternoon, my discomfort with him had become too much.

"He's been an ass," I told my mother, "and he's being really annoying, and I can't get him out of my room, and this needs to stop. Please, Mom. I need some help."

My mother paused. "Oh, Stefanie," she responded, brushing me off. "You know what he's like . . . There's nothing I can really do about it, and I'm at work right now. Let's wait until I get home to talk about it . . ."

It was not the response I needed, and we didn't talk about it later.

That evening, I got the sense that she was avoiding the conversation with me. I was too embarrassed to tell my mother that this wasn't a one-time inconvenience, that it was occurring repeatedly. I never fully explained what was going on, in large part because her response was so discouraging.

I'd gotten the message: She couldn't protect me, or wouldn't, and I was left with a lingering shame.

That phone call was the first time I realized that even my mother was fallible. I was vulnerable, and she wouldn't or couldn't step in on my behalf. Yes, it made me angry, I just didn't understand that yet—and I've missed her ever since.

But before all of this, before her illness, before my mother's remarriage, we played games. And those days at the kitchen table, watching her concentrate and practice and learn, I was still a child who wanted to be like her. The idea of playing bridge together now was appealing.

I'd signed up for lessons the year before I began working as a MAiD provider, taking classes at a local senior center, where I met a couple named Glen and Louise. They were in their mid- to late sixties and among the youngest people in the room. He was funny and clever, she was warm and kind, or maybe it was the other way around. We met every Friday at twelve-thirty in one of our homes with Ann, another woman I'd teamed up with. My work calendar reflected this "meeting," and I guarded that time slot fiercely.

Since I'd started work as a MAiD provider, bridge had become my version of self-care. I loved the game and the friendships it facilitated. When I played bridge, its total use of my brain required a complete break from every other aspect of my life. As soon as we started to play, I was able to forget that just a few hours ago, I might have been kneeling at someone's bedside and administering medication through an IV catheter as a dozen family and friends said goodbye to a loved one. For two hours, my telephone was off and my emails unchecked. There was no birth, no death, and no family demands, just three friends, four suits, and a whole lot of concentration, me trying hard to remember which cards had already been played and what the heck it meant when Ann bid two-no-trump on the second round after opening with a minor.

———

After we returned from the mall, I watched, somewhat amazed, as my mother picked up the phone and arranged a game for the next day. With few words but clear intention, she explained exactly what she wanted. Whomever she was speaking with took over the task from there.

The next day at two p.m., we found ourselves sitting at a bridge table for four in a common area of her facility. My mother sat across from me as my bridge partner, and we were joined by Clara, a slow-moving eighty-two-year-old with a cane and a pronounced kyphosis (an excess curvature of the upper back), and Susan, a woman in her sixties who had suffered a debilitating stroke and was confined to an electric wheelchair. Like my mother, Susan was one of the younger members of their facility, and she'd been an active member of the academic community until only very recently. I'd met her on a previous visit, and she'd been keenly interested to hear about my career shift. I suspected she'd be looking for an update, and she was.

"So now that it's been a few months, tell us, what has it really been like for you? Have you experienced any backlash? Have you encountered any roadblocks?"

I was happy to have this conversation, but it felt a little weird. These were questions I wished my mother had asked, information I had hoped to share with her. But I never knew how much she wanted to know about assisted dying. She'd made it clear that she was supportive of my work, but she didn't inquire further, and I never knew if it was due to her communication challenges or emotional reticence, or perhaps just a general discomfort. My mother cared what others thought, and I suspect the Jewish community in Halifax, like the one in Victoria, was mixed in its reception of MAiD. Orthodox factions had made it clear that such actions were unacceptable in their faith, even if I knew of several progressive groups that were much more understanding of patient suffering and supported acquiescing to personal needs and wishes. I doubted my mother paid too much heed to what the various clerics were saying; nevertheless, I welcomed Susan's questions as a way to bring up what I was thinking and doing.

I noticed my mother listening to my answers as she and I played a hand on defense.

"It's been fairly incredible," I told Susan truthfully, but speaking as if to my mother. "We're expecting some pushback from various groups, mostly religious, if I'm honest, but in the meantime, the work has been challenging and much more meaningful than I expected. Helping someone to fulfill their final wishes can be quite . . . well . . . profound."

My mother seemed interested in what the others asked about and even more so in what they thought.

"I think it's so important what you're doing, Stefanie," Susan emphasized.

We played for almost two hours. No one kept score, but each team held their own, and when my mother bid and made a contract for five diamonds, I was genuinely impressed. I noticed Susan used a wooden card holder and wondered if that might be an idea for my mom. Her tremors sometimes made it hard to put the correct card down without losing one or two others to the floor, but I suspected she'd be resistant. Even so, bridge seemed an ideal game for her—so much of its communication was silent— and she was as sharp as ever.

After the card game, back in her living space, I thanked my mother for the idea to play bridge. Just like when I was younger, I felt like we'd had a conversation over a hand of cards. I think she must have felt it too. When I said I hoped we could do it again, she seemed awfully pleased.

Before I left her apartment that evening, she stunned me with a complete non sequitur as I was getting up to go.

"Stef . . ." Her head was bobbing rapidly, even more than usual. I knew she was exhausted, but she was making an effort to speak slowly and clearly. "I'm proud . . . your work . . ." She smiled and looked right at me. "Really!"

I might have always known it, but it sure felt good to hear it.

"Thanks, Mom," I said as I kissed her good night. "I'll see you tomorrow."

It had been a good visit, but I returned to Victoria without having broached the difficult topic of end-of-life care with my mother. I felt blocked, unable or unwilling to confront her. I wasn't sure why. And at the same time, I couldn't help imagining myself in the scene. What if it were my mother on her deathbed? What would I hope to say or have said? Was it that I loved her, that I thanked her, that I forgave her? Which one of those was the truth, and which words had I yet to utter?

What, if anything, was holding me back?

CHAPTER 14

IT WAS NOW OCTOBER 2016: four months since the law had changed in Canada, and a great deal had already happened. I'd met with thirty-six people about the possibility of obtaining an assisted death. Of the twenty-eight who had filled out the formal paperwork, I had found eighteen eligible. I had already helped twelve of them to end their lives, and there were four other patients whose medically assisted deaths were pending. I'd gone from being a beginner in a new field of medicine to feeling more certain of what I was doing and more comfortable with how I wanted to do it. I was becoming known among local family practitioners and specialists for my work in assisted dying, and the number of referrals to my office continued to climb.

That month, I got a call from Dr. Whitmore at the Victoria Hospice Unit, a local hospice society that runs an independent facility with seventeen beds, physically attached to the local hospital but funded in significant part by donations from the community. The team cares for approximately 350 patients at various stages of illness out in the community at any given time. The society primarily supports people in their homes, but they also admit patients for respite care, help in managing acute symptom flare-ups, and of course provide end-of-life care for people close to death. The goal of any hospice or palliative care center—and there are thousands of them across North America and around the world—is to optimize the quality of life that remains for patients, whether by good symptom management such as pain control or bowel care, or through emotional and spiritual support such as bringing music to the bedside, allowing pets to visit, or facilitating the writing of legacy letters to loved ones. In myriad creative ways, palliative care teams make a world of difference in the comfort of a person at the end of their life, and I am a strong supporter of expanding access to palliative care across all settings and communities.

Dr. Whitmore wanted to tell me about a specific patient in her care:

He has open wounds across his abdomen as well as in the inguinal region. He reports them under his scrotum as well. There are multiple nodules all over his body, many are open and weeping. The largest one is in his right axilla. It's draining a large amount of pus . . . really, this guy looks like he's been shot in the chest a dozen times. And he's in incredible pain.

The patient's name was Ray, he was sixty-two years old, and he had been diagnosed with metastatic lung cancer fourteen months earlier. A school janitor for over thirty years, he had never married and didn't have children but had a small group of close-knit friends. He first noticed a lump in his right underarm and ignored it. Then he developed a lump on his left flank and a smaller one on the front of his abdomen. None of this stopped him from working. When the largest one on the right finally broke through the skin and began weeping murky fluid, he decided to see his doctor. A biopsy proved it was cancer, and more testing discovered the original culprit in his lung. New lumps began appearing every week, and they were increasingly painful. He had radiation aimed at the largest offenders, shrinking them in size and temporarily easing his discomfort. At age sixty-one, Ray decided it was time to retire, and he agreed to begin a course of chemotherapy.

Despite his treatment, the cancer continued to grow, and as new nodules appeared, he experienced more pain and less ability to function. Ray told Dr. Whitmore that during that time he felt a little like he was playing whack-a-mole; he would have one nodule irradiated only to have three others appear. Second-line chemotherapy was equally unsuccessful. Ray's pain went up and his weight went down. The third choice of a chemotherapy drug was simply too toxic, so he stopped there. That was two months ago, and the home care nurses could only do so much. By the time Dr. Whitmore called my office, Ray was cachectic and weak and covered in lumps at various stages of growth and discharge. He had been admitted to the hospice unit four days earlier in what was aptly referred to as a "total pain crisis," and he was asking for an assisted death.

I met with Dr. Whitmore first, in the room behind the nursing station. She was a fast talker, like me, and didn't mince words. She introduced me to the resident, to a nurse in the room, and to one of the counselors who popped in to grab a chart.

I had heard disturbing stories from my colleagues in other cities of obstructive physicians and of entire hospice facilities opting out of offering assisted dying. Many faith-based institutions had made it clear they would not be providing this care based on the teachings of their church, but even some non-faith-based palliative care facilities were not willing to be involved. Despite our alignment on the importance of quality end-of-life care, the primacy of patient-centric decision-making, and the goal of reducing patient suffering, MAiD and palliative care folks somehow seemed to diverge when it came to the specific option of assisted dying.

Across the country and around the world, many palliative care clinicians have made it clear they will never participate in assisted dying, in any form. They often quote the World Health Organization's definition of palliative care, which includes a line declaring palliative care "intends neither to hasten nor postpone death" and is interpreted quite definitively. But the patients who fall under the auspices of palliative care are often the most interested in pursuing an assisted death. This is a conundrum for all involved, and not a small one. Any overt exclusion of assisted dying from within palliative care creates conflicted administrators, frustrated clinicians, and worst of all, confused patients. The primacy of patient needs appears to get lost in the philosophical debate.

Dr. Whitmore cut straight to the chase. "We're glad to have you here, Dr. Green," she told me. "Our medical director speaks for all of us when he states that he feels it's important to respect a patient's right to know all of their care options. But I must let you know that none of the members of my team are willing to assess for or provide assisted dying."

The good news was that, unlike many other hospice facilities, Victoria Hospice wouldn't stand in the way of *my* providing information about MAiD to patients within their facility; nor would they stop me from providing MAiD to those who requested it and proved eligible. They just didn't want to play any further role.

"The team is struggling," Dr. Whitmore reported. "We're likely going to lose a few staff members over this new 'liberal' policy."

Since we started this work in 2016, many palliative care physicians across the country have become involved in MAiD, and some have even become providers, but resistance to assisted dying within the palliative care community has continued. My colleagues have reported holding MAiD consultations in bus shelters, on busy street corners, and in bustling cafés when not allowed to do so within a facility that objects to assisted dying. "Forced transfers"—when a health care facility requires a person requesting assisted dying to go off-site to receive or even be assessed for MAiD—continue to impose unnecessary suffering on patients who are dying and, by definition, already suffering intolerably. In order to endure these transfers, patients often require significant amounts of analgesia that can compromise their ability to provide their final consent. Tragically, some have died in transit, a far cry from the autonomous, dignified death they fought so hard to achieve.

After our conversation, Dr. Whitmore took me to meet Ray.

"I've seen a lot of people. And I've seen a lot of pain," she told me before we entered his room, "and we usually do a really good job, but this has been extremely difficult to control. We've thrown absolutely everything at him. I mean, he's on a ketamine drip, for God's sake."

What do you do when the Cadillac of pain control is not enough? I was finding that pain was rarely cited by patients as the reason they were requesting an assisted death; significant reduction in quality of life or an inability to do anything that brought joy or meaning to their lives were the reasons I heard most often, and international evidence told a similar story. For the most part, modern medicine and palliative care do a good job in managing pain. But Ray seemed to have the experts stumped.

"I know we might be able to help him a little bit more, but sometimes I just don't think we can do enough," admitted Dr. Whitmore. "This is one of those cases. I'm all for your helping him if you think he qualifies. He's a lovely guy in just a horrible situation."

In his private hospice room, Ray was sitting up in a soft recliner, eyes closed, feet planted, hands gripping the armrests, dressed in light blue pajamas and a bathrobe. Although there was a eucalyptus aromatizer on the bedside table, it was no match for the unmistakable smell of rotting flesh that pervaded the room. A slight man, Ray had a large dressing under his pajama top that covered the multiple lesions scattered over his abdomen. He appeared to be sitting rigidly so as not to move. It appeared that even breathing was painful.

———

Back in Montreal, I had completed a partial fellowship in palliative care after my family medicine residency and before extra training in infant and maternal care.

This experience provided me the opportunity to spend more time with patients who were suffering at end of life, and I began to see that people could experience similar symptoms in completely different ways. The development, for example, of peripheral neuropathy—a numbness in the tips of the fingers secondary to chemotherapy—might be perceived as an unfortunate side effect by a teacher or a catastrophe by a guitar player. My newfound appreciation for context and framing turned out to be helpful as I went on to practice maternity care. I heard a lot of women complain of pain during labor, but building on what I had learned in palliative care, my years in maternity care reinforced for me the distinction between pain and suffering.

Pain is the feeling we have when something hurts—a cut, an electric shock, perhaps a disease-related, aching inflammation. I've seen a lot of women in pain during labor and delivery. Suffering is more about the *experience* of pain, the story we make up about it, how we understand it, and what we believe will become of it. If I pinch three people in the same room with the same pinch, they will all experience similar pain. While one person may find it strange to be pinched and then move on with their day, another might be more upset. The second person may become anxious that I will return to pinch them repeatedly, perhaps with an instrument, perhaps with a desire to draw blood. I might inflict scarring, permanent damage, or worse! This second person suffers more than the first. And pain need not be limited to the physical. Emotional pain can also lead to a tremendous amount of suffering. It's very individual and very personal because suffering is informed by our own histories, our own experiences, and our own interpretations.

When dealing with women in labor, I learned that one of my most effective roles in treating pain was to look for and help alleviate fear. I've seen women in labor who are convinced they are dying. Epidurals and pain medications all have their place, and I have used them liberally when requested, but for a laboring woman, reassurance that all is going as expected and that her baby is quite well despite what she is acutely experiencing is usually more effective at reducing suffering than most medications. "I know this is hard and might seem crazy, and it's probably pretty scary, but you're doing just great. Everything is happening just the way it should. I promise. You've got this! Your baby is doing fine, your body is working hard. Listen to what it needs—you want to squat? You're doing great! I'm really impressed."

Reassurance, empowerment, reduced suffering.

Now, with my work in MAiD, I was discovering that I could help reduce suffering in patients who were dying by listening carefully, offering choices, and empowering decision-making. Taking the time to understand whether a patient is suffering and, if so, from what is the great challenge of the work I do. "I hear your brother arrives tomorrow. I know you haven't seen him in eight years; you must have so many mixed feelings. I'm glad your daughter is staying with you in the meantime. I see the palliative team has drawn up some extra morphine for you to use in between your regular doses, if needed. They showed your daughter how to give this to you, so if you feel like you need something more for the pain, you just ask."

Reassurance, empowerment, reduced suffering.

Palliative care teams, in my experience, are experts in reducing suffering, and I have developed a tremendous respect for the work and its practitioners. However, those who work in end-of-life care know that there are times when, despite all efforts, we are unable to adequately relieve pain, just as we are sometimes unable to relieve shortness of breath or terminal delirium. At times like this, palliative care clinicians may offer what's known as palliative sedation. Ray had already discussed this option with Dr. Whitmore, and he'd made it clear that he wasn't interested.

Palliative sedation is used when a dying patient is suffering in a way that cannot otherwise be controlled. It typically involves a continuous infusion of a strongly sedating drug. If you've had a loved one die in hospice or in a hospital—or at home with the help of hospice care—you're probably familiar with this type of terminal sedation. You might recall that the medical team suggested that death was expected shortly, that there was no longer any need for food and water, that these might make symptoms worse by encouraging excessive secretions. It was likely recommended that all fluids be discontinued. You will have witnessed your loved one slipping into what appears to be a peaceful sleep, with death typically arriving a few days later. Your hospice team likely reminded you that palliative sedation is an option of last resort, a way of controlling your loved one's final symptoms, but it does not hasten death in any way, as per their credo. Of course, the combination of fatal illness, strong sedation, and the cessation of hydration may hasten death: perhaps not the direct intention of treatment, but a well-known, fully expected, and, if we're honest, often welcome result.

The decision to begin what is properly termed "continuous palliative sedation therapy" (previously known as terminal sedation) is one that is generally taken by the patient's medical team, often in conjunction with the family, and commonly when the patient is suffering unbearably and is no longer capable of providing consent. Death may take hours, days, or rarely, one to two weeks. Palliative sedation is widely accepted and a measure for which many people are grateful; it is also, for the most part, unregulated, unreported, and unmonitored.

By comparison, MAiD is a wholly regulated, closely monitored, and carefully outlined process that can proceed only with the explicit consent of a competent adult patient. And death does not take days. Yet assisted dying is generally considered controversial and is less universally accepted. I'm still trying to figure out why it isn't the other way around.

———

Ray bluntly told me that he found the idea of palliative sedation "just stupid, it's not what I want." As much as he wished for the pain to stop, he wasn't interested in lingering for some time in unconsciousness. He wanted his life to be over. Ray had been asking for an assisted death for several weeks, since before his admission to hospice, and despite appreciating the best efforts of his medical team to manage his unrelenting pain, he wanted to proceed.

"Ray, I believe you are eligible for an assisted death," I said, "and I'm willing to sign the paperwork stating as much and to assist you. It's important you've been able to consider the different possibilities, but I hear you loud and clear."

"Do you think Dr. Whitmore will be upset?" he asked. "I don't want her to think I don't appreciate all she's done."

I reassured him that Dr. Whitmore would understand his decision, and I pointed out it was she who'd called me to meet with him in the first place. Ray looked relieved. We agreed to call Dr. Whitmore into the room to review his decision and to formulate a plan together for moving forward.

What was happening in the hospice in Victoria reminded me of the kind of integrated end-of-life care practiced in Belgium. Palliative care began developing there in the early 1980s, around the same time as the drive for the legalization of assisted dying. Belgian pioneers of palliative care held the view that access to proper palliative care should be a pre-condition for assisted dying becoming acceptable and available; they felt that assisted dying and palliative care could and should develop together. The idea was that by ensuring excellent palliation, every opportunity of comfort care would be afforded the patient prior to any decision to request an assisted death. This approach has been widely accepted by the Belgian public, local palliative care clinicians, other health professionals, and legislators alike. Despite the Church remaining wholeheartedly against any support of euthanasia, even the Brothers of Charity, a religious order that runs many of the mental health facilities in Belgium, have publicly stated they will allow assisted dying in their facilities for those whom they cannot adequately palliate. Just as important, data suggest that since the legalization of assisted dying in Belgium, access to and funding for palliative care have risen substantially.

Within twenty-four hours, I confirmed Ray's eligibility and received his properly completed paperwork. In collaboration with the hospice team, we set the date for his procedure in forty-eight hours' time. When I stopped by his room, he seemed grateful for the hospice team's ongoing support even in light of the decision he'd made. Unlike some other hospice facilities in other parts of the country, this hospice didn't require transfer to any other location or secrecy around his decision.

Ray's death was a simple affair in the hospice's rooftop garden, attended by three of his closest friends. His nurse wheeled his bed up through the elevator, to the fourth floor, and out onto the manicured rooftop. She brought along his IV pump to deliver continuous pain relief. Ray thanked his friends for always being there for him, and they wished him a comfortable journey to wherever he was heading next.

"I realize this might sound ridiculous, Dr. Green, but I feel like you saved my life. Thank you for making this happen for me."

They were his last words.

As I left the hospital after Ray's procedure, I turned out of the parking lot and onto the main road to head home. I switched on the radio. There was a catchy, toe-tapping, popular tune playing, and I began mindlessly humming and then singing along with the music. I was rhythmically smacking my steering wheel and kind of dancing while driving. It took a minute, but I became aware of myself and then of how I was feeling.

I wondered if it was inappropriate to be happy at that moment. A patient I had cared for had just died, after all. I checked in and found myself feeling rather . . . upbeat, not so much from the music but more like how I felt after delivering a baby. I was startled at this discovery, almost confused. I stopped tapping my toe, turned off the music, and pulled over into a curbside parking spot. Upbeat? Well, yes. I felt like I was a little hyped up on adrenaline. This can't be right, I thought. But there was no denying it. I did feel good. I felt very good. More accurately, I felt like I had done something good: like I had given a gift to a dying man. Ray had been in a lot of pain, extreme pain, in fact, and we had helped him. The hospice staff and I had joined forces, worked as a team, and listened to his wishes. We had helped someone fulfill his own journey with dignity and compassion. And we had done so through a model of integrated end-of-life care, combining the best of palliative treatment with the patient's wish to receive MAiD. What I was feeling was gratification that I was in a position as a clinician—as a person—to offer this assistance.

But it occurred to me that I probably shouldn't tell anyone. What would they think? "I helped someone to die today, and I feel really great about it." I might be seen as a psychopath. Not long after I got home, I took it to the email group. I began by updating them on how it had gone with the hospice. Then I asked the touchier questions.

"So, I'm wondering how you feel as you leave a MAiD procedure you've just facilitated. Are you sad, satisfied, confused, numb, proud? . . . What is it you're experiencing? Obviously every case is unique, I get that, but . . ."

And then I related what I was feeling earlier in the day. I completely trusted this space and these colleagues. If I couldn't be honest with them, with whom could I be?

Within forty-five minutes, I found three responses already posted. People were encouraged by what had happened with the hospice team and wished they could have such positive experiences in their own communities. More comments followed shortly, and the discussion persisted for one or two days. And as I anticipated, it wasn't only about working well with hospice. A colleague from another province wrote that he also felt good about his work in assisted dying, that compared to his otherwise often frustrating general medical practice, it brought a huge amount of meaning to his life and to his work—but at the same time, he too felt the need to whisper this truth.

In emails that were visible only to us, we talked openly for the first time about how the work made us feel. We each acknowledged that our experiences were not universal and each context was unique, that not every case represented such a high level of collaboration, but that nevertheless, our new jobs were routinely bringing us a sense of meaning, a sense of satisfaction, and yes, its own form of reward. In this, I'm happy to share, I was not alone.

CHAPTER 15

THAT SAME FALL, MY COLLEAGUE Jonathan Reggler repeated a comment he'd previously made within our growing email group: "More than just an email group, we need a truly national organization to support us."

I had always agreed, and so did the rest of our colleagues: It was time to form an association to represent those of us who worked in assisted dying. We needed more than just professional collegial support, coming as we did from a wide range of fields—including family medicine, anesthesiology, nursing, and palliative care—and the multidisciplinary nature of the work (we routinely worked with colleagues from social work, pastoral care, speech-language pathology, and administration). As Nevin's story demonstrated, practitioners required consensus on the interpretation of the legal criteria for MAiD. There was a need to establish adequate training resources, to create medical standards, and to encourage the standardization of care across the country. In other words, we needed a national body of MAiD experts, mentors, and educators. So far, though, no one was taking the reins.

I knew the original five of us from Vancouver Island would help teach a full-day workshop on MAiD for the health care community at the end of the month in Parksville, BC. I spoke privately to each of my colleagues in advance and asked if they would be willing to sit on the board of a national organization. I convinced Tanja to be in charge of membership; Jonathan and Jesse would tackle standards and guidelines; Konia could lead on education. It was easy to call up Ellen in Vancouver and have her agree to take on research. By the end of that day in Parksville, I had six willing board members, and we all shared a vision.

Charged with administering the paperwork, I incorporated a national organization, a nonprofit association that would support and give voice to the professionals doing the work of MAiD across the country. Our main goals were threefold: to support those doing the work of assisted dying; to educate both the public and the health care community about MAiD; and to become a leading voice in establishing medical standards for MAiD in Canada. We gave ourselves the name of the Canadian Association of MAiD Assessors and Providers—CAMAP—pronounced *Ka*-map, and with my colleagues' encouragement, I took on the title of president.

It would be another six months before we were fully realized on paper, but the work to connect and support the entire MAiD community began immediately. That winter, I created a newsletter featuring stories of program development and overcoming hurdles from different regions of the country, sharing data, raising thorny issues, and presenting hypothetical case histories as a teaching tool. Our new board of directors decided to develop a website where we could post a library of resources and even a few family testimonials. Work began on the writing of clinical guidelines for our membership. We began organizing research and connected with academic centers for collaboration. We cohosted webinars with Dying With Dignity Canada in which we shared personal experiences and lessons learned from challenging cases. And the email group, now hosted by the University of British Columbia and a formal online forum, continued to flourish.

"Any suggestions for assessing a person who has full capacity but cannot speak? What have you done when family members are divided and angry about a patient's decision to have an assisted death? Has anyone ever had children as young as six years old attend?"

There was more and more to do. And what did I know of running a national nonprofit? I was learning as I went, seeking help from friends, family, acquaintances in my community, and anyone and everyone I could tap.

Not long after the official formation of our group, I began to envision a national conference on MAiD. I convinced Jean-Marc to be the event planner. He had remarkable organizational skills, and together we worked out a concept for the event. Our keynote speaker would be the distinguished lawyer Joe Arvay, who had successfully argued the *Carter* case in court. The conference would take place on the first anniversary of MAiD becoming law in Canada, in June 2017.

———

Even in Victoria, where it's temperate year-round, it was beginning to feel like we were rounding into winter. Holiday decorations were popping up everywhere. Instead of summer flower baskets hanging on city streetlamps, now there were tinsel replicas of candy canes and reindeer. I was looking forward to some family time. Sam was due to return home from his first year away at university, and Sara would have several weeks off from eleventh grade.

I was curious to see if there would be a slowdown with MAiD around the holidays. Things had seemed to be picking up, and I wondered if it reflected ongoing growth of the program or if the workload was going to be cyclical. Certainly there had been busy times of the year in maternity care: Springtime was always the most hectic, and in Victoria, home to the Canadian Navy's Pacific fleet, we maternity practitioners always knew when a ship that had been away for over six months finally redocked—nine months later, we saw a predictable spike in babies being born. With MAiD, I hardly knew what to expect.

Requests for assisted dying had been increasing month after month, but with the holidays drawing closer, patients kept telling me one of two things: They either wanted to die before the holidays so their families wouldn't associate the season with loss; or they wanted to share one last holiday together and hoped to schedule their death early in the new year. Quite a few people proceeded in early December. But as families began to gather for the holidays, there was an understandable inclination to want to stick around. Several people delayed their plans and hoped to tough it out. Not all could make it through. A number of patients declined quickly and needed urgent care. Unfortunately, some of those cases were over the holidays.

As it turned out, December 2016 was the busiest month for MAiD on record within the Island Health Authority. In the first four months after the law was changed, our entire region (encompassing a little under eight hundred thousand people) was averaging six MAiD deaths per month. For the months of October to January, the average had grown to twenty. For me personally, my holiday work evolved to make January 2017 the busiest month of my practice for a long time yet to come. I was busy at the office, busy at the hospital, busy in my home, and busy trying to start our new national association. To be honest, I felt busy in my sleep.

By the time Gordon's nephew Rick called my office in January 2017, Gordon had been asking about MAiD for almost two months. It had been difficult for Rick to find the proper information on whom to call for help. Gordon's family physician had wiped his hands of "this stuff," and the idea of calling someone at the local health authority hadn't occurred to the family. In the end, a friend of a friend of theirs read about a talk I gave at a local community center and tipped them off to my name. The Internet took care of the rest, and I agreed to see Gordon within twenty-four hours of their request.

I often heard accounts of similar barriers: "My doctor didn't know anything about it," "My doctor said he doesn't provide this type of care," and the heartbreaking "I didn't feel comfortable asking my doctor . . . I've known her for twenty years and thought she'd be upset with me. I didn't want her to think she'd failed me." Stories like these and Gordon's inspired me to give more public talks, even if some colleagues in the local medical establishment were reluctant to have me speak at medical rounds for the entire hospital department. I wasn't exactly sure why that was. Many local colleagues were curious and sought information, but there seemed to be some discomfort around organizing the provision of information on assisted dying within certain segments of the health care community. By contrast, the public demand for information was considerable. Suffering patients had requested and driven the change in the law. Perhaps it was the patients who would have to enlighten their doctors rather than the other way around.

Gordon lived in a condominium downtown; on the day of our appointment, I drove over to see him. Rick buzzed me into the upscale building, and I took the elevator swiftly up to the tenth floor. It was warm in the condo, which was flooded with sunlight. Gordon was lying half clothed in a hospital bed set up in his living room, sleeping. He was very thin, and at six-three, he had the look of an emaciated giant. As I walked over to greet him, I spotted the familiar blue binder of information from the palliative care team sitting on the coffee table. I noticed an empty urinal container hooked to the foot of his bed and an unopened package of adult diapers partially hidden underneath. I counted five bottles of pills lined up on the counter leading into the kitchen. Before a word was spoken, I had a sense of what was happening—palliative care was involved, multiple pain medications were routinely dispensed, and Gordon was bedbound, not even up to using the commode anymore.

Rick and Gordon's wife, Mary, stayed in the room to listen while we spoke. The large cancerous growth in his cheek and jaw made it difficult for Gordon to talk, but after a few minutes, I could better understand his altered speech.

I learned he was eighty-four, a retired engineer, a world traveler, and a lifelong supporter of the right to die with dignity. He had been diagnosed with a Merkel cell carcinoma, an uncommon form of skin cancer that had already spread to his lungs, scalp, and abdominal wall. Gordon understood his cancer was incurable. In the last few weeks, he had become bedbound with fatigue. Unable to eat solid food, he required help with absolutely everything, from getting dressed to getting to a commode. Gordon had given up on the former and dreaded the latter. He told me he just lay there, waiting to die.

"This life is a misery," he declared on the morning that we met. "If I had a revolver, I'd take care of it myself."

He spoke those words with such sincerity that I could not stop an image of the ugly aftermath from coming to mind. Thankfully, Gordon went on to explain that he'd prefer something less traumatic for his wife's sake.

Rick explained that when awake, Gordon was still very much himself: He had real wit and lucid thoughts. But his recent decline had been significant. He was asleep during the day as many hours as he was awake. The narcotics had his pain under control, although his periodic confusion was upsetting to everyone. Gordon's circumstances served to reinforce for me that it's not for lack of adequate care or support that the majority of people ask for assistance to die. They ask because all quality of life has gone and they no longer can find meaning in living.

Gordon had filled out a request for MAiD, but I noticed it was improperly completed, with witnesses signing on two different days and neither on the same date as his own signature. We arranged for the request to be redone. I told the family that, in my opinion, Gordon was eligible for an assisted death, and I promised him I would work hard to quickly find a second clinician to assess him and fulfill all the requirements of the process.

Normally, there was a mandatory ten-day waiting period after the written request in which the patients can reconsider their choice, but I had the authority to shorten this requirement if both assessors agreed the patient was imminently dying or imminently at risk of losing the capacity to make this decision. In Gordon's case, I was concerned enough about his recent decline that this might become necessary. We explored his feelings about palliative sedation versus obtaining an urgent assisted death. Gordon stated his strong preference for MAiD, so pending the conclusion of the second assessor, I planned to return in seventy-two hours and assist him to die.

As the elevator doors opened once again onto the tenth floor three days later, I sensed there was a problem. Maybe it was the sound: It wasn't the calm, silent hallway I was expecting. Gordon's door was open two doors down on the right, and Rick was straddling the threshold. I could hear people milling about deeper inside. Head down, with his hands stuffed in his pockets, Rick appeared to be mumbling to himself and subtly shaking his head. He looked up as I started toward him, but he seemed unsure whether to come and greet me or to wait a moment longer until I crossed the thirty feet to where he stood.

As I drew closer, Rick explained that Gordon had had a tough day or two, and the palliative team had suggested he take higher doses of morphine, which Gordon had gratefully accepted. The pain was once again under control, but now he was sleeping almost continuously. Once I stepped inside the apartment, Mary quickly introduced me to the gathered family and then reported that she'd not been able to speak with Gordon for over eighteen hours.

I found Gordon in the same place, in the same bed, and under the same sheet. As with my last visit, he was sleeping when I arrived, only this time I couldn't rouse him. I tried every method—touch, loud voice, pressure on his breastbone—all to no avail. It had been over eight hours since his last injection of pain medication, but there was no sign it was wearing off. At one point, Gordon opened his eyes and seemed to briefly look at me, but he said nothing. He couldn't blink, squeeze my finger, or respond to my questions. He could not communicate with me in any way or let me know if he understood what was happening.

Shit.

I wasn't sure what to say, but I knew what had to happen or, rather, what could not. I knew I could not act. I needed Gordon's consent, and there was no way he could give it. I dreaded facing the family, and they were all there, watching and waiting. I turned to look at them, but Rick spoke first.

"Before you say anything, Dr. Green, we just want you to know we all understand what's going on here. You were very clear about the process and the procedure, and we understand we're in a bit of a pickle. But we also know Gord, and we know what he wanted. And he told you so himself. So, before you say anything, I think I speak for everyone here when I say no one would say a word, to anyone, ever. If you would just consider going ahead . . . We all know it's what Gord wanted. And it's the right thing to do. Please . . . just go ahead. We'll all vouch for his consent."

Five pairs of eyes looking at me, pleading, hopeful.

This situation felt like the most difficult I had faced so far. Yes, I'd been frustrated about the lack of clarity around my ability to assist Nevin, but this time I wasn't debating details over email. I wasn't a plane trip away. I was standing right there, in the living room, with the family, next to a patient, a person I had promised to help.

For a moment, I considered going ahead. Who would ever really know?

But I knew I couldn't. As much as their argument made sense to me, as ridiculous as I thought the situation was, it would have set a dangerous personal precedent, and it was a line I was not willing to cross. For some, the job is to advocate for change in the law. For me, the job is to work to the best of my abilities, and to the highest of standards, but always within the law.

It's hard to describe what it felt like to stand in Gordon's living room trying to explain to his family why I could not proceed. Of course I knew what his wishes were. Yes, he had followed all the correct procedures. No, he should not be punished because he came to me so late in the course of his illness. I fully understood their position, but it didn't change the regulations: a procedural safeguard determined by politicians . . . with nothing to do with standards of care.

"I understand everything you are saying," I told them. "I might even personally agree with you. But I cannot take the law into my own hands. This practice is new and requires standards, regulation, and oversight to ensure it is carried out safely. I'm so sorry, but I cannot proceed." I decided to take the burden of responsibility off the family and accept it as my own. "I know the situation seems absurd, but I just can't take the risk of going to jail."

There was no more discussion after that. I packed up my things in silence. I said goodbye to Mary, wished her strength in the coming days, and left the building.

Some may argue that in "the good old days," this was when doctors might have intentionally increased the dose of the pain medication and patients could have slipped away under the guise of appropriate pain control. Perhaps in some places they still do. I maintain that this is where providers of MAiD demonstrate we are accountable to a system that strives to balance autonomous wishes and action with protection of the vulnerable. There is a necessary if imperfect piece of legislation in place to which we are all beholden.

I shared my experience with my colleagues on our online forum. They were deeply sympathetic and offered up their own stories of similar scenarios. Calling off a procedure due to the unanticipated loss of capacity of the patient—I was horrified at how common this was.

"Seven months in and we're still not getting consulted until too far along in a person's decline," one person said. "I'm not clear whether it's the patients who aren't asking, a difficulty in finding an assessor, or health care practitioners who are unwilling to refer in the first place, but it's really tough on everyone when this situation occurs."

"What drives me crazy is that we know it was what the patient wanted"—I was venting my frustration—"it was just the final consent before we began that I wasn't able to confirm."

Requiring final consent immediately prior to proceeding is a measure to ensure the patient can change his or her mind at any time, right up until the moment of the procedure. This is a safeguard built into the legislation to help assure that it is the patients themselves who provide the consent to assisted dying, and to help reduce the risk of abuse among vulnerable populations, meaning nobody can ever consent to MAiD on anyone else's behalf: no power of attorney, no health care representative, no angry spouse or greedy child.

In seven months, I had seen many people fearful of losing their ability to consent. Some patients refused to accept adequate pain control in the days leading up to their procedure for fear they might become too sleepy. This resulted in increased pain and suffering. Even more worrisome, I was hearing of some terminally ill people who were choosing to end their lives with MAiD earlier than they would have liked for fear that their illness might progress more quickly than expected and rob them of their ability to decide to die as they wished.

"I really wish there was a way to consent in advance," someone argued on the online forum after I shared my experience with Gordon. "For people who get referred to us too late in the process, for those who've already been assessed for MAiD and deemed eligible, but especially for people with dementia."

A firestorm of commentary ensued. The subject of assisted dying in patients with dementia was always intertwined with the topics of final consent and advance requests. Although I hadn't yet met with any patients who had dementia, I could see that assisting someone with memory loss would be complicated. If a patient has a diagnosis of dementia, by the time he or she is in an advanced state of decline, does that patient still have the capacity to make a request for an assisted death?

Some say dementia patients should be able to ask for an advance request *before* they lose capacity. There had been tremendous public support to create such an option. I wasn't convinced it was that simple.

"I'm not sure I could ever provide an assisted death to someone who couldn't look me in the eye on the day of the procedure and consent," began one colleague on the CAMAP forum.

"As a geriatrician," answered another, "I work with patients at all stages of dementia, and I have seen what this disease can do to a person. In its advanced stages, it is a devastating, horrible disease. If it were legal, I would definitely honor an advance request by someone wishing to avoid such a fate."

When Canadian law was amended to allow for MAiD, three issues deemed too complex to initially legislate were slated for further study: the possibility of MAiD in mature minors (those under eighteen but deemed capable of making their own health care decisions); a request for assisted dying when a mental health disorder is the sole underlying condition; and the notion of an advance request to consent for MAiD. My instinct told me it would be important to find a safe way to allow advance requests for MAiD for people with dementia, but to this day, there remain critical questions to which I don't have all the answers. Primary among them is who should decide when criteria are met, and with what measuring stick? And how would we determine if the patient is suffering? Would that still be necessary?

Many people suggest if they were given a diagnosis of Alzheimer's disease, they would like to be able to make an advance request for MAiD. They would like to outline the conditions that, once reached, would trigger fulfillment of their wish to die. People often cite a time when they can no longer recognize family as a typical criterion. But who should be responsible for declaring when these conditions have been met, and at what point can one determine that the criteria have been fulfilled? No one would suggest proceeding to an assisted death the first time a family member is not recognized. The second time? When it's consistent? Over how long a time period?

And what if this person, let's say it's your mother, who has said her whole life that she would want an assisted death if she could no longer recognize her family, is now living comfortably in a specialized health care facility where she seems unlike the person she used to be—she doesn't recognize you as her child, and she acts significantly differently from the chatty parent who raised you? Perhaps she doesn't communicate much anymore or seem particularly connected to anyone, yet oddly seems to enjoy a rousing game of bingo every Wednesday morning at ten-thirty (didn't she used to hate bingo?). Even if she meets the pre-outlined criteria for when she would want an assisted death, I am not certain I would be comfortable providing one for her. What would I say when she smiles and asks who I am, why I am visiting, and says, "No, thank you, I don't like needles, so please don't start an IV in my arm right now, I'm heading to bingo"? The essential component of suffering appears to be missing. And whose suffering should we take into account? The person who was or the person who now is? It's simply not so simple.

But I do think we can find a way. And for people like Gordon who have capacity and who meet eligibility requirements, for those who've been fully assessed and formally approved and have already set a date to die, I strongly believe there should be a special type of advance request, one that would allow them to proceed with MAiD even if they lose the capacity to provide their final consent. Such an allowance would not address the larger complexities of advance requests for patients with dementia, but it would help people like Gordon and his family who found themselves in a predicament that was not unique, according to my cross-country colleagues. Exactly who would have been harmed by allowing Gordon to proceed?

The palliative care team ensured that Gordon was comfortable and well sedated until his death. He died seventy-six hours later, in his living room, surrounded by his loved ones. Rick called to tell me they were glad to see he hadn't suffered. They understood and respected my position but, he pointed out, those seventy-six hours had been a grueling eternity for the family.

Rick and the rest of Gordon's family might carry some guilt for not having helped him achieve his final request; they definitely shouldered an extended period of suffering while they awaited his final outcome. I was torn between my professional duty to reduce Gordon's suffering and the necessity of staying within the law. Ironically—although it wasn't what he wanted—I believe Gordon, in his unconscious state, might have been the least affected of us all.

Part 4

SPRING

CHAPTER 16

THE FEBRUARY SKY WAS FILLED with broad gray clouds, and it was beginning to rain, but my dog still needed a walk. In spite of my complaints about the wintry weather, I always found morning walks with Benji to be grounding, a tiny capsule of sanity in an otherwise crazy world. Despite a significant dog allergy, I'd come to love our four-legged family member, and I was constantly amazed at how he instinctively sought out whoever most needed his companionship at any given moment. We were headed to the beach, so I turned my cell phone to vibrate. I had pledged to keep my time there cell-phone-free, but I couldn't bring myself to shut off the outside world completely.

When we got there, Benji ran ahead and quickly found the stick he wanted to play with, tail wagging, excitement obvious. There was no arguing with him at this point. A walk to the other end of the beach was not on his agenda. It was time to catch, to dig, or to chew, and I acquiesced to his alternating preferences until it was time to go.

A few minutes after we left the beach, my cell phone began to buzz. I dug my phone out of my jacket pocket and was surprised to see the name on the screen.

It was Dr. Vass, a senior physician from the community palliative care team, so I decided to answer the call. He asked if I would see a patient of his named Edna. He'd been caring for her for several months. I hadn't worked with this doctor before, and I was simultaneously flattered that he had called—I respected his expertise—and apprehensive about what his personal opinions about assisted dying might be. Then again, I knew he wouldn't be calling me if he hadn't come to terms with his patient's request.

Edna was having worsening symptoms of her multiple system atrophy, an uncommon neurodegenerative disorder that was affecting every aspect of her life. Two weeks earlier, Dr. Vass had been visiting with Edna when she'd asked him for MAiD by scratching out letters on a whiteboard. It was one week after her seventy-seventh birthday, just after she'd returned home from a hospitalization, and she had repeated her plea several times since. Dr. Vass was calling me to ask if I would assess her for eligibility. Edna had a daughter and a fairly large extended family, but her youngest sister, Mindy, was the point of contact. I was already booked for most of the day, but I assured Dr. Vass I would be able to see her soon.

Back home, after I fed the dog and changed my clothes, I sat down at my desk to look into Edna's medical history. Reading the records never gave me the full story—you had to be in the room with the person to learn that—but it was an important step in my process.

Edna managed a slight smile upon my arrival at her home a few days later, but her eyes seemed locked in a blank gaze. I noticed that her frail body was strapped into her padded chair to stay upright. Her care aide told me they were just about to get her to the commode and then back into bed for my visit. I stepped outside and listened from the hallway as the mechanical lift was recruited to help. I heard friendly but firm instructions from the care aide, then I heard cries of discomfort from Edna. About twenty minutes later, I was seated at her bedside, the commode wheeled away, the care aide having made himself scarce. Before I even began, Edna was already scratching something on the whiteboard. I waited for her to finish, three letters that said it all.

"D-i-E"

She knew why I was there. I was surprised and thankful she was still able to write. She stopped and looked up, and I thought she was done. She uttered a sound I didn't understand and then brought the marker down forcefully, drawing my attention to her message and simultaneously dotting the exclamation mark.

"D-i-E P-L-S-!"

Request received.

Edna was close to her sister, and with Mindy filling in the details, I learned that Edna had been a pioneer for most of her life, one of only two women to graduate with a bachelor's degree in biology from her college back in 1960. She taught high school science for almost two decades, did a few stints as the principal of two schools, and then retired from her post as superintendent at the age of sixty-eight. An avid hiker and a supporter of women's rights, Edna had remained active and involved in a variety of volunteer positions until her diagnosis overwhelmed her.

Edna had slowly deteriorated over the past eight years and was now unable to walk or talk. She'd lost coordination of the movement of her legs and eyes. Her arms were slightly more functional, but the left one was difficult to control, and she'd become wholly dependent on others for care. More recently, she'd been losing the ability to swallow, and she had landed in the hospital last month after aspirating food into her lungs. There was now talk of surgically inserting a feeding tube into her stomach. She'd decided she didn't want that. She saw no reason to prolong her life as it was, but she did not wish to starve to death: thus her request for MAiD.

It was difficult to reconcile the woman before me—gazing blankly ahead, unable to speak—with the same trailblazing woman I was learning about. But the next time I visited, a week later, I got a small glimpse of Edna's indomitable spirit when she used that valuable whiteboard.

We were once again meeting in her bedroom and talking about what might come next. "A feeding tube is a simple device," I said, "and easy to arrange. It could buy you some time to consider your options."

"NO," she wrote in her erratic print. "ENuF!"

Edna was understanding when I told her I thought she was likely eligible but that I needed to dig a bit more through her records, to read the specialist reports, to get a more fulsome picture of her trajectory and care.

I spoke again to Dr. Vass and reached out to her neurologist. Two weeks later, I returned to Edna's bedside with the news that I was convinced that she was eligible, and I was willing to help her if she felt the need to go ahead.

She drew a happy face . . . no eyes, just a smile.

We then turned to practical matters. Edna had been raised in a religious home and still had family who were deeply faithful. She'd been worried about their possible reaction, so she'd kept much of the decision-making to herself. Now that she knew she was eligible, she would share her decision to proceed, and she hoped they'd be willing to join her on the actual day of her death. With Mindy's help, we discussed some of the obstacles she foresaw, and I arranged for a hospice counselor to facilitate what everyone expected would be a difficult conversation.

It didn't go well.

I received a phone call from the counselor after the meeting to give me the "heads-up" that there were strong feelings and dissent within the family. The counselor told me she had encouraged people to express their feelings and to listen to each other's points of view, but that much of the meeting had felt like a sermon. Edna had contributed little to the conversation.

"As her brother was talking," explained the counselor, "she took the time to write out 'CHRiStN ANtAgONiSM.' I'd say she's determined to proceed."

When I returned to meet with Edna so we could talk about choreographing the day of her death, she informed me that her relatives would not be joining us for her final moments. There was a clear difference of opinion regarding her final decision, and heated words had been exchanged. Edna was disappointed but set on going ahead, and I reassured her that I would be there with her. Mindy explained Edna had lost her son to melanoma (a skin cancer) nearly ten years earlier and that her daughter preferred to say good-bye the night before the procedure. Edna's brother and sister-in-law had refused to attend, and Edna's nephew Andrew and his wife had also chosen not to be present. Mindy confirmed that she alone would be with Edna.

By then I understood that being present for a loved one's death is harder on some people than others. While it's true, at least from my experience, that most family members prefer to be present, the final images of a loved one's death cannot always be easily erased, so some choose to remain present until their loved one has fallen asleep and then excuse themselves for the final few moments. I always explain what people can expect to see, offer a few options of when they can step out, and then let them decide for themselves. With Edna's family, I understood there was a more specific reason they did not wish to be present—a deeply held religious belief system that could not accept her decision.

I thought it would be a quiet affair. But on the afternoon of Edna's scheduled death, I arrived at her home to a chaotic scene. I could hear a man's voice yelling as soon as I opened the front door. It was Edna's nephew Andrew and his wife. They were standing at the foot of her bed, pleading with her to reconsider. Two care aides were standing outside her door, looking frightened and unsure what to do.

"They have poisoned your mind!" Andrew thundered. "The Church will never condone this. Your soul will never rest. You know that . . . you simply cannot do this!" His anger was mounting. "*We* will never condone this!"

They switched tactics, begged to stay with her, pledged to do whatever was necessary to keep her comfortable. They threatened to leave if she went forward with her plan.

I'd been under the impression that everyone's goodbyes had been scheduled for the night before and that the family wouldn't be present today, so I hadn't prepared for the possibility of such a scene.

"Good afternoon," I announced loudly. The yelling stopped immediately. "I'm Dr. Green," I added in a more normal voice.

Edna looked calm, but her face was hard to read. Andrew looked exasperated. I asked if we might talk in another room, and he and his wife followed me to the living room, where I gave them an opportunity to explain their point of view. I listened and nodded and heard them out. When they were done, I told them I respected their position. I explained that I understood the basis of their faith and meant no disrespect with the following comment, but it really didn't matter what they wanted or believed. "This decision is Edna's and Edna's alone."

They had thoroughly stated their concerns, and Edna had heard them. I had too. And while I speculated that this decision might never be right for them, Edna had reached a place in her illness and, most importantly, in her suffering, where she believed it was right for her.

"You are welcome to join us if you can contain your emotion, but you are not welcome in her room otherwise."

Andrew lapsed into momentary silence. He stood up abruptly, then sat back down. "How can it be possible that, as a close family member, my arguments won't be taken into account?" he asked.

I assured him that his arguments were important but only in relation to his own health care and no one else's.

"But this is unconscionable!" he began ramping up again. "If you proceed, I will call the police. In fact, I will call them anyway . . . this must be stopped. You cannot just kill my aunt . . . and if you won't listen to me, you'll have to listen to them."

I remained unfazed. I was concerned to see him so upset, but this was not one of those legally or medically complex cases. Unlike Nevin's, Edna's diagnosis was clear, and there was no doubt she was on a trajectory toward death. And unlike with Gordon, I had gotten here in time. There was nothing questionable about it: I had a patient who was eligible for MAiD, and she had made a voluntary formal request. The law in this case was clear: She was entitled to my assistance. I was confident in my role and in her rights. I felt sorry for Edna's family, I understood they would need support, but I would not be bullied out of my responsibilities, nor would I let them bully Edna.

"You can call," I answered. "Go ahead. I suspect they will be helpful in enforcing the law and escorting you out of this house." Then I checked my tone, dialed down the rhetoric, and took a breath. "It would be a shame if that were Edna's final memory of you."

We stared at each other in silence. I could tell Andrew was weighing his options.

"I see," he said, and stood up once more. "Alice, we are leaving. Our work here is done. We've done what we could. Aunt Edna will pay the price. I will not attend her murder."

And with that, they walked out. Mindy was just arriving, but they did not stop to talk. I was a little saddened to see them go—I had hoped they would rally to support their aunt—but I was also relieved.

In an odd twist of fate, I was alone at this procedure. There had been a conflict in scheduling, so Jessica had come by earlier to start the IV and then left. In the end there was just Edna, Mindy, and me in the bedroom, and Edna provided her consent.

Once the whiteboard was put to the side, I set up my medications on the night table and sat on the edge of the bed. Mindy was on the other side, holding Edna's hand. When I asked if she was ready to begin, Edna grunted and nodded slightly. She couldn't quite meet my eyes, but she grabbed my hand and squeezed quite firmly, three distinct squeezes in a row. Then she let go, reached over, and laid her hand over Mindy's. I didn't really know what her hand squeezes meant, but they felt like a thank-you to me. For a woman who couldn't speak anymore, for someone who'd had others try to speak for her, I thought she'd communicated beautifully. I began.

Later on, alone in the protective confines of my car, I ran over the events in my mind. Andrew referring to Edna's death as a murder had been upsetting to me even though I knew it was purposeful hyperbole. I had to remind myself it was Edna's disease that was killing her, and my role was only to facilitate her free will. I returned the medication boxes to the pharmacy, stopped by my office to complete and fax the paperwork, and drove home. I was promptly greeted by a happy little dog, whom I rewarded with an extra-long scratch under the chin, after which I'm pretty sure we both felt a little bit better.

I asked my colleagues online if they'd ever encountered such resistance, and I'm sorry to say I wasn't alone, but there were remarkably few instances of anything similar. Much more common were friends or family members who respectfully declined to attend, citing differences in values, but remained respectful of their loved one's right to do as they pleased.

I spent several weeks worrying about whether Edna's event might lead to a complaint about my actions to the professional licensing body. I was confident any such complaint would be settled in my favor, but I dreaded having to go through the process. I took comfort in the fact that in the end, Edna died with dignity, holding the hand of a person who loved her, confident in her decision, and empowered to follow through with it by a rights-based legal system. I'm happy to report no complaint was ever made.

CHAPTER 17

AFTER NINE MONTHS OF PRACTICING MAiD, I was comfortable with the medical aspects—the technical practicalities and the physical processes. But what was less straightforward were the family dynamics, both in the buildup to a death and on the day itself. Although I had only once encountered family members as vehemently opposed to my work as Edna's, I was continually reminded that my patients weren't the only ones who were suffering, that their loved ones were going through their own pain. As time went on, I began to devote more thought to the people left behind—their loss, their grief, and their not always obvious needs.

When the law changed in Canada allowing for MAiD, we had focused so much effort on building the required infrastructure to support the clinical care that we hadn't spent enough time thinking about support systems for the loved ones left behind. By the end of my first year in this practice, we would start to see some development in MAiD-specific bereavement resources, but back in those early days, I had to rely on my (still-imperfect) instincts.

Most families rallied to support their loved one. Even if there was an initial difference of opinion about seeking an assisted death, it was unusual to see families divided and arguing. What was much more common was seeing people struggling to say goodbye. Some friends and family members just didn't know how. MAiD offered no magic bullet in that sense. It did give people an opportunity to express their true feelings before it was too late, which often facilitated closure. But saying goodbye is never easy. Even when I had helped everyone involved to prepare—they knew what would happen, the order of events, how long it would take, and what they would see—death often still seemed like a shock, and I had become aware of the importance of helping people navigate the aftermath once I pronounced someone dead.

A pronouncement of death may sound like an ending, but in truth, it marks a beginning. For those left behind, it's the start of a new chapter, a time of life without their loved one. For many, this can be tremendously difficult. Every relationship is unique, so every reaction is unpredictable. I was still learning how to guide people through those first moments after a death with professionalism and sensitivity.

I had come to help Joseph, but it is his wife, Stella, whom I will remember most vividly.

When I first met Joseph, he and Stella had recently moved into a new high-end retirement community in Sidney, a small municipality just outside of Victoria. It was a time when he knew his lung cancer would be responsible for his death, but he could still slowly walk the stairs to pick up their mail. We met that afternoon on his living room couch, surrounded by unpacked boxes, with Stella sitting next to him. At his request, I explained the process, the paperwork, and the details of the procedure. I answered Joe's questions and asked a few of my own: "If you ever get to a point where you request an assisted death, where do you think you would like it to happen?"

"Here, at home," Joe answered without having to think. "Would that be all right?"

"Certainly," I responded. "That makes a lot of sense to me. And have you ever thought of whom you might want to have with you in the room at the time of your death?"

These were routine questions, and responses were often some variation of: "Just my immediate family and maybe a close friend or two." But Joe seemed stumped. He didn't answer at all, so I rephrased the question: "I won't hold you to it, but what would it look like if you could have anything you wanted? Music? Spiritual guidance? Any particular family or friends?"

Stella, who was sitting silently next to Joe, shifted uncomfortably.

"No," answered Joe. "None of that, I don't think." He spoke quietly while looking directly at me.

There was a pause in the conversation. I wasn't certain I understood, so I looked to Stella for confirmation. "Stella, will you be there with Joe?"

"No," she said. "No, I won't."

As answers go, it was pretty definitive. And since they had been married for fifty-five years, it was unexpected. Stella offered no explanation, and Joe didn't seem at all surprised, so I didn't probe deeper.

Although I'd met several patients who wanted to "protect" their loved ones from the sight of death, spouses and adult children usually insisted on being present. I always encouraged the conversation about who would be in the room. I found that while some people had strong feelings, most hadn't ever considered the options. The final decision was left to the patient most times, but those ensuing discussions were valuable, offering family members a chance to consider decisions I hoped they would feel good about in the future—and these consultations frequently resulted in additional people present at the bedside.

But that was not what happened with Joseph.

Three months after that first meeting, on the day of his assisted death, I was sitting on the edge of a rented hospital bed in a side room set up for him. He was lying flat in his bed, looking frail—he looked easily ten years older and ten pounds lighter than the first time we had met.

"They are not going to join us," he reminded me about his family. I still wasn't sure if this was Joe's wish or that of his wife.

Joe informed me that Stella and their son, Stephen, would stay together outside his room to support each other while he died. I went along, believing it wasn't for me to judge or interfere with their decision at such a late juncture. When I left the bedroom to speak with Stella and Stephen, she again confirmed that she didn't want to be present when Joseph died, and that she'd appreciate her son's company. I asked if they wished to remain in the apartment or perhaps go outside for a walk. Stella said she'd prefer to be outside, and so the issue was settled.

Once Joseph's IV was in place, I invited Stella and Stephen to go into his room to say a final goodbye while Adele and I stayed in the living room. Adele had recently joined Jessica as one of two nurses primarily working with me to provide IV services for MAiD. Barely five-two and always sporting the largest smile, she was the head of the IV team at the Royal Jubilee Hospital and, coincidentally, as I would soon find out, the neighbor of a good friend (in Victoria, we joke about there being only two degrees of separation). Over the next few months, I would come to learn that Adele was a steady, compassionate woman with a great deal of nursing experience who believed strongly in the idea of assisted dying. She was someone I could count on to support the program, the families we dealt with, and, when necessary, me.

Adele and I couldn't make out much of what was said inside the bedroom, but after Stephen came out, I overheard Joseph talking to Stella. "And thanks . . . for a great fifty-five years."

It didn't sound all that intimate, but it was heartfelt nonetheless. Stella came out, quiet and reserved, sat down, and began to methodically change her shoes.

She was not young, not lithe. She was deliberate and slow, dealing with one strap at a time, out of her Velcro sandals and into her tie-on sneakers. She eventually walked over and took her coat from the closet. She put it on and turned once, over her shoulder, to silently wave goodbye. Stephen was visibly upset as they left the apartment together. Stella seemed . . . numb.

I asked Joe if he was ready to begin, and he was. I suggested he imagine a special memory. I began administering the medications, and he quickly slipped from consciousness. Within minutes, the procedure was over.

As if on cue, Stella and Stephen returned. I quickly closed the door to the bedroom, assuming they did not want to see Joseph in death. I was wrong.

"May I go into the bedroom and take out Joe's hearing aids?" Stella asked me. She wondered if I'd already done so, and I admitted that I had not. "I left them in place so he could talk with you," she explained, "but they have to be stored away properly."

I offered to go in and do this for her, but she seemed determined to do the job herself. Stella opened the bedroom door just a crack and took a peek inside, while I took a seat at the kitchen table to continue filling out my paperwork.

"He looks just like he's sleeping, like he looked the last few nights," she observed, "just resting with his mouth open, under the covers."

Stephen joined his mother at the bedroom door and poked his head inside, then returned to the living room sofa. I watched through the open door as Stella went in and removed Joseph's hearing aids, carefully putting them in the container on the nightstand. I saw her pause afterward to look at Joseph. She placed her hand on his chest, and I assumed she was saying a private, silent goodbye. She stayed like that for a minute or two, and then she joined me at the kitchen table, where she remained standing.

I explained that the procedure had gone smoothly, that Joseph had been very comfortable and had simply slipped into sleep.

"Did you have to close his eyes?" she asked.

An odd question. I answered that I did not. I explained that I had asked him to think of a wonderful memory, and I had encouraged him to close his eyes in order to do so. "He told me he would be thinking of a particular visit to Spain, of a festival of lights the two of you had stumbled upon: a magnificent evening in many ways, I was told." I smiled.

Stella seemed to recognize the memory but only nodded. I went through a somewhat standard debriefing—I talked about available bereavement resources and suggested that she and Stephen had given Joe a gift by being as supportive as they had been. She seemed to take this all in calmly, completely unemotional.

It wasn't until I had finished all my paperwork that Stella voiced her true concern. "Are you absolutely certain? I mean, I'm sure I saw his chest rise and fall. Are you sure that he is dead?"

I realized then that this was why she had stopped and touched his chest. She had needed to check.

Part of the procedure when assisting someone to die is to pronounce the patient dead. That's the medical term for what we do. You hear it thrown around on TV: doctors who "pronounce" the patient. If you ask a teaching physician what's involved, you might get an answer that includes checking pupils for position and response to light, checking response to tactile stimuli, checking for heart sounds and pulses, and finally, recording the time of death.

When administering lethal medications, there is that predictable physiologic pathway: The patient falls asleep, then goes into a deep coma; breathing stops, the patient pales, lips will often turn a bit blue. Most times, I can see a pulse in the neck. It slows. If I look carefully, I can see it become irregular, fibrillate, and eventually stop. There is often a remnant of a heartbeat even after it can no longer be seen in the neck, so I usually wait another minute before I listen with a stethoscope to ensure that cardiac arrest has occurred. If necessary, I tell the family it will be another minute or two, and we sit together. I often hold the patient's still-warm hand. We sit in silence, or we tell stories involving the person who is dying, whichever seems most appropriate.

I've had more than one patient emphasize "Make sure that I am dead" when planning his or her scheduled death. Whenever this happens, I always promise I will do so, and I reassure the person that I won't allow him or her to wake up halfway through the procedure. I make sure to talk explicitly about my work, the finality of the process, and my determination to make the dying process smooth and comfortable—and complete. I have always been diligent in confirming the patient is dead, holding off from informing the family that their loved one is gone until I am 100 percent certain this is true.

"But are you absolutely sure that he is dead?" Stella asked again.

In the millisecond after she asked that question, I replayed the steps I had taken to verify if Joseph was indeed dead. "Yes, I am sure."

But I could tell that Stella needed me to go and check.

One important lesson I've learned throughout my years in medicine is that you must try to meet people where they are, whether it's by using appropriate language or matching the mood and style of speaking. The more others feel you are hearing them, the more likely they will be to listen. This is not something restricted to medical practice. When a friend shares good news, we raise our voice and speak quickly. When it's bad news, we speak more slowly and quietly. But it's not limited to one's manner of speech.

I wanted to meet Stella wherever she was. I assumed she was grieving, and I suspected she was having trouble letting go. And yes, a very small part of me felt it would be wise to go and double-check, just in case. I suggested we go back into Joseph's room to have a look together.

In the bedroom, I placed my hand on Joseph's chest and noted there was no movement. She placed her own hand next to mine. I waited while she assessed things, but she still seemed doubtful. I gently explained to her how I determined if someone was dead—a lack of heartbeat, a lack of reflexes, a lack of response to pain. I pointed out the discoloration of his lips, the changes beginning to show in his fingertips. She nodded but seemed to need more. When I mentioned the stethoscope, assuring her I had already listened for a long time, she whispered yes, I should check that again. So I went through the motions of listening at three different areas of his chest. At some point, I offered the earpiece to Stella, and she listened for at least fifteen seconds. I could tell she was unconvinced, so I placed the stethoscope on my own chest and took a medium-size breath and then paused. I was certain she could hear the airflow and my heartbeat, and she must have been able to contrast this to the silence emanating from Joseph. I placed the stethoscope back on his chest and waited another minute to ask if she noticed any difference.

"Yes." She spoke quietly, looking down. "I thought I heard something the first time, but"—what was that emotion I heard in her voice: hope? fear? disbelief?—"but now I see I was hearing noise from outside. I see now . . . Thank you."

"It must be difficult to say goodbye," I suggested. It was fifty-five years, after all.

Stella didn't say anything. I left her with Stephen and wished them both well, but I was unsettled by her noticeable struggle.

There's no doubt in my mind that the day of a scheduled death is harder on the family and friends than on the patient. I see it over and over: a person ready to die, eager for an end to suffering, satisfied with the decision, and grateful for the ability to proceed. These feelings are not always shared by their loved ones. Louise's son, Pete, was a good example. I've seen a variety of reactions and coping mechanisms. There is the confusing emotion of relief for their suffering loved one and, yes, for themselves. There is guilt, maybe the belief that they could have done more. There is sadness, pure and simple, true grief at the loss of a life partner, disbelief, stunned silence, anger, gratitude, all of these and more. I was learning how best to absorb these reactions, how best to validate them, to hear them, to help those who feel them. This wasn't my area of expertise; nor, technically, was it my responsibility to follow up and support people after the event. But I understood by now that reactions were a crucial part of the death and not always entirely predictable.

As I left her home that day, I wondered if Stella had needed something else from me and didn't know how to ask. In the weeks to come, I often thought about Stella, whether she was coping, and if she had begun the long, slow process of acknowledging that her husband of fifty-five years was really gone.

I couldn't shake the feeling that I hadn't handled Stella's emotions well, so I went to my colleagues at CAMAP online. I changed the names and several details to keep it all hypothetical, but I told them what had happened with Stella after Joseph had died. The first response was supportive and assured me that I'd done my best in an unusual situation. The second response was from a newcomer to the community with a question about whether others routinely stayed with the family until the funeral team arrived (few did). It was the third response that chilled me: "From what you describe and the way you describe it, it sounds to me like she was a victim of spousal abuse. I suspect she was checking to see that her abuser was actually dead."

Everything shifted just slightly. I replayed my interactions with Stella with that lens in place, and it all fit just a little too easily.

"Of course, I don't know this family," my colleague continued, "or any of the real details, but I have some experience in this field. I'm not suggesting you do anything. I'm just adding my first impressions for your consideration. And, if I'm right, your reassurance after the fact might have been exactly what she needed."

I'll never know if it was true, and there's no legitimate way for me to find out, but the possibility haunts me to this day. "Fifty-five years of marriage" took on a whole new meaning.

CHAPTER 18

LATE IN THE WINTER, I received a referral directly from the fledgling local MAiD office. This was a program based in an Island Health facility set up to help support the public as well as the practitioners. It was not nearly as robust as similar offices that fully coordinated care in other regions, but they did their best with what they had, leaving the bulk of the administrative work to the practitioners. I called to get some background information, but the woman I talked to didn't have many details, only that she had interacted several times with a soft-spoken man, originally from Britain, named Edwin, who seemed alone and in need of some help. She admitted it wasn't clear what he was suffering from, but he had specifically called the MAiD office and talked repeatedly about assisted dying, so she thought an assessment was most likely in order. I agreed to do a home visit within the next ten days and asked Karen to prepare a chart. I made a note to gather Edwin's medical records, but I had trouble locating any background information.

On the day of the home visit, I parked my car on the street in front of an old apartment building on the fringe of the same family-friendly neighborhood I'd lived in when we'd arrived in Victoria. I punched the apartment code and was buzzed inside. The lobby had a low ceiling and was wrapped in fake-wood paneling that looked like it had last been updated in 1975.

So far, the collective experience from all other jurisdictions—in the

U.S. and Europe both—was proving true in Canada: The patients I met who were asking for an assisted death were predominantly white, well educated, elderly, and of a higher socioeconomic class. Certainly this had been the experience across the border in Oregon and Washington, the two states with the longest experience with assisted dying in the United States, and it also reflected a large portion of the demographics of Victoria. Was this due primarily to the distribution and dissemination of information about assisted dying? Was it due to the issue of opportunity or access to health care in general? Or did lack of uptake in certain ethnic and indigenous communities reflect cultural norms? My colleagues and I were hesitant to be proactive within marginalized communities lest we appear to be pushing an agenda upon a vulnerable group of people, but some of us began coordinating qualitative research to ascertain attitudes and levels of interest from a variety of community settings, including prisons and low-income neighborhoods. Although I guessed that Edwin was white, I began to suspect this day's visit might be an opportunity to serve someone outside the typical socioeconomic demographic. I entered the elevator, and when the doors slid slowly open a minute later, I was welcomed into a dimly lit hallway.

I was still knocking on the door when Edwin opened it. A thick cloud of cigarette smoke billowed out from behind him. It was difficult not to cough as I stepped inside his apartment. He quickly looked both ways down the hallway, muttering, "Sometimes they listen outside my door," then closed and locked the door behind me. I noticed three handwritten messages taped to the back of the door, reminding him to keep the door locked and to check for mail once a week.

Edwin was disturbingly thin, dressed in oversize threadbare yellow pajamas, and barefoot. He looked to be well into his seventies. His nails were long, his beard was ragged, and he smiled quite a bit, but his teeth were in need of some care. Neither he nor his clothes appeared to have been washed recently. None of this had any bearing on his eligibility for MAiD, but I began to sense something else might be going on.

He guided me into his small apartment along a cardboard floor runner made of flattened boxes. We went straight into the small living space, which had a kitchenette on one side. The walls were pale beige and bare. I saw the windows were covered by cardboard squares that were securely duct-taped in place, preventing any light from entering the room, and I felt a twinge of concern in my chest. Something here was off. A small electric fan swirled the smoke-filled air, and a well-worn brown chair faced an old couch that stood against the wall.

Edwin offered me the couch and sat in the chair, all the while beaming in an excessive, almost childlike way. He was clearly excited to be hosting this encounter. Before I said a word, he began talking incessantly in what some clinicians might refer to as pressured speech—a medical term for when a patient feels the need to share all their thoughts, at an accelerated pace, with an urgency that often seems inappropriate to the situation and is difficult to interrupt.

"I am very honored you are here today. She was so nice to me on the phone, she said you would visit, and now you are here. The others said you wouldn't come but you are here. So very good you are here. I hoped they were wrong. They're sometimes wrong. I can't always tell when they're wrong. I have no more doctors now. I need a doctor, you know? Yes, I need a doctor. I think I should die, it is time for me to die."

He spoke in an unending flow, his gentle manner doing little to calm my mounting unease. This type of speech is common but not exclusive to mania or bipolar disease. His mention of "others" suggested possible family or friends but the equal possibility of voices or auditory hallucinations.

I noted that I was closer to the door than Edwin was, and I tried to remind myself of who might know I was with him, wondering if Karen or anyone else did. I admonished myself for not telling anyone where I was going and tried to focus on what Edwin was saying. I couldn't help coughing from the smoke, but I politely declined his offer of a glass of water.

While I considered how to take charge of the conversation, Edwin explained why he wanted to die.

"I am old now and I am in pain. My feet especially, my ankles, the bones in my feet, they all hurt now. I am so thankful you are here. And this part of my arm too. Really, it is a lot of pain I have. I am old. It is time for me to die. I have thought a lot about this. I am really ready."

Edwin was listing his various pains and telling me of his troubles. To my alarm, he slid off the chair onto his knees and crawled toward me. He stopped directly in front of me and shook his hands to emphasize certain points he was trying to make. He showed me various joints and bruises in explanation of his problems, thrusting body parts in front of my face one after the other. He remained squatting in front of me for what felt like a very long time but was probably only really a minute or two. Although I admit I considered bolting, I didn't actually feel physically threatened. He wasn't particularly angry; I guessed he didn't see the need to observe the usual physical boundaries. When I recrossed my legs to create a slight barrier between us, he turned and crawled back to his chair, continuing his uninterrupted story.

I had stopped listening to the details. By then I was fairly certain Edwin had a mental health disorder. I interrupted and started to ask how he got his food, whether he could care for himself in his home and in the washroom, and if he had a close friend or two on whom he could rely when needed. While Edwin began answering, reassuring me that he was absolutely fine in all of these matters, I began planning my exit strategy. I didn't want to anger him, but I didn't want to lie. I also didn't want to suggest I would assist him with MAiD if I suspected it might not be true. What I wanted was to get someone more experienced in mental health to come and see Edwin.

I thought of my colleagues in another region who had received death threats from a psychiatric patient after they told him he was ineligible, and then I pushed the thought away.

Instead, I began to answer Edwin's questions about MAiD, which he seemed to find intensely interesting. He decided to share with me the various plans he'd made over the years to die by suicide. He stood up to find and then show me the electric knife he kept in its original box in his kitchen cabinet, and he explained that he'd once considered using it to cut his own neck. That was the final straw. Looking back, I'm pretty sure there was no threat intended, but in the moment, it occurred to me that there was a potential weapon in his hands and it was time for me to leave his apartment.

I told Edwin I was glad that he hadn't used the knife on himself, and I moved on to explain that I wasn't certain if he met all the criteria for an assisted death. While I was thinking there might be a question about his mental capacity to make a request for MAiD, I decided to focus on the likely more palatable fact that he might not meet the criteria of his natural death being reasonably foreseeable. I explained that despite his seventy years and despite his stated suffering, which I did not discount and assured him I believed was real, the law was the law, and I didn't believe I was allowed to help him in this way at this time. I also mentioned that the law might evolve one day and his medical condition might change, and he was free to stay in touch.

I was beginning to hear my husband's voice in my head, the conversation we would likely have if I recounted the details of the afternoon's visit. As I imagined his anxiety, I recognized it as my own. I was alone in a strange man's apartment, I was uncertain about his mental stability, and there was a knife in the room. I wanted to get out.

Although intuition is important, and I've learned over the years to trust my own, I was also a little ashamed of how I was feeling. I knew Edwin was in need of help, I just didn't think I was best qualified to provide it; nor was I convinced that remaining in his apartment was necessarily safe. I prepared myself to lie or stall if necessary, if he became angry or tried to stop me from leaving.

I made a mental note that from now on, I would always do a thorough read-through of medical records before visiting anyone at home. I decided Karen and I should share a calendar so she always knew where and with whom I was. And I swore to myself that if there was any indication of an untreated mental health disorder, I would not go alone, or I would ask for a call ten minutes into the appointment as a safety check. All of this was being decided in my mind as my mouth kept talking about MAiD and why Edwin may or may not qualify, and why I now had to leave and how I would review his records and, once things were clarified, I would get back to him.

I walked back to the door. Edwin followed, then unexpectedly took my hand. His hand was warm and soft, almost delicate, the only reason I was able to stop myself from reflexively pulling away. He was smiling, thanking me for visiting, assuring me he understood everything we'd discussed, so grateful I had come to see him, wondering when I would be back. He kept my hand in his, his eyes searching my face, imploring me to answer. He was standing very close to me again, too close for my comfort level. I could feel my heart beating in my chest. Stay cool; he is harmless, I told myself. I'm almost there. I extracted my hand, unlocked the door, opened it, and stepped into the hallway. Only then did I turn back to Edwin.

"I'll call you next week after I review your records in more depth. I'll have more information for you then."

He thanked me again, bowed a few times, and I left, bypassing the elevator and heading straight for the staircase at the end of the hallway. I needed to keep moving. As I descended, I started going faster. I burst out into the lobby and hustled out the front door, taking deep breaths of fresh air, and walked quickly to my car. I got inside but couldn't sit still. I got back out, took in more air, and realized how scared I was.

I called the MAiD office and relayed my experience to the person who had sent me here. She was silent, then apologetic. We agreed we needed better triage in the future. There was still so much we all had to learn. By the time I had relayed my entire experience, I felt calmer, able to get in my car and move on with my day.

Edwin was my last appointment. Before returning home, I drove to the beach, parked near the edge, sat in the car, and watched the ocean. I often sought out the water's edge in order to clear my mind and refocus.

I was conscious of not wanting to bring work-related stress directly back into my home, and I wasn't feeling entirely settled. I wondered if I had overreacted, if I'd never been in any real danger. I asked myself whether I was letting Edwin down and not properly advocating for him. Each time I questioned my reaction, I circled back to the same unsatisfactory conclusion . . . I just wasn't sure. I needed more information, and Edwin needed more than I could offer. It was so much more straightforward when people had terminal physical illness.

Edwin's diagnosis was unclear to me, and his capacity to make a request for MAiD was certainly in question. By their very nature, some mental health disorders affect how we think, understand, and experience our world. How can a clinician separate a rational request to die from suicidal ideation secondary to mental illness? How do I determine whether a request for MAiD is based on facts and personal values or driven by irrational motivation? I know it can be done—I am aware that mental illness does not routinely mean a loss of capacity to make your own health care decisions—but I suspect there might be situations in which this distinction can be challenging.

Managing patients with mental health disorders is extremely complex in regard to MAiD. It was not one of those issues for which I could create a new protocol as I encountered it for the first time. Does a mental health patient have the right to refuse treatment? (We know that answer can sometimes be yes.) Can a mental health disorder ever be considered irremediable? (There's a lack of consensus on this.) A person with both depression and cancer can be treated for depression, and once their mood is stabilized, if they're still desirous of an assisted death, they might be found eligible for MAiD. But what if the mental health disorder is their sole underlying condition—a thirty-year history of treatment-resistant depression or a conversion disorder? Is it ethical to allow those with mental health disorders a pathway to access assisted dying? Are they not particularly vulnerable and deserving of enhanced protection? Several safeguards were in place, but the law did not specifically exclude mental health patients. Should it? On the other hand, blanket exclusion from accessing MAiD based solely on one's mental health diagnosis might be considered discriminatory and ethically unacceptable. In the larger legal and clinical landscape, these issues remain unsettled to this day.

As I watched the waves, I thought about all the things I promised myself I would do differently going forward. I pledged to share my new security ideas with my colleagues and to call the community health unit to seek out some help for Edwin. Feeling better with the comfort of a plan of some sort, I finally drove home, although I'll admit I refrained from telling Jean-Marc all the details of my day . . . at least until I'd put some of those new protocols in place.

CHAPTER 19

NOT LONG AFTER THE APPOINTMENT with Edwin, I made another trip to Halifax to see my mother, this time to celebrate her seventy-fifth birthday. Jean-Marc was away visiting family in Europe, but both of my kids, along with my brother and his family, would be joining for the festivities. My brother and I had thrown my mother a large party the year she turned sixty-five, but she'd refused one the year she turned seventy. We'd been contemplating what to do to mark this new milestone when she informed us she'd already decided to throw a party for herself. Though she was now residing in a supported living environment and unable to carry on a full conversation, my mother rented a medium-size room in a local hotel, chose the menu for a luncheon, issued invitations to approximately twenty-five friends and family members, and arranged for flowers and balloons. She'd had some help, but I was impressed.

We arrived in Halifax a few days before the luncheon. All four of her grandchildren were going to be present. Three were at university and would be flying in separately to join us—my nephew, my niece, and Sam—and Sara would be traveling with me. With our nine immediate family members spread across five different cities, it was a great excuse to come together. My brother agreed to emcee the event, which left me in charge of "saying a few words," a task I no longer minded, except that I wasn't sure what to say.

During the cross-country trip, I thought about my mother and our

203

relationship. Since becoming a mother myself, I had been determined to be more emotionally available to my children than my mother had been to me, to provide them the stability and sense of safety that this period in my life had lacked. As my children grew older, I moved through various stages of deeper insight and understanding about my mother and our relationship. I began to recognize the sacrifices she had made to keep my brother and me in our home. I considered whether her decision to remarry might have been about companionship, stability, and building a family around us as much as it might have been for love. I understood through my own parenting experience that clarity and two-way communication with children were not always easy to achieve, but I had yet to make it all the way through to forgiveness for her failings.

In whatever I would say at her party, I didn't want to rehash familiar family anecdotes or cite the volunteer work she had done in the community when she was younger and more vibrant. Likewise, I didn't want to color my remarks with any emotional baggage or lament her more recent physical decline. What exactly could I focus on? After Sara and I got off the last of our flights, I still had no idea.

Turning in to the hotel driveway on that familiar Halifax corner of Spring Garden Road and South Park Street, walking up the steps into the lobby of the Lord Nelson Hotel, catching a faint smell of ocean on the breeze and the sound of the maritime accent in the welcome of the doorman, in the conversations happening across the lobby, in the voice of the staff member behind the reception desk . . . reminded me I was home—no, I was back—no, I was visiting. This place always mixed me up. It was as familiar as my childhood and as foreign as any place you haven't lived in in over thirty years. I was straddling two worlds—my childhood and my adult world—whenever I visited my mother in Halifax.

We checked in and unpacked before settling into bed. With a four-hour time difference, the clock was telling me it was one a.m., but it was impossible to fall asleep. In the wee hours of that morning, I finally landed on what I wanted to say at my mother's birthday celebration.

In the past, when I thought about my mother, I had tended to focus on her weaknesses, her physical limitations, and her inability to protect me enough as a child, but as I grew older—and even more so since I'd begun working in assisted dying—I'd started to recognize her strengths as well. My mother had gotten divorced with two children in 1979. As one of the first in her social circle to do so, she was a trendsetter in that regard. When she remarried at the end of 1981, the term "blended family" was far from familiar, and there was no road map to guide our rocky transition. Less than ten years later, she was diagnosed with her neurological condition, which stole her independence and slowly chipped away at her self-esteem. And yet she remained undeterred—continuing to travel and socialize as she could, eventually hiring the help she didn't want. Today my mother remained determined and defiant in the face of her illness. While she couldn't participate in most conversations, she was content to sit among family and friends. Her vision and hearing were starting to fail, but she was still able to hold cards, played cribbage almost daily, and could still beat most opponents at Scrabble. Yes, of course, I'd seen and spoken to her on her bad days, but she always seemed to bounce back.

In my mother, I saw the seed of my own emotional fortitude. I'd had a turbulent childhood at times, and I'd learned at an early age to protect myself by building some emotional armor, some emotional walls to help keep the intensity at bay. Although this coping mechanism had not always been helpful in my personal relationships—making me more cautious about becoming vulnerable—it was perhaps due to this inner toughness modeled on my mother, and the lessons in protecting myself from difficult feelings, that I was able to compartmentalize my life, such that I could do my MAiD work and not be wrecked or overwhelmed by it.

In my speech, I decided to talk about my mother's strength, her resilience, and her tenacity.

I walked over to see my mom the next morning, leaving Sara to sleep in. By the time I arrived at her place, my mother was already up, dressed, and had eaten breakfast. Her care aide, Marguerite, had been there since seven-forty-five a.m. getting her ready, and they'd done a good job together. My mother was well dressed, with a spot of makeup and a fun pair of earrings. She was eager to go out for a "walk" in her wheelchair. Marguerite and my mother chattered away as we rolled. Actually, Marguerite mostly chattered, my mother nodded, and they filled me in on the hoops they'd had to jump through in order to organize the luncheon.

I understood Marguerite had done most of the groundwork, but they had this wonderful dynamic: She brought every decision to my mother, who was as stubborn and opinionated as always. How many balloons at the front of the room and what color should they be? What should be used as a centerpiece on each table? How many tables in total, and who was and wasn't invited? Marguerite was the voice and the driver, but my mother was calling the shots. It was remarkable how they functioned as a team, and the best part was how they always made each other laugh. The role of lighthearted facilitator of my mother's demands and comedienne for her amusement wasn't one I could easily play, and I was grateful that she had found someone to fulfill it.

On the morning of the luncheon, we got to the hotel thirty minutes early so my mother could see that the room had been arranged correctly. Everything looked festive, elegant, and inviting. She asked that we take a few photos together before her guests arrived. My kids and their cousins were in their element. All between the ages of seventeen and twenty-one, coming into themselves—the once-clean-shaven boys with long hair and beards, the girls chattering away and happy to see each other—they were hamming it up for the camera, striking kooky poses, and making their grandmother smile.

My mother's guests began to filter in, each greeting her where she sat and offering some wishes on the happy occasion. When the time was right, my brother welcomed everyone and thanked them all for coming. We ate our appetizers and lunches to a constant background chatter and a steady number of visitors to my mother's table. I was seated across the table from her and marveled at the kindness of her closest friends. One after another they'd pull up a chair, speaking slowly but loudly over the background noise, leaning in close to be able to hear her. At first I was grateful for their efforts, but I soon realized it was also a mark of the person she was to them; that they cared about her enough to go beyond her limitations in order to connect.

Before the cake, my brother asked me to say a few words. I looked around at the faces of men and women I had known all my life, people who were well aware of all that my mother had been through. I noticed the aging faces of the family and friends and understood that everyone had been through their own ups and downs.

"Luckily," I began, "my late grandmother Betty taught me that a speech should never be more than two to three minutes, so I promise you this won't be long. My mother has no idea what I am going to talk about, and she may or may not approve in the end . . . I'm sure I'll hear about it either way . . ."

There was a murmur of laughter from the crowd.

"I am not going to stand here and recount her contributions, of which you are all well aware. What I want to shine a light on is the stuff she doesn't like to talk about . . . some of her challenges. My mother doesn't like to discuss her hardships, past or present, but I believe this is the stuff that showcases her true essence. What I want to talk about is my mother's resilience."

I mentioned how trendsetting she had been in her time and the obstacles she'd overcome. I recognized she was not unique in this respect but that her illness (which I knew she rarely spoke of) placed extra burdens on her and those around her. I noted the friends who'd fallen away, the ones who were not with us to celebrate, because I suspected they were unable to cope with her restrictions.

I began wrapping up. "Others in my mother's situation might have folded up the tent along the way, but not my mother. She has faced all her challenges with tremendous fortitude, a stubbornness, even, that I believe is worthy of great respect."

I raised my glass to her and asked others to do the same. Around the room, faces of everyone my mother loved turned in her direction in acknowledgment.

It wasn't exactly forgiveness—there was still a tender part of me that felt bruised by her distance during my teen years—but it was a sincere appreciation of her strengths. And I realized it wouldn't have happened without my work in MAiD. It was maybe the first time I understood that working in assisted dying had provided me a new perspective: on life, on my own life, and on the life of my mother. I'd met people with far less challenging symptoms than my mother asking for help to die, and I had a newfound respect for the efforts I saw people make, both to continue living, even past the point of what they had thought would be acceptable, and ultimately to choose their end of life. All of this cast my mother's ongoing efforts, her persistence, in a new light. She was indeed a survivor, as she'd always told me she was. Sometimes survivors had to make choices that were tough on the rest of us, but the goal was to live another day, to do better the next time. My mother was indeed fallible, but she was absolutely doing her best. What more could I ask?

I flew home feeling good about this new perspective and insight into the seeds of my own strengths, but it was only a matter of time before I was reminded that I was far from invulnerable.

———

Bev was relatively young at sixty-seven, but she was terminally ill with metastatic colorectal cancer. When I first met her, she was already thin and tremendously weak, but she welcomed me to her bedside with a warm, wide smile, and she gave the immediate impression that, when well, she was the one accustomed to giving unto others. Bev was a woman of faith, and she was at peace with the knowledge that her life was ending. It was no longer a question of if but of how soon, and of how much more decline she was prepared to endure.

"I just want a little more time with my children," she told me. "My eldest is flying in from Australia, and then I want to die."

Bev emphasized how grateful she was for her husband and all he was doing to keep her comfortable, but despite the incense he'd set up in her room, the pungent patchouli could not mask the particular indignities of a disease of the rectum. I imagined this reality was not lost on Bev, and I suspected it was a special source of suffering.

When I arrived at Bev's house on the afternoon of her death, I watched Adele drive up, and we walked in together, descending the stairs to the basement, where we found Bev in the bed that had been set up for her there so that her husband had more room to care for her. There were people sitting and people standing, some talking with Bev and others talking among themselves, perhaps ten in total. There were glasses of half-sipped champagne on the nightstand and a few more on the floor, as well as an empty bottle with a pink ribbon tied around its neck off to the left. There was a pleasant, quiet hum about the room, and the patchouli was as strong as ever.

I acknowledged those who turned at the sound of my entrance. "Hello, I'm Dr. Green." Everyone stopped talking, and not for the first time, I brushed aside my discomfort at feeling like an interloper. Bev introduced me to everyone, helping prove her clarity of mind and giving us all a moment to adjust to one another. I was considering the awkwardness of meeting her family in this way when I heard Bev say, "And this is my mom."

These are not words I often hear at a scheduled death. The average age of those I have helped is seventy-five, so Bev's introduction caught me off guard. There, in the chair at the foot of her bed, was an elderly woman with a dark raincoat, oddly, still on. She was deep into her eighties and holding hands with a young woman, a granddaughter, it turned out, who was doting on her. My eyes lingered for an extra second on this novelty—a parent at the bedside—then I restrained my surprise and moved on to the next steps.

Soon enough, we were gathered around for the event. I was sitting on the large mattress to Bev's right, with eight syringes lined up and in order next to me. Adele was standing in the back of the room, out of the way, armed with pen and paper and waiting to record the exact times I administered the medications.

"Does anyone have anything else they want to say before I begin?" I asked.

One by one, Bev's loved ones stepped forward. Bev's daughter Jennifer walked around and sat on the other side of the bed. She took her mom's hand, leaned in close, and thanked her for everything she had done for her. "I love you and I'm going to miss you dearly, but I know you're doing the right thing for yourself," Jennifer said. Then she hesitated, eyes closed, shed a few quiet tears, and placed a last lingering kiss on Bev's forehead before stepping back. I was touched by this tender selflessness.

Jennifer's partner, Rob, a stoic-looking young man in his early thirties, stepped forward toward Bev and softly but confidently promised he would love and care for her daughter forever. Bev smiled, holding his gaze. "I know you will," she told him. She reached for his hand, which he offered and she squeezed, then he bent forward, raised her fingers to his lips, kissed them, and stepped back, a gracious knight.

Others approached Bev and took their turn. This process of saying goodbye, though far from universal, was exceptionally moving, and I tried to stay as insignificant as possible during these precious final moments. I was conscious of being the voyeur, and I wrestled with the feeling that I had intruded while recognizing my role as the clinician in charge. I instinctively looked away as if doing so might provide a greater sense of privacy, but I was mesmerized by what was happening right in front of me.

I was drawn out of all these thoughts when Bev's mother, who had been silent until then, spoke up. "I want to say goodbye," she declared.

I watched as she struggled to get out of her chair. Her granddaughter helped her to stand, but then Bev's mother shrugged loose of the support in order to approach Bev on her own. The old woman leaned down, reached out unsteadily, and held Bev's face with both hands. Her exaggerated knuckles and her crooked purpled fingers contrasted vividly with Bev's pale, smooth, steroid-induced cheeks. She kissed Bev firmly on the right cheek, then kept her face close by as she spoke her simple farewell: "Goodbye, my darling, my dear."

It wasn't so much what was said as the thought of what was happening that affected me. How does an eighty-eight-year-old woman say goodbye to her daughter knowing she herself will remain behind? How does a mother say goodbye to her child? It was unnatural, unfair, not the order in which things should happen, and I wasn't prepared to consider it. I couldn't help projecting myself into the scene . . . what if my mother were asked to say goodbye to me? Or worse yet, what if I were asked to say goodbye to my daughter? I could hardly bear it. For a moment I couldn't breathe, and a cold sweat passed through me as I involuntarily imagined the mind-numbing horror of what her death might feel like. After more than forty assisted deaths, it was the first time I felt tears that I simply could not hold back. I wanted to look away to break the narrative running through my mind, but I couldn't take my eyes off the two of them. I wasn't exactly unable to move, but I didn't feel completely in control of myself.

When my tears began to fall, I forced myself to look down at the bed to compose myself. I breathed in deeply. I was unaware I had been unable to until then. I was conscious of the family sitting close to me, and although I suspected they were caught up in their own experience of loss, I wondered whether they'd noticed that I was so struck. I knew of no guidance on how to behave in such a situation: the clinician moved to tears, stumbling through projection. I was conscious of wanting to move this event forward, for myself as much as for Bev, but I was at a complete loss as to how to do so respectfully.

Luckily, Bev took care of it for me. "I want my monster here!"

She was asking for her dog.

The energetic black poodle bounded up onto the bed and immediately came over to sniff me and my syringes. She allowed me to stroke her, which calmed me, and then she nuzzled in close to Bev. Now we were all ready, no more excuses for delay. Bev caught my eye and asked me to begin.

Ten minutes later, she was gone.

I did my debrief with the family, hugged them goodbye, but didn't speak a word as Adele and I left the house together. I was still reeling from the overall emotion and didn't want to speak until we were well out of earshot. At my car, I put my bag down and looked at Adele before opening my door. "Well, that was quite something," I started, and I wondered if it was just me or if she too had felt the impact.

"It certainly was," Adele replied. "Stefanie, can I ask you something?"

"Of course," I answered.

"Can I offer you a hug?"

I nodded, and before I knew it, Adele embraced me with a firm, supportive squeeze. I must admit, it felt great.

Remaining professional is part of the job—patients expect it, standards demand it, and I had known this when I went into the field of medicine. Doing so in the midst of joy and especially tragedy was something else I had learned in my maternity days. It was not appropriate to remain behind and share in the celebrations after a baby was born, nor was it for me to break down or withdraw at the birth of a stillborn. But it turns out all these emotions go somewhere, and every once in a while, a crack forms in the retaining walls, and the feeling slips out.

CHAPTER 20

SPRING COMES EARLY IN VICTORIA. By the beginning of March, the tulip bulbs have burst through the earth, the buds on the perennials have opened, and our annual flower count begins. Tourists start streaming in to see the cherry blossoms that line the streets, a stunning legacy of the vibrant Japanese community who once flourished in our city. It's the only time of year that the deer seem to be less visible; they are breeding and due to give birth soon.

As the new season came around, there was a noticeable increase in the demand for care. The uptick around the Christmas holidays had become the new norm, and I was routinely seeing several patients a day, accepting four or five new assessments a week, not uncommonly providing more than one assisted death within the same week. Consultations were coming in from general practitioners, hospitalists, oncologists, neurologists, or patients and families directly. I was also managing the patients I had met previously by following up, reassessing, and providing care when the time was right. Looking back, I wonder if I might have been testing my limits, curious to know if I could continue to cope with a continuously expanding workload.

And it wasn't just me. Across the nation, interest in assisted dying was climbing, and my colleagues were equally busy. I was amazed by how many people didn't seem to know it was now legal while more and more people were requesting and receiving help. In the first six months of MAiD in Canada, 0.6 percent of all deaths were reportedly by assisted dying (this is compared to 0.3 percent in the state of Oregon, where assisted dying for terminally ill patients had been legal since 1997). In the second six months, that number rose to 0.9 percent. No one knew how many MAiD clinicians there were within Canada or, just as important, how few. All I knew was that I was busy, and that here on Vancouver Island, with fewer than ten clinicians involved in the work, we were providing more than three times the national average of medically assisted deaths.

At times I thought I had seen it all, but new patients had a way of surprising me.

My first response to hearing the news about Liz was: if it could happen to her, it could happen to me, and that was a sobering thought. Liz and I were acquaintances more than friends, but we were both in our late forties, married with kids, and initially knew each other from my semiregular attendance at a hot yoga studio. We'd gone for coffee once, and I learned about her family, her work in interior design, and that she was hoping to move to my neighborhood. One year later, she and her husband, Mark—a quiet architect with no interest in yoga—invited us to a BBQ. They'd recently successfully relocated, so I got a peek at her new house, her home life, and her three children—two boys and a younger daughter. Since then, my attendance at yoga had diminished, but we waved when we saw each other in the neighborhood, knew we could borrow an ingredient if in a pinch in the middle of a recipe, and found ourselves at a few of the same holiday parties every December.

Liz had been preparing dinner in the kitchen one night when, quite out of the blue, she'd had a seizure. The rumor that circulated was that she had brain cancer. I heard it first from another yoga buddy who knew Liz better than I did. Within a week, the information was updated and clarified—the cancer had originated elsewhere. Liz had stage IV melanoma, and no one understood how it had gone undetected for so long. Cancer was found in her lungs, her liver, her lymph nodes, and her bones, but Liz discovered she was sick only when it wreaked havoc that day on her brain.

I wanted to know more, of course, but had no right to ask. If someone mentioned Liz or fed me details, I was eager to listen, but I felt too removed to ask about her health.

One day that spring, I was on the hospice unit to meet with a new patient when I happened to see Mark at the ice machine. I nodded respectfully but kept moving. Mark—with his sandy brown hair and boyish face—was the foundation of Liz's world. I had no business knowing that his wife was ill enough to be in hospice. It's always a test when I run into someone I know on the hospital campus, and it has been my whole career. The reflexive "What are you doing here?" is always on the tip of my tongue. I try to catch myself. Everyone is entitled to their privacy.

Nevertheless, I began to wonder if Liz was considering an assisted death, a natural question for me. I also knew that assisted dying wasn't for everyone. There are those who accept the inevitable, but others need to fight to the end: It's who they are, how they cope, and I respect that. If I were facing a terminal illness at this stage of my life, I would fight with everything I've got. But I can also envision that a time might come when I'd prefer to end things on my own terms. If I were no longer able to communicate, if I'd already said my goodbyes, if my lingering were only causing more pain for my loved ones, and if I were facing only further decline, I can imagine I might be thankful for the ability to decide when.

I was tempted to pay Liz a visit, but Dr. Whitmore, the hospice doctor I'd worked with many times in the past, reminded me I had not been invited. "It's inappropriate to drop in simply because you noticed she's here," she rightfully pointed out.

I left the unit saddened to know Liz was in decline and properly chastened for my well-intended plan. It was clear I had no role in her care.

Then, three weeks after I saw Mark at the ice machine, I got a new referral: "Hoping you can see this very pleasant woman with metastatic melanoma. Married, mother of three teens, she's been palliative for some time now. She's requesting MAiD and wants to talk with you about making this possible in the very near future. She continues to decline here on the hospice unit. Family mostly on board."

I checked the name twice, surprised to be holding a consult for Liz in my hands. I was aware of what this referral meant, but I needed to be certain that she realized it was me—her yoga acquaintance. At the studio, I used my married name, so I asked the palliative care doctor to double-check before I accepted her case.

"One hundred percent," Dr. Whitmore announced. "Her exact words were: 'That would be awesome. I'm glad it's someone I already know.'"

Liz asked to first see me alone. She was dressed in a hospital gown, wore no makeup, and had her hair cut into a bob and down around her face instead of up in her signature ponytail, a far cry from the limber leader I knew from the hot room. She seemed to have reduced movement on the right side of her body, and her disease had robbed her of some of her words, but she appeared eager to talk.

"I want . . . MAiD . . . it's what *I* want. Anyone who doesn't like it . . . they don't have to." She seemed slightly agitated. "I want . . . you . . . to help me. I know . . . I know what I'm asking."

She smiled. She seemed satisfied that she'd said it all correctly. "I'm sure," she repeated, "don't listen to them . . . if they disagree. I am sure."

She told me Mark understood and was supportive. She informed me that her extended family was welcome in the process, but she explained that she would not tolerate them questioning her decision. She was determined to end her life before her illness took her personhood. "While I'm still me," she emphasized, "while I still can."

Her goal was to prevent her children from ever needing to grapple with a mother who did not recognize them.

While Liz had made her wishes clear, she also wanted to know how it all worked, so I invited Mark to join us for the broader conversation. It seemed like her decision was harder on Mark than Liz had expressed. He was supportive but bewildered—he kept asking her if she was sure. I answered as many questions as I could. The big question seemed to be about whether the kids would attend her death or not.

They were most concerned about their eleven-year-old daughter's possible reaction. I recommended as much open communication and honest sharing as possible. How much did their daughter understand about Liz's illness? I suggested resources they could tap and reminded them to validate whatever feelings the kids might bring up. I'd had little experience to date with teenagers at the bedside during MAiD, and I wondered whether knowing me would make the situation easier for them or harder. I was relieved to hear the family had an appointment with a hospice grief counselor in two days.

A week later, Mark called me—could we talk, just the two of us? We arranged to meet at hospice in the small meditation room, a soothing space with a window, a couch, a yoga mat, and a singing bowl. I entered the room wondering if I was out of my league; I was not a trained grief counselor, and I knew Mark less well than I knew Liz. Again I wondered if our familiarity would be a benefit or an obstacle.

We sat on the couch. I listened as he spoke.

"Everyone's been so amazing . . . I mean . . . really, amazing. I haven't had to cook in forever. Food just keeps showing up on our doorstep."

He seemed uncomfortable. He wasn't looking at me. There was something on his mind.

"I don't know," he continued. "I mean, I don't know how much people know." He shrugged a little, looked a bit sheepish, then turned away from me. "Liz told a few people she was thinking about this . . . about assisted dying and all. I think it's tough to understand. I mean, I'm struggling with it myself, you know?"

He looked back at me for an answer, but I waited, sensing there was more.

"I mean, I'm not really *for* this, right?" he said. "I'm going to support her, but I don't want her to do it. I just . . ." He looked away again. "I . . . I just don't want her to."

By now, I'd helped only one or two people under the age of fifty. Most of the younger patients I had seen and assessed had never quite gotten to the point of asking me to help them die. I suspect it was simply too hard. To ask to die when you're in the prime of your life is counterintuitive. Mark's reaction reminded me how different this process felt when helping an eighty-nine-year-old making an autonomous decision at the end of a full life compared to assisting a forty-eight-year-old in the middle of raising a family.

"And my mother," Mark continued, "my mother is really upset about it. She doesn't understand it at all. She keeps telling me I can't let Liz do this."

I told Mark that sounded incredibly stressful and said maybe he could help by contextualizing things for his mother. I suggested he needed to do this for his kids as well, and in an age-appropriate way.

"Yes," he confirmed, "they know. They understand Liz is dying, that she's staying here in hospice, and that she won't be coming home." He was looking down.

"One way to frame this for them might be to remind them that MAiD is a choice," I said. "A difficult choice. Maybe even a courageous choice. You can explain that Liz has a disease that will lead to her death, but she is choosing to die on her own terms, in a way that she chooses, at a time that she chooses, and surrounded by the people she loves. Do you think they could understand that?"

"Yeah, that's a good way to say it to them, maybe. They'd see their mom as strong instead of weak. I like that." He was absentmindedly nodding.

I carried on. "And what about you? Do you see it that way?"

"I can see that. I just don't like the whole idea."

"No, there's nothing here to like." I looked straight into his eyes. I could see the grief brimming there. I softened my voice a little. "There's no good way to lose your wife, Mark. And there's never a good way to lose your mother."

We sat for a while in silence. I couldn't imagine. More accurately, I could. Liz was my age. This could be me. Mark could be my husband. But I didn't want to identify too deeply. Instead I hid behind my professional mask, relating to his predicament but keeping a safe emotional distance.

On the morning of Liz's death, I woke up at four-thirty. It was quiet in the house, and it was pitch-dark between the slats of my window blinds.

I rarely woke up before my alarm. I was prepared for my day in practical terms, but lying awake in my bed, I began to wonder if I was ready psychologically. I worried that because I knew Liz socially, there was a risk I might become distracted or overly emotional in the room. I allowed myself to consider the awkwardness of the situation, and I wondered how I would feel the next time I was at the yoga studio and heard someone talking about Liz. How would it feel to face her friends? What would I say when I saw them? Something? Nothing? Did I expect their thanks, or did I fear their scorn? And how about Mark and the kids? What would they feel when they drove past my house or saw me on the driveway?

I remembered an old sailing truism: "If you're wondering whether it's time to put on a life jacket, it means you already should have." All morning, I considered calling Adele to join me for Liz's procedure. I knew she normally worked at the same hospital. I wouldn't need her for IV support that morning, the hospice unit had other resources available, so she'd technically have nothing to do. But I felt better imagining this event with her by my side, so I decided to send a text: "Hey, Adele, you working at the hospital this morning?"

She texted back right away: "What's up?"

I was aware of other MAiD programs in the country that ensured at least two members of the clinical team attend each event for mutual support. In the community setting, I always had a nurse with me, but in the hospice unit, I usually worked alone. Who was I kidding? This had to go smoothly. I called Adele to explain.

Thankfully, she didn't hesitate. As I walked in, I was relieved to see her standing next to the nursing station. We met briefly with the hospice team and Dr. Whitmore, and then we headed into Liz's room.

We introduced ourselves to the family, and Adele accompanied them all to the solarium while I sat with Liz and chatted privately. She told me that for all her bravado, she hadn't been sure she would follow through or whether she could leave her children, but she knew she would be leaving them regardless, and she felt the time was right. Over the past week, with the help of a friend, she'd written several letters to family members and created some special mementos for her kids. Last month, she'd made a video for when her daughter turned eighteen. "There's so much more I wanted to do . . ."

Liz made me promise I'd be successful.

The solarium was now completely full, with more than a dozen gathered guests. Liz's sister let me know that everyone wanted a chance to say a personal goodbye, and so began a long procession of last visits.

I waited in the hallway. Some people took just a quick minute. Liz's siblings took quite a bit longer. Finally, Mark and the kids went in together, and I made sure the door was closed behind them. I had no words to offer as they walked past me. I knew of no way to soften this blow.

After they were finished, Mark cracked open the door, signaling that anyone who wished to do so could come back into the room. I could hardly look at him as I set up my medications on the table to Liz's left. His eyes were red, his shoulders sagged; there was profound sadness etched on his face. He sat next to his boys on a vinyl couch behind me. His daughter was in his lap, curled up to his chest, and his arms were wrapped around her. He was staring straight ahead and didn't say a word. The rest of us gathered around Liz, and I asked if she was ready to begin.

"Now?" I heard the daughter ask from behind me.

I turned. I had seen a variety of tokens of love handed to, held by, or worn by the dying person. This day, Liz's eleven-year-old daughter left her father's embrace and broke through our circle to approach her mother for the last time. She solemnly showed her a hand-painted heart-shaped pendant that looked like they may have made it together. She ceremoniously kissed it and placed it gently to Liz's lips for the same, and then she put it in Liz's left palm.

Liz mouthed "I love you" to her daughter, closed her fingers around the pendant, brought it to her chest, and closed her eyes. As she smiled, a single tear escaped the side of her eye, and the girl returned to her father's embrace.

Then I made a cardinal mistake. Wanting to contribute in some way to the solemnity of the moment, I remarked out loud how lucky Liz was to have such a loving and supportive family. I instantly realized I had hit a nerve when Liz's teary-faced fifteen-year-old son angrily spat out that nothing about his mother's circumstance could ever be considered lucky. Fair enough. I nodded agreement in his direction, but he buried his face in his father's shoulder.

"Please"—it was Liz—"let's begin."

I asked for her last words and she smiled. She wished everyone love and to have love.

A young girl's voice called out from behind me, "I love you, Mommy!" and I began.

When I tried to guide Liz to a favorite memory, she instinctively closed her eyes once more, then immediately reopened them. "But there are so many to choose from!"

It was a moment of striking contrasts. I was an outsider sharing an incredibly intimate scene. I was ostensibly guiding the procedure while, all around me, Liz and her family were showing me how it should be done. Her death was invoking a deep and palpable sorrow, the expression of which was creating a remarkable showing of love.

Liz closed her eyes one last time. She fell asleep with the first drug, deeper still with the rest of the medications. There was a very gentle snore for just a few moments, then nothing but the sobs of her family. It happened in seven minutes. And I took another full minute to be sure. I needed to be sure. I had promised.

It was the only time I didn't voice the actual words. I felt like it would be disruptive, or maybe that's a justification. The truth is, I didn't trust my voice. I looked up and saw Liz's sister looking directly at me. She knew it was over but needed confirmation, so I nodded. Then I packed up my medications and left the room, touching Mark's shoulder as I passed him on the way out.

I went to the quiet room behind the nursing station, and I was comforted to see that Adele, who had followed me out of Liz's room, was there chatting with the other nurses as I began to fill in the paperwork. I took a deep breath and tried to concentrate.

By the time I finished, I was feeling more composed. I told Adele I was fine and that I was thankful she had come. She said she had not really done anything, but we both knew she had done a lot.

It wasn't until I climbed into my car that I let my guard down. The professional work was over, but the sorrow that had permeated the room stayed with me. A mother was being taken from her young family, and no one wanted her to go. It felt unfair, unnatural. And it was all a little too close to home.

Part 5

SUMMER AGAIN

CHAPTER 21

MY EXPERIENCES WITH LIZ AND Bev, where I had felt gripped by emotion, had surprised me. They'd broken through my ability to compartmentalize and, honestly, caught me off guard. I knew my feelings were only natural, but I didn't like losing control, and I found those moments unsettling. I wondered if I was pushing myself too hard, if these were signs that I was becoming overwhelmed.

On the other hand, Liz and Bev were breaks from the norm. True, my experience with Edwin had been particularly stressful, but again, it had been an outlier. The rest of the time, I worried I was becoming a little bit too blasé about my MAiD work. A certain normalcy had developed around what I was doing. In and of itself, that was to be expected. But how was it that I could assist someone to die in the morning and go on to a meeting, another consultation, or out to dinner the same night without even batting an eyelash? Was there something wrong with me that I could help someone to die and then play bridge in the afternoon, chatting and joking with friends and not even mentioning what my morning entailed? I remember the first time I assisted two people on the same day, I wondered if I could be emotionally fully present with both families; if I could provide each person what they deserved. It turned out that I could. But was this something I wanted to become so terribly comfortable with? Or was I in denial about the toll the work was taking?

So far, for the most part, I'd been able to honor the promise I'd made early on to my family and myself: no MAiD assessments or deliveries on weekends or after five p.m. Balancing my own needs with those of my patients had been challenging for me. Not working weekends or evenings meant some people died before I could arrange to meet with them. Other times, patients I had already seen and assessed went downhill so rapidly over a weekend that I wasn't able to get back to them quickly enough. By the time I saw those patients on a Monday morning, it was too late, and they were no longer capable of providing consent, similar to Gordon. I felt absolutely terrible in these instances, and I had to work hard not to carry them as personal failures. Sometimes I had to remind myself that MAiD hadn't always been available, and other quality options existed. I was lucky in Victoria, we had excellent palliative care teams, and there were now three other providers of assisted dying, but they were busy running full medical practices of their own on top of caring for their MAiD patients. We covered for each other when we could, but it wasn't always possible. There were so few of us doing the work that I was often tempted to make exceptions, but so far I'd done so only once, when I helped the mother of a good friend to die on a Saturday afternoon.

While I'd put parameters around the days and times I was prepared to work, I hadn't put any limit on the number of new patients I was prepared to take into my practice. I often saw as many as four new patients each week because the demand for consultations was so high. I hadn't felt overburdened, but could I tolerate it all at this pace? Helping Liz had been especially tough. Was my reaction a sign that I had hit my limit? Was that why I'd become overwhelmed with Bev? Or was the fact that other cases *didn't* make me so emotional a warning sign of repressed feeling? I couldn't decide if I was handling it all exceptionally well or if I was on the brink of burning out.

I checked in with everyone who mattered.

"I think what you're doing is important," my daughter told me. "And yes, I absolutely think you're around enough."

It was somewhat reassuring, but what sixteen-year-old wants their mother around more often?

"Well, I'm a little concerned about you, Stef," said Jean-Marc when I asked what he thought about my schedule. "You're definitely around more than you were with maternity, but you're working every evening until bedtime and getting up earlier every day. I know you care deeply about what you do, but can't you delegate some of what you're doing? What about your CAMAP work? Surely someone else could take over part of that?"

It was a fair question, but I had no intention of slowing down the growth of CAMAP. We were finally incorporated on paper. Membership was growing weekly, I was getting close to publishing our second newsletter, and plans for the conference in June were in full swing.

I talked with my own doctor at my annual visit, and she asked how my new work life was going.

"Honestly," I answered, "I find it very rewarding, but I'm working far more than I expected."

"I imagine it's fairly intense," she replied. "Don't forget what you used to tell your maternity patients when they were staying up day and night . . . you can't take care of your family unless you yourself are well."

She reminded me to exercise when I could, make time for some downtime, and not let hobbies go untended. It was stuff I already knew, but it carried more impact coming from my own doctor.

After that visit, I decided to try cutting back on the number of new patients just a little bit, to give myself room to breathe. After all, the work was no longer new—I'd been doing it for close to a year. "It's a marathon now, not a sprint," a wise colleague pointed out. If I were going to be in this for the long haul, I needed to pace myself. Karen would be able to do some of the triage, I realized. She knew from my maternity days that I found it hard to say no to patients. She'd be able to be more realistic. If my roster was full, my roster was full. End of discussion.

We looked at my calendar and agreed to leave only four spots for new patients over the next six weeks, and I asked Karen to make me stick to it.

One afternoon not long after the schedule reduction, I found myself with an unexpected half day off, so I took my kayak out for the first time in over six months. It was glorious, and I wondered why it had been so long. Yes, I was coping well with the work overall, but that didn't mean I could give up on moments that reconnected me with nature and with myself. Hadn't Liz taught me how precarious life could be?

Out on the water that day, paddling past the beach where I walk with Benji and onward, past the rocky point where the local boat launch sat empty, I felt free and rejuvenated. Reducing my schedule had been the right thing to do.

But that didn't mean I didn't have occasional lapses. Another fine morning, after realizing I had a few hours to relax, I noticed I was missing a chart for the next day's visit to one of my few new patients. Instead of taking out the kayak, I decided to walk to my office, a thirty-minute jaunt, while I listened to the electrifying sounds of the *Hamilton* score, my newest musical obsession. My intention was to pick up the chart, quickly check my inbox, and then head straight back home. This would count as self-care, as far as I was concerned.

It started off well. Then, when I got to the office, I noticed some papers sitting in the fax machine. I couldn't convince myself to leave them there for Karen, especially knowing she wouldn't be in for forty-eight hours. I turned the papers over and began to read.

The first page was an urgent consultation from the office of one of my previous maternity partners. She had a patient, a middle-aged woman with glioblastoma, a brain cancer. The woman had been diagnosed only two months earlier but had already suffered a period of significantly decreased cognition. She had temporarily recovered due to the effects of some steroid medication, but everyone knew her time was quite limited. Incredibly, she'd lost a close friend to the same disease five years earlier, so she knew exactly how this was likely to progress. She wanted to discuss MAiD soon, and she wanted to be prepared to act. Could I please see her within a week?

The second referral was from a colleague who worked exclusively within the hospital and was considering becoming a MAiD provider herself. She was asking if I would see a man she was discharging home that same day. He was the patient of a family physician friend of hers and the first MAiD case from within that physician's practice. They were all needing some support. Her physician friend had asked for the name of an experienced practitioner, and she had suggested mine. It would be a favor of sorts to slip this into my schedule, but she was a colleague I wished to encourage and help. The patient in question was deteriorating but not immediately urgent, could I please see him within ten days?

The final two pages were from a local doctor whose name I did not recognize. It was a new referral of an eighty-year-old man with myelodysplastic syndrome, a cancer of the immature blood cells in the bone marrow. In this illness, blood cells do not make it to maturity. He had been fully dependent on biweekly blood transfusions for over four years, but they were becoming less and less effective, and he was becoming more and more symptomatic. Two weeks ago, with the full support of his wife, he had made the decision to stop all further transfusions. He was becoming predictably weaker, and although he was receiving good palliative care, he was also asking for MAiD, urgently if possible, in an effort to avoid the last few weeks of decline before death. Could I please see him this week?

———

In a perfect system, assisted dying should never be an emergency. There should be a timely referral for information, a rigorous process to determine eligibility, room for consideration and exploration of all other options, and then, if required, careful planning of the procedure itself. There were many possible reasons why this wasn't always so. Nonparticipating facilities and faith-based obstruction aside, inadequate awareness of assisted dying in the public and within the health care community meant people sometimes came to me too late in their illness: too late for them to consider their options, too late for them to provide consent, too late for me to assess them before they died or to offer an alternative to their imminent, natural, often unnecessarily uncomfortable death. Low numbers of clinicians willing to be involved in assisted dying work meant limited access to assessors and providers of care, and yes, personal boundaries sometimes imposed limits on when those few clinicians were available. All of this meant that when I got inquiries like these, it was very hard for me to say no.

I checked the online calendar and discovered that Dr. Trouton, the other MAiD physician in town who did possibly even more MAiD work than I did, was away for the next ten days. The physician who normally handled any overflow was in town, but he was already swamped. And to be honest, I was flattered by these personal referrals. Karen wasn't here to shield me from the requests, so I sat down and started investigating. I reviewed the medical records I had been sent. I looked up a few more from the hospital record system, then looked at my schedule, removed a half day I had on hold for personal time, and shuffled a less urgent follow-up appointment with a known patient to a few days later. After ninety minutes, I had a plan. I called Karen, told her we were taking on three new people in the next seven days, and had her help me confirm the appointments. Then I walked home wondering what I'd just done, or undone.

I was walking fast, feeling a mixture of stress and adrenaline. I was glad to be able to help out but questioned if I had made a mistake. I could hear Jean-Marc's voice telling me to pace myself. I could hear my doctor's voice reminding me I needed to build in regular opportunities for stress release.

The eighty-year-old man had already lost capacity by the time I saw him twenty-four hours later. He died eight days later in hospice, his body simply unable to function, his organs shut down one by one. He was comfortable and well cared for. His wife was understanding.

The woman with brain cancer stabilized on steroids. She got her MAiD paperwork in order, she updated her will, and she died with my help five weeks later as she requested: at home and with family by her side. She hosted a farewell party for close friends two days prior and told me it was one of the best parties she'd ever attended. "Everyone was so very nice to me, and everyone important was there!"

The patient of my colleague's physician friend was glad to see me when I arrived at his front door within a week. He had a widely metastasizing lung cancer, a new inability to get out of bed, and a firm commitment to never again set foot in a health care facility. He rewatched most of his favorite movies, spoke with his brother a few thousand kilometers away on FaceTime, and chose to die at home with my assistance two weeks later with only his wife of thirty-three years by his side.

In the end, I felt good about taking on these cases. I realized it was only because I had created some openness in my schedule that I had the ability to jump in when I wanted to. Was there a message about life here, about staying open so that I could be flexible when something new rushed in? I would have to keep balancing my choices, block off time for my own needs once in a while, and allow for some last-minute changes.

I was still figuring it all out.

CHAPTER 22

WHEN I RECEIVED A REFERRAL for a patient named Anne during that first year of providing MAiD, I couldn't help but think of my mother.

"Please assess this woman with multiple system atrophy. She has deteriorated steadily over the past ten years and feels ready to consider assisted dying."

The similarities were uncanny. Both Anne and my mother had uncommon neurological diagnoses. Both illnesses were slowly progressive, although Anne's had evolved more quickly, and it had become even more profound.

When I first met Anne, I recognized the slurred speech right away. I was probably nodding as her husband told me about her tremors, her inability to write, her difficulties with walking, and her risk in swallowing. I learned that their illnesses weren't the only thing they had in common. Both were determined to fight their disease, to remain in their home, and to be as independent as possible.

Anne's application was one that had taken a long time. Her illness was complex and not well understood, so I secured extra neurologic opinions. When I was eventually able to inform Anne that she was eligible, I was surprised to hear that she wanted to wait before proceeding. A great-grandchild was due to arrive in just over two months, and Anne wanted to hold that child at least once. The baby arrived, but Anne delayed again, and I began to question her intentions. When I arranged to speak with her alone to explore how she was feeling, she made clear she was under pressure from her family not to follow through. She was eager to proceed with MAiD, but they were not ready to let her go, and she was torn about what to do. I suggested some family counseling, and Anne and her family agreed to a session to air their respective feelings. I wasn't in attendance, but afterward, everyone agreed it had been helpful. My colleague's note was appropriately vague about certain details, but she noted some long-standing tension between Anne and at least one of her daughters.

It wasn't for me to ask more, but it felt somewhat familiar.

As her family struggled with letting her go, Anne got steadily weaker. Finally, nearly nine months after I first met her, she told me she was ready. I made the arrangements, counseled and consoled the family, and on the day of Anne's scheduled death, made the long drive up the island to assist her.

The distance made it a little trickier than usual, but I arrived close to our scheduled time. The clock on my dashboard read 1:23 p.m. as I pulled up and parked in her driveway. I had planned Anne's death for one-thirty p.m. and was acutely aware that walking in early would likely be frowned upon. For most families, every last minute was precious. Arriving late was likely to feed patient anxiety, so I'd developed the habit of being quite punctual for my visits, particularly when arriving for a death.

At one-thirty p.m. sharp, I knocked on the door, and Anne's husband, Lawrence, a big bear of a man, let me in. He'd been her primary caregiver for many years, and I knew this was going to be difficult for him. We set up in the living room with Anne in her favorite recliner. The family gathered around her and prepared to say their goodbyes. Lawrence sat next to Anne on a small chair and held both her hands in his. He was forcing a supportive smile on his face but was clearly shattered by what was happening. Anne's two daughters were on either side of their mother, gathered in close. I guess I was expecting some loving goodbyes, so I was surprised when I heard Anne's younger daughter, Jill, begin.

"We haven't always seen eye to eye, Mom." She looked nervous, like she was unsure whether she should be saying this. "I'm sorry we spent so much time arguing."

Anne kept her face turned toward her husband.

"I just want to say—" Jill tried to continue.

But Anne had already had enough and cut her off. "Let's not make today about you, dear."

No one had any difficulty understanding *that* speech.

Jill remained silent after that. Her sister glanced over sympathetically but chose not to say a word. Lawrence remained focused on his wife, seemingly oblivious to the dynamics at play around him.

It seemed there was little more to add, but I went about my usual routine and asked if anyone had anything else left unsaid. This time no one spoke. I asked Anne if she had anything she wanted to say. She shook her head.

"Then are you ready to begin?" I inquired.

"I am."

I attached the first medication to the IV tubing and slowly began the injection. "I'm beginning the first medication," I announced. "You might not feel anything at first, Anne. But soon you will feel relaxed, very comfortable, and eventually pretty sleepy."

"Larry," Anne suddenly began, "I just want to thank you for everything."

I cringed. I knew she would fall asleep in under a minute; I really encouraged last words before we started. I didn't want her interrupted or unable to express what she wished, but here it was happening anyway. I only hoped that was both the start and the end of it, that she'd already said everything she had wanted to. Lawrence kissed both her hands and just smiled, looking steadily into her eyes, as the tears streamed down his cheeks.

"And, girls . . ." She shut her eyes as she struggled to continue. "I wasn't . . . I always . . ." There was a short pause, and her head bobbed. "Aaaaall . . . waaaaaysss . . ." I knew she wouldn't finish, she couldn't. It was a terrible realization.

But then I heard Jill, steady, loud, and clear.

"I forgive you, Mom, for all of it."

I am certain Anne would have heard those words—hearing is often the last sense to go as we die. I stopped what I was doing and looked up. I wondered if Jill had offered this statement as a gift to her mother or perhaps as a gift to herself.

My question was answered two seconds later when she followed up with a much quieter "I really do."

Her sister reached out and the two women squeezed hands, acknowledging some understanding between them. Jill seemed much calmer now, almost radiant. Her chin was raised, and she looked at peace as she closed her eyes and allowed her own tears to release. No one said a word after that.

Not for the first time that day, I thought of my own mother . . . and father. What a contrast this outcome seemed from my experience at my father's death, where so many of our feelings were left unsaid and, at least for me, unsettled. I was impressed with the gentle closure this daughter had sought and found, the higher ground she had taken. But how late the effort had come. Was I destined for a similar last-minute resolution with my mother, or worse, would I never find one?

Once again, my patients and their families were prodding me to try to do better in my own life.

———

The next time I was in Halifax to see my mother, we sat in her apartment, me on the love seat across from her, she in her electric easy chair, the light from the generous north-facing windows filtering in to brighten the room. We'd shared a quiet morning, looking at old photos and reminiscing, organizing a drawer or two, and throwing out some old paperwork she was no longer required to keep. I was preparing to leave her alone to rest for a few hours when she announced: "I think I might be dying."

Her frankness caught me off guard, coming from a woman who never talked about her own mortality.

I could feel my heart start to race just a little. The familiar rationalizations began to form—I should go and let her rest now, I thought. We could always talk about this later. It would have been a whole lot easier.

Instead, I decided to stay. My view of my mother had been shifting. I understood that her fortitude had taught me early on to find distance from some of my emotions and, in turn, that emotional armor had helped me to carry out my work. But working in MAiD had also called the maintenance of this barrier into question. Seeing people so deeply connected—watching Harvey and Norma say goodbye, forehead to forehead, whispering their final words, or listening to Bev's family expressing their love—had thankfully pierced that armor. These and other examples showcased the richness of some of the relationships I saw. They made me question if I was lazily accepting some superficial relationships in my life when what I wanted (needed?) was something more meaningful. They inspired me to deepen the connections with some of the people around me. Why are we so afraid to really know each other, to let ourselves be known? I wanted to be more open, to receive and to look for more rapport, and that meant being more available for both my mother's physical needs and her emotional struggles. Here was an opportunity not to run away but to purposely dig in and connect.

I took my lead from her pronouncement and opened the conversation.

"I hope you're not," I responded carefully, "but maybe we should talk about what you'd like to see happen if you ever do need to be hospitalized; what you'd hope to transpire if you ever get more seriously ill. Can we do that?" I was asking permission. "Can we talk about what you'd want me to say if someone asks me to speak on your behalf?"

"I don't really know . . . They gave me this form to fill out . . . What do you think?" she asked.

I took the paper she was holding and unfolded it, then quickly understood what was happening. It was a standardized form from her assisted living home requesting a check mark be placed next to her preferred level of intervention in case of serious illness. The form provided three different levels of possible care: full resuscitative efforts; hospitalization and medical treatment (but no ICU) for conditions considered likely reversible; or no transfer to any hospital, only comfort care within the assisted living facility itself. I learned that her care home asked its residents to update their preferences annually. Why had I never seen this before?

"Which one do you think I should choose?" my mother asked.

"Well," I said, recognizing what was being asked of her, "I guess we should make sure we understand what each of these means before *you* choose what you think is best."

"So tell me," she said, "what exactly do they mean?"

She wasn't eager to discuss all the details, and yes, it was slightly uncomfortable, but it also felt good to start the conversation. I went through the items with her one by one. I tried my best to explain what they meant, what the ramifications were. As I left that day, I turned back and saw my mother sitting in her easy chair, a tremor apparent in her head, rereading the words on the paper. She didn't look up as I walked out the door; she seemed focused, I expect contemplative, and determined to make a careful decision. This felt like a step in the right direction. It's so important to start the conversation. And I knew we could build on it in time.

CHAPTER 23

IN THE EARLY SPRING OF 2017, I was asked to be the keynote speaker at the annual general meeting of Dying With Dignity Canada. In the course of a year, I had gone from the neophyte, standing nervously on Peggy's doorstep for my first consultation, to the expert, asked to speak at a national meeting about my work. I was grateful for so many aspects of the work—the camaraderie of my CAMAP colleagues, the opportunity to spend more time with my family, the many lessons I had learned from my patients and their families about life and how to better live it, and now this acknowledgment from others within the end-of-life movement. Being keynote speaker was a tremendous honor.

It also meant I had to prepare a speech, a task that necessitated reflecting back, not just on my work over the past year but my career in broader terms. By now, the parallels between my work with delivering babies and my work with assisted dying were clear to me.

Back in the days when I was caring for pregnant women, I once delivered a colleague, a nurse from the hospital maternity ward with whom I had worked on multiple occasions. Amy was determined to have an unmedicated birth and to labor at home for as long as possible before presenting to the hospital. We labored together there for a while before eventually migrating in. She was strong, determined, and focused. Her husband, Myles, by contrast, was a bundle of jitters and concerns. It wasn't uncommon for a partner to nervously pace between bedroom and kitchen, offering sips of water and repeatedly asking how to help, but Myles was particularly panicked.

As it happened, Amy's was a textbook natural delivery, the kind we don't see as often anymore, and it was exactly what she had hoped for. I can still remember the joy I felt placing baby Fiona, wet and crying, directly onto her mother's bare chest. Amy was shaking but excited. Myles's hands were on top to steady hers. Both of them were wide-eyed and speechless.

After a few minutes, I took the baby to examine her and confirmed she seemed perfectly healthy. As I announced this, the nurse was helping Amy into a clean gown, so I offered Myles a chance to hold his daughter for the very first time. I wrapped Fiona up in warm flannel blankets and capped her with one of the hand-knitted hats our ladies' auxiliary provided every newborn in the hospital. There were small wisps of red hair poking out from underneath when I handed her gently to Myles. I directed him to sit in the vinyl chair in the corner. He couldn't take his eyes off her, he was in absolute awe of his little bundle and clearly falling madly in love.

Two months afterward, I was seeing the whole family in my office for a final visit before sending them back to their primary care physician. As we were saying our goodbyes, Myles surprised me by asking a question: "You know what it's like when you're out on the road in the middle of nowhere and it's after midnight and your car breaks down? You know what I mean, Dr. Green?"

"Yes, unfortunately, I know exactly how that feels," I answered, smiling.

"Then you call for roadside assistance and wait, right?"

"Yes."

"And you wait, and you wait. Then you finally see it. You see the headlights of that truck coming round the corner and heading toward you. And you know it's all going to be okay. Dr. Green, you were like those headlights. Once you arrived at our house that night, I knew it was all going to be okay. I was so scared before you arrived. I can't thank you enough for everything you've done for us."

I sometimes think of Myles when I tell people they're eligible for

MAiD because I've seen it's often just the promise of help, the *possibility* of assistance, that reduces fear and suffering.

Both maternity care and MAiD are intense, intimate, emotional experiences that call up family dynamics and require me to respect personal choices. Both challenge me to be at once fully present and then, fairly quickly, to graciously withdraw. Both birth and death are obviously significant life events, passages, transformations, or transitions of a sort, but not just for the baby or the person who is dying. I can see now that significant change comes to everyone involved.

Transition is the "passage from one state, stage, subject, or place to another." During my work in maternity care, I tried to guide those transitions through experience, shared knowledge, reassurance, and patient preparation. I tried to understand each individual's goals and needs. I learned the difference between pain and suffering, and I watched, sometimes mesmerized, as people evolved from panic to focus, from person to parent, and from couple to family.

But I could say something similar about my work in assisted dying. Patients at end of life also see me as their guide. Not unlike my role in maternity care, my job in MAiD is to stay focused on what patients need, listen for their intentions, understand their goals, and help steer them and their loved ones through what I hope can be a slightly more empowered transformation from partner to caregiver, from person to patient, from life to death.

My role also goes through transition during these events—as I place a baby on Mom's chest or as I pronounce out loud that a loved one has finally died, and I am immediately aware that my role has shifted from a helpful guide to a respectful witness.

Every one of my patients' transformations will happen with or without me; I understand that I am superfluous. But transitions can be frightening, so I like to think I can help, that perhaps I can sometimes be those headlights comin' round the darkened corner.

I wondered how I could ever begin to convey all of this in a keynote address to a roomful of professionals.

———

It was Sunday, May 28, 2017, and I was in my hotel room in Toronto the morning before giving my keynote speech. As I lay drowsing in bed, an exciting text came through. It was from a *New York Times* reporter named Catherine Porter to say that her story on assisted dying in Canada had made the front page of the newspaper. As it was still dark in my room, the brightness of my cell phone forced me to squint to see the picture she'd sent.

I clicked on the link to the article and began reading. The seven-thousand-word story was an intimate account of one of my patients, John, who had died with my assistance, and it included photos of the people involved and several video clips of him speaking. It was big, bold, and beautifully written.

I had been the subject of some Canadian press in the past, but when the *New York Times* contacted me wanting to write a story, it was the first time my work providing MAiD had attracted international interest. Catherine had hoped to follow a patient from a decision to pursue MAiD through the final procedure. Could I make some introductions? This was a significant request and a difficult one to fulfill. Most people were either too ill or completely uninterested in sharing the fleeting final moments of their lives. For all the positive experiences I had witnessed, most families were omitting any mention of assisted dying in the obituary, and many were sharing their true plans with only a close circle of friends. To participate in this project would invite a public scrutiny most families did not welcome, and I never would have asked most of the people I worked with to consider going public with their story. But Ms. Porter's timing was fortunate. I immediately thought of John.

John Shields was a remarkable man with a remarkable story, and I suspected that he would be open to this opportunity. Twice a husband, once a stepfather, and a friend to a great many, John was an Irish American man who began his adulthood in the Catholic Church as an ordained priest posted to Vancouver, BC, from New York in 1965. His break from his faith only four years later led him to an eventual career in social work, where he focused on helping disadvantaged youth before presiding over British Columbia's largest labor union, for whom he secured equal pay for women and advocated for workers' and First Nations' rights. Later in life, he played a significant role in protecting large swaths of wilderness in BC. John had deep connections to BC's Indigenous communities, led a men's circle, and became a spiritual cosmologist, believing the universe was conscious and that everything was inextricably connected.

John had been suffering with amyloidosis, a rare disease that meant there was a buildup of abnormal proteins in various organs of his body that were wreaking havoc with his function. In an uncanny coincidence, this was the same disease that had probably been afflicting Nevin. Unlike Nevin's, John's diagnosis was not in doubt. By the time I met him, he was numb from his toes up to his shins and from his fingertips up to his elbows. He had significant trouble walking and needed help to dress. He had evidence of amyloid in his gut, his heart, his skin, and his kidneys, and it led to a change in his voice, trouble swallowing, bowel and bladder problems, and infections. John suffered from tremendous amounts of pain and knew his symptoms would only become worse as time went on.

When I confirmed his eligibility, John told me it was the first time he had felt some hope since he'd received his diagnosis, and he set out to live his final weeks with purpose and with clarity. He and his wife, Robin, decided to develop a public workshop called Living Well, Dying Well, to encourage people to speak freely about death and dying.

John's dedication to open communication on the topic of end of life coincided with Ms. Porter's goal of bringing this story to a wider audience. When I asked John if he would consider sharing his death and his decision with a journalist, he was quiet at first—I could tell he was thinking—then a broad smile appeared on his face. Despite the enormous impact he'd had on others in his life, John suggested that dying openly, publicly, and wholeheartedly without fear could be his most meaningful legacy.

I put him in touch with Catherine. He allowed her several interviews and eventually granted her the privilege of attending his death. I hoped she would do him justice.

The night prior to his assisted death at the Victoria Hospice, Catherine Porter watched as John orchestrated and attended his own Irish wake. There were dozens of admirers in attendance, plenty of beer, music and poetry, and many goodbyes. The event was at once festive and poignant. When asked to explain John's journey with assisted dying, Robin summed it up that evening as follows: "We're befriending death. We're holding it, we're witnessing it, we're taking it back into our own hands."

The next day, I assisted in John's death. Also present were Catherine Porter, John's wife and daughter, two close friends, and a woman named Penny, a certified life cycle celebrant who served as officiant. She and John had worked together to design a ceremony drawn from cross-cultural wisdom traditions, resonant with John. Over the course of the thirty-minute ritual, Penny invoked the ancestors, and his friend Heather read the Prayer of Saint Francis of Assisi: "Lord, make me an instrument of Your peace; Where there is hatred, let me sow love." At one point, we all joined John as he began singing his favorite Gershwin tune, "I Got Rhythm," with its familiar refrain: "Who could ask for anything more?" For all his emotional availability, John was a stoic man. I had yet to see him cry. But when his wife told him that fires were burning for him on several different islands, and that Native elders were playing drums for him farther north on Vancouver Island, he closed his eyes and wept.

I had known the *New York Times* piece was pending but hadn't been sure when it would appear. After Catherine texted, alerting me to the fact that it had made the front page, she began sending me some of the readers' comments.

There were already so many. John's story had clearly touched a nerve. There was a handful of criticisms, including an expected comment that physician-assisted death was a "poor substitute for palliative care." This, of course, failed to take into consideration the point that John was receiving outstanding palliative care within a palliative care facility when he chose assisted dying. There was a more thoughtful comment suggesting "we must try our best to remove suffering, but we should not add to the grief of death the grief that it wasn't a 'better' death." This reminded me of my maternity patients who'd be upset when their birth plans were not strictly adhered to in the face of medical emergencies and the surprising disappointment they sometimes felt at not having achieved their "perfect" birth. I was saddened to consider that some people might feel pressure to create a perfect death or any suggestion that John's story was the bar against which all deaths should be measured. Not all assisted deaths could be like John's, but I felt it important as an example of what *could* be achieved if one lived in a society that allowed such events to occur.

The most memorable criticism I read was one from a discontented reader who wrote: "I think it very unethical for *The New York Times* to publish such a personal story. Who am I to know any of Mr. Shields' friends and their last comments about him? Who am I to look at the women weeping at his hospital bedside? I am not Mr. Shields' friend." But that struck me precisely as part of the value of John's gift. He was willing to share these events, to air his thoughts, to model his journey, to show how it looked to "befriend death"—essentially allowing people to see those celebrating at his wake and weeping at his bedside. He did not wish the reader to be afraid of death or uncomfortable or feel the need to turn away. And his sharing had a profound effect.

The article sparked many conversations; others began sharing their own stories with MAiD; and in my experience, more people began to talk more openly about their wishes at end of life. When I had begun this work a year ago, I'd been determined to do it in the open, to not be secretive. I wanted to educate and to inform. But I had also needed to be protective of my clients—all of them deserved my discretion, and many had explicitly asked for it. They didn't want their choices to be made public. By sharing his story in such detail with a major news outlet, John had cracked open the door.

———

In my speech later that morning in Toronto, I told the story of my patient Ed, the free spirit who was also a clown. I spoke about what the work meant to me, why I thought it was important. I made a few links to my work in maternity. Word had gotten out about the *New York Times* article, so there appeared to be added excitement in the room. People seemed appreciative of my candor and asked questions.

After I left the event and boarded the plane to go home, it dawned on me that it had been exactly one year since I'd been in Amsterdam, sitting squarely in the audience, seeking information at a conference on assisted dying. Over the course of the intervening months, I had learned the ropes and come to appreciate in ways I never could have imagined the paradoxical nature of the job. I orchestrated events, but I was a witness to their unfolding; I was knowledgeable about the medicine, but I was always learning about people; I was called to act, but I often couldn't help feeling; I'd become confident in my role, yet I was endlessly humbled by the trust my patients placed in me.

Since the Canadian law had changed, over a thousand Canadians had received an assisted death. There had been no rush to misuse or abuse the regulations, no charges leveled against any clinicians, no strikes of lightning upon my head. Instead there had been gratitude and empowerment and robust discussions about death and dying. Awareness of the issue was growing, and I felt certain John's article was going to help address the lingering stigma around assisted dying and maybe even put the topic on a more global radar.

I had also met a team of extraordinary colleagues. Together, we had worked to organize and support the small but growing number of clinicians across the country who were beginning to do this work. CAMAP was fostering professional growth and emotional resiliency and had given us a platform to lobby for the highest standards of care, whether through the production of guidance documents for our membership or through ongoing educational events. We were forming productive relationships with local, provincial, and national medical organizations. We were negotiating remuneration for clinicians, lobbying for access to better medications, and providing a platform for researchers across the country.

Once home, I plunged into finalizing the details for our own conference on assisted dying, due to begin in under a month. Amid all the decisions and the organizational tasks, I received an unexpected email through the CAMAP office. Health Canada, a branch of the federal government, had reached out and wondered if we could talk.

It turned out they wanted to find out about our organization, where our members were coming from, and how we saw ourselves evolving over the next two years. There were three federal employees on the call. At first I felt a bit like I was at an unanticipated job interview, being grilled by the boss's team. But then they asked if they could set up a meeting with our board so we could advise on issues around our practice. Of course I said yes. As if that weren't enough, I boldly invited them to join us at our upcoming national conference, which was happening the following month, to coincide with the first anniversary of MAiD. To my surprise and delight, they said yes.

It felt as if CAMAP, our group grown from small beginnings, had officially arrived.

CHAPTER 24

THE CITY WAS ONCE AGAIN enjoying its long days of summer. The cycling paths were filled with leisurely sightseers among the athletes. The eaglets had finally hatched, their early growth and feeding were well underway, and if I was especially lucky, I might look up to the sky and watch as they learned to fly. But for Meg, the wife of my patient Richard, the season was irrelevant. Richard had taken a turn for the worse, and she was more and more concerned.

I had been meeting with Richard and Meg for several months. It wasn't common that I saw a patient on a Monday and assisted in his or her death only a few days later. Often it took many weeks and multiple visits before I could establish eligibility or before they felt "ready" to proceed. The visiting and assessing that led up to a death constituted the true bulk of my work, with the actual procedure taking up a smaller portion of my time. While a straightforward case of someone with end-stage terminal illness might take three or four hours to fully assess, speak to everyone involved, and document my findings, a more complicated application for MAiD might take dozens of hours, require multiple visits, liaising with multiple specialists, research into uncommon diagnoses, and discussions with MAiD colleagues.

At Richard's initial consultation, which had taken place in January, I had assumed we were meeting for the first time. It was only when he extended his hand to shake mine that I recognized him.

"I told you we would meet again," he said, his eyes smiling.

His waxed white mustache and hair were distinctive. It was the same Richard—the elderly man in the debonair suit, the one with the fancy walking stick for a cane—who had taken my business card at the talk I'd given at the United Church back in November. That evening, I had wondered if he might need my help someday. It appeared now that he did.

Richard was dressed in his signature jacket and tie, and I learned he was a retired accountant. His condo featured art on the walls and sculpture in little nooks, and everything was orderly and in place. I surmised that Richard was a meticulous man, and the way he told me his medical history only confirmed my initial impression. He explained he was beset with the usual ailments of eighty-three years—a little heart failure, some hypertension, a touch of gout, and significant hearing loss. More crucially, he had been diagnosed with metastatic prostate cancer three years earlier. Richard had managed well enough through the early treatments of hormonal injections and surgery. The cancer was slow-growing but persistent, showing up in his vertebrae to explain the mounting pains in his back, appearing as painless spots in the ribs on his right, and unfortunately blossoming deep in his left hip, making it more and more difficult to walk. Radiation was helping to reduce these lesions, and enzalutamide was offering the promise of more time, but he knew the interventions would ultimately fail, and he wanted to be ready for the eventuality.

This was a second marriage for both Richard and Meg, and despite their age difference—he was twelve years older—one of the many things they had in common was having nursed their first partners through cancer and death. Richard had watched his first wife suffer the ravages of ovarian cancer, and he noted that despite his good care, her death was "far from good."

"I will not subject myself or Meg to such an ending," he told me.

Richard was a strong supporter of the notion of dying with dignity, and Meg was a strong supporter of Richard. When I asked Meg what her thoughts were about Richard's request, she explained: "We both feel very lucky to have found each other later in life. I'll be absolutely devastated when it happens, but we've talked a lot about this, and Richard has my full support."

By his own admission, Richard was not yet truly suffering, and I had noted he was not yet in an advanced state of decline. We reviewed the process of MAiD, where he fit into it at that time, and agreed to speak again in three months.

When we met again in April, despite some obvious decline, he still wasn't ready. Richard's case was not atypical. What he wanted was what we in the email group referred to as "MAiD in the back pocket"—the reassurance that MAiD would be possible and everything was lined up and ready, without making an advance request, which was still forbidden by law.

When Meg called me back that summer, however, I sensed that things were shifting. Over the last few weeks, Richard had been in more pain, using more medication, and requiring a walker. What truly scared Meg was that Richard had fallen out of bed the other night, and she had needed to call 911 to help get him back up. His family doctor had arranged to have him registered with the palliative home care team. Meg thought this all warranted an update.

"I do not wish to die in a hospital," Richard explained as we explored the conditions he thought might trigger his request for MAiD. "In fact, I never want to go back to a hospital, no matter what. If I collapse in the middle of the night, leave me here. If my pain becomes intolerable, I will ask for your help to hasten my death. And I'm a proud man. If I can no longer get myself out of bed or back in safely, I'll be ready. I'm not sure I can list all the things that would make me call and ask for your help, but I'm certain I will know when it's time. Is that all right?"

It was. By then I had observed that my patients tended to know when their time had come, when their suffering had become too much. I always encourage those in my care to trust their instincts. In the end, many decide to live well past the conditions they thought would be intolerable; discovering that not being able to get in and out of bed isn't always as terrible as expected. Perhaps some folks delayed for the sake of their loved ones, but mostly, I believed they did this because they found inner strength and resources they didn't know they possessed, a deep desire to live as long as they could possibly bear it, and yes, at times a bit of hope.

Ten days later, Richard had what Meg believed was a significant heart attack. She called to tell me he had experienced terrible, crushing chest pains but refused to let her call an ambulance. She'd called the palliative response team, and the nurse had instructed her to give him nitroglycerin and morphine.

I agreed it was time to complete the paperwork, and Richard filled out an official request form. I spoke to his family physician, who agreed to be the second assessor, and we both determined Richard to be eligible. I suggested to Richard it was time to tie up any loose ends.

Two days later, I heard from Meg again. Richard had had more chest pains, more moments of confusion, and he had fallen yet again, the previous night, slipping from bed while trying to get up to the washroom. As he sat on the floor with severe pain running up his back, he'd broken down and cried, and he'd told her he was done.

"I don't want another week of this. I'm ready. Call Dr. Green."

On the day of his scheduled death, Adele agreed to accompany me. I used the short elevator ride up to his condo to familiarize her with Richard's circumstances, supplementing the medical background by noting the orderly nature of the home and Richard's preference for jackets and ties. With those details fresh in mind, I expect we were both all the more surprised when Meg answered our knock in her bathrobe and bare feet. She looked smaller and somewhat younger than usual with her hair in a simple ponytail, the comfortable white bathrobe tied at the waist. Meg let us in and asked us to remove our shoes. She told me Richard was in the bedroom, so I made my way in for our private conversation.

Walking into someone's bedroom always feels intimate. The bedroom is the inner sanctum and the private decor can speak volumes about style and personality: the scent of the closet, the products on the night table, the most beloved, more personal photos. Richard and Meg's bedroom featured a king-size bed at its center. There was a framed anniversary poem for Meg on the side wall, a stack of books on her bedside table, and a collection of medication bottles on his.

What was most surprising was Richard himself. He was sitting in bed, covered from the waist down but otherwise naked, propped up with several large pillows; glasses off, hearing aids in place, and white hair childishly askew. The sharply dressed accountant with waxed mustache, suit, and tie was gone, the layers finally peeled back. I was slightly taken aback at his transformation, but then, what else was I expecting?

Richard smiled when he saw me approaching, double-checked that he was modestly arranged, and thanked me for coming. We had our talk, all was in order, and I went out to chat with Meg. When Adele returned to tell us Richard's IV was in place, we all walked back in together, and Meg immediately took charge. "I hope you don't mind if we're naked, in bed, together."

Meg unties her robe, folds it over a nearby chair, and heads to the window to draw the curtains. She turns off the room light and switches on a small lamp. She plumps up her pillows and climbs into bed, the room now lit with a warm amber glow. I am struck by her steady confidence. She is in her seventies and he is eighty-three. I watch with a sort of envy as Meg arranges herself to be sitting sideways but reclining, turned toward Richard, arms reaching out and around him, pulling him into her embrace. He leans in, wrapping his arms around her, and places his head upon her shoulder, their bodies clearly familiar with each other's contours. He looks up at her and they kiss a few times, her hand on his cheek. She strokes his face, his shoulders, his arms, and they kiss some more.

"What good memories we have," Meg begins, "how lucky I have been to have had you for this long."

They speak of their love for each other, of the wonderful years they have shared, mentioning a few cherished memories. I am stunned at the simplicity of the script and moved by the tenderness of this scene. She cradles him as she continues to kiss him, and he speaks of his complete happiness in being with her. I am silent as I sit at their bedside, watching this love scene unfolding in front of me. It takes my breath away.

Before I even think of saying anything, I hear Richard whisper, "Now, please."

They maintain their embrace as he falls asleep. Meg holds him tightly, rocking him slightly, as his breathing slows and then stops. She shifts only an elbow to allow me to check for his absent heartbeat. I excuse myself quietly and then head to the living room, leaving them together for a final farewell.

———

People often ask me what I do for a living, a question usually intended as a benign conversation starter.

"So, what do you do for work?" they ask at the cocktail party, the school event, the festive holiday gathering. How exactly can I explain?

In that instant, I am passing a baby girl, wet and new, onto Amy's chest, her eyes wide in anticipation, her arms trembling from exhaustion. My heart is pounding as I open the door to enter Harvey's home. I'm carrying a bag of lethal medication. "I'm a little scared," I hear him say. The reel starts to speed up: I see the tumor in Gordon's cheek, the nodules covering Ray's chest, the skeleton that was Charlie's body. I hear the absence of Joseph's heartbeat. The long pause. The reel slows. I'm confused as I hand Stella my stethoscope. There is turmoil in my chest as I watch an eighty-eight-year-old in a raincoat reach down and hold her daughter's face for the very last time. A black poodle jumps up on a bed and I am grounded, the smell of patchouli in the air. Faster again, my nostrils fill with smoke and I see Edwin's beaming smile. I hear Andrew yelling at his aunt and Helen yelling at her grandson. "Who could ask for anything more?" we sing. I'm in a room in a crowded farmhouse. I can almost taste the strawberry jam. I feel upbeat as I enter my car. I feel helpless in my kayak, thinking of Nevin. "I feel like you saved my life," said Ray.

"So, what is it you do?"

I begin to smile as I see Ed in his clown suit. He chuckles as he turns his head back to a comfortable position and falls asleep. He falls asleep. She falls asleep. They thank me and then they all fall asleep.

"I help people."

I offer them choices. I empower my patients by letting them know they are eligible for an assisted death. This doesn't mean they have to do it, and it doesn't mean they will. It means they can proceed if they ever feel the need to, and the result is a reduction in suffering.

How do I feel when I do this work? As if I have been a part of something profound. As if I have had the privilege of helping someone in need.

"Really . . . thank you." I hear Harvey's weakened voice and try to understand his complicated gratitude. I picture the blank stare of Liz's three children: incomprehensible what is transpiring in front of them, the end of their childhood in an instant. I feel Edna's squeeze of my hand three times, and I know she is certain of her choice. I picture Meg cradling Richard in their bed, and I believe that I have learned what love can look like.

For me, the work is less about how people wish to die than it is about how they wish to live.

What's most important for you?

Have you shared this with someone you love?

While none of us is exempt from death, I have learned we can make the choice to embrace our life at any time, even its final moments.

EPILOGUE

IN THE TIME SINCE MY first year of providing assisted dying in Canada, much has evolved—my understanding and the interpretation of our law, the infrastructure to support its administration, the community of professionals involved—as has the field of assisted dying itself, locally, nationally, and internationally.

CANADIAN UPDATE

When I first began this work, phrases like "a reasonably foreseeable natural death" and "advanced state of decline" were new, unclear, and untested. In the years since, our understanding of the law has matured. Disputes remain and standardization is still lacking, in my opinion, but some things have been clarified. In June 2017, Justice Perell of the Ontario Superior Court handed down a decision that would significantly bolster the way clinicians and others would interpret the language of the national MAiD law, and in doing so, he changed how assessors and providers of care would practice.

A plaintiff known as AB (her identity remains protected) was a nearly eighty-year-old woman who had been battling severe progressive osteoarthritis for twenty-five years. Despite multiple surgeries, joint replacements, and medical treatments, she had become wholly dependent on full-time care and suffered terribly from uninterrupted pain. Clinicians could not agree on whether she met the eligibility criteria of her natural death being reasonably foreseeable, so she sought clarification from the courts. In an effort to interpret the law, Justice Perell clarified that a person needn't be terminally ill for his or her natural death to be reasonably foreseeable or to qualify for MAiD. A person need only be on a trajectory toward death—"taking into account all of their medical circumstances, without a prognosis necessarily having been made as to the specific length of time that they have remaining"—to meet this particular criterion, and the determination, he emphasized, is meant to be a clinical one, to be decided by a clinician . . . not a lawyer and not a court. Neither the federal nor provincial governments appealed the decision, and this interpretation became the national standard. It allowed an easing of the more conservative interpretations many had been erroneously using up until this time, opening the door for people with degenerative illnesses, with longer prognoses, to potentially qualify for MAiD. This was especially helpful to those with neurological conditions like multiple system atrophy or Parkinson's disease, whose trajectory is unfortunately clear but whose timeline until death remains imprecise.

Nevertheless, the requirement of a reasonably foreseeable death remained controversial because many argued it shouldn't have been imposed in the first place. The original Supreme Court decision that struck down the prohibition of assisted dying in Canada, the *Carter* case, did not mandate that a patient be near or at end of life, only to be a competent adult suffering intolerably from a grievous and irremediable condition. Inevitably, in September 2019, another long-awaited decision in a MAiD-related court case arrived.

Jean Truchon, a man with severe cerebral palsy, and Nicole Gladu, a woman with post-polio syndrome, had successfully argued that the law, colloquially known as Bill C14, violated their Charter rights because it was too restrictive, specifically because it *required* a person's natural death to be reasonably foreseeable. Justice Baudouin of the Quebec Superior Court agreed and, in a strongly worded decision, determined this eligibility criterion must be struck from the law. She suspended her decision for six months so government could amend legislation or consider new safeguards. Importantly, neither the provincial nor federal governments chose to appeal the outcome. The Quebec government allowed the decision to take effect— removing the requirement that natural death be reasonably foreseeable in the province of Quebec (and simultaneously ending a unique provincial requirement that a person be at "end of life"). The federal government pledged to align federal law with the provincial decision.

Once they understood they would be updating the law, the Ministry of Justice decided to consider other possible amendments, and in February 2021, the federal government introduced a package of potential changes commonly referred to as Bill C7. After gathering feedback from a variety of stakeholders across the country, proposed legislation would not only remove the criterion of a reasonably foreseeable death but also make procedural improvements, dropping some safeguards and adding others.

One of the most important changes in Bill C7 was that it allowed some patients who had already been assessed and found eligible for MAiD to waive the requirement of granting a final consent. This would permit clinicians to proceed with MAiD, in certain specific circumstances, even if capacity was unexpectedly lost, as was the case with my patient Gordon. Other changes included removing the ten-day waiting period for those whose death is reasonably foreseeable, and the addition of extra safeguards for those whose death is not foreseeable—a minimum ninety-day assessment period; the mandated input of a clinician with expertise in the condition causing the person's suffering; and the required information about, offer of, and serious consideration of a trial of all reasonable and available means to reduce suffering, including mental health and disability support services, counseling services, and palliative care.

Lawmakers also recognized that no longer requiring foreseeable death meant that more patients who were suffering exclusively from a mental health disorder (such as treatment-resistant depression) might now qualify for MAiD. In C7 they proposed to exclude this entire category of patients (those suffering exclusively from a mental health disorder) from access to assisted dying, citing concerns about irremediability and vulnerability. The Senate perceived this ban as discriminatory and amended the bill so that the exclusion would be automatically repealed after eighteen months, allowing time to develop protocols and guidance and operationalize any additionally required safeguards. The House of Commons accepted the sunset clause but amended it take effect in two years. Bill C7 became law in March 2021, meaning the exclusion of those with solely mental illness will end in March 2023.

Meanwhile, a federally mandated review of the issues surrounding possible access to assisted dying for mature minors (those under eighteen with decision-making capacity), advance requests for MAiD (after diagnosis but before significant decline, such as for people in the initial stages of dementia), and the implementation of MAiD for patients with mental health disorders as their sole underlying illness began in May 2021. Findings are due to be reported in 2022. There is no shortage of challenges that remain or solutions to be discovered as MAiD practice continues to progress in Canada.

AMERICAN UPDATE

Evolution in the field of assisted dying has not been restricted to Canada. Significant change also continues to appear within the United States.

In 2016, when I first began providing MAiD, there were five states that allowed some form of assisted dying in the U.S.—Oregon, Washington, Montana, Vermont, and newly, California. Since that time, five other states—Colorado, Hawaii, New Jersey, Maine, and New Mexico—and the District of Columbia have all passed statutes to allow for assisted dying. Some legal scholars even suggest that, similar to Montana, where MAiD is not specifically legalized but is not prohibited under current law, North Carolina could also allow for assisted dying. Taken together, the populations of these twelve jurisdictions total eighty-four million people, or 25 percent of the U.S. population, with potential access to MAiD.

As was pointed out in a recent review of the various assisted dying laws in the U.S. by legal scholar Thaddeus Pope:

> The expansion of MAiD (in the USA) is notable not only for its size but also for its pace . . . Seven of today's twelve MAiD jurisdictions enacted statutes within the past five years, two of which were . . . in 2019 alone, and half of the remaining forty states considered MAiD legislation in 2021.

All of the new statutes in the U.S. are based on the original end-of-life model from Oregon, but as Pope's paper emphasizes, the various state laws are not all equivalent, each differing slightly in process, safeguards, or eligibility requirements. He goes on to further suggest:

> During the first two decades of U.S. MAiD, policymakers placed heavy emphasis on safety at the expense of access. Today, more states are working to recalibrate the balance . . . Two innovations are particularly likely. First, all states now require the . . . clinician to be a physician; however, some states will probably extend MAiD to advanced practice registered nurses (APRNs). Second, all states now require that the patient be terminally ill with a prognosis of six months or less, but some states will probably extend that to twelve months or longer.

The other significant evolution within the U.S. is in some creative thinking. While the MAiD statutes in the U.S. uniformly require patient self-administration, they use different verbs to describe how the patient may take the drug. In the five states where MAiD legislation uses the specific term "ingest," it is clear that the route of administration of medications to be used for assisted dying must be via the gastrointestinal tract. The most common way to achieve this is through drinking a liquid, but it is now understood that there are other ways to ingest medication.

> For those already dependent on artificial nutrition and hydration, a patient may press a plunger on a feeding tube to administer lethal medications. Others might press the plunger on a rectal tube.

These acceptable options of ingestion (defined as the use of the gastrointestinal tract) negate the necessity of being able to sit up, hold a glass, or swallow.

GLOBAL UPDATE

Since my first year providing MAiD, attitudes around the world toward assisted dying have continued to shift. In June 2019, what is known locally as voluntary assisted dying (VAD) came into effect in the Australian state of Victoria eighteen months after state legislation was passed. The Victoria model is based on the Oregon one of requiring a terminal illness and prognosis of six months or less, and the state of Western Australia followed suit and passed a similar law the same year. Three more Australian states—Tasmania, South Australia, and Queensland—all passed assisted dying legislation in 2021. Meanwhile, a VAD law also passed in New Zealand in 2019, went on to successful national referendum in 2020, and came into effect in 2021. In February 2020, a five-year-old law banning professionally assisted suicide was rejected as unconstitutional by Germany's top court. In a decision reminiscent of the Canadian saga, the Constitutional Court of Austria, in December 2020, found the ban on assisted death unconstitutional and a violation of an individual's right to self-determination. And on March 18, 2021, Spain's parliament passed a law to legalize assisted dying, which took effect three months later, making it the fifth country in Europe where terminally ill patients can legally obtain help to end their lives. At the time of publishing, both the Scottish parliament and the British House of Lords are debating similar legislation.

COVID UPDATE

While there have been many important shifts both nationally and internationally, there have been some new factors that haven't been as welcome or expected.

In March 2020, the novel coronavirus, or COVID-19, swept through the world, bringing our lives to a shuddering halt. Here in Canada, some expected an increased demand for MAiD and others questioned if we could even continue to provide it. Many services came to a standstill, resources were rationed, hospitals prepared for overload, and no one knew what to expect. In some regions, community MAiD programs temporarily shut down as facilities assessed their resources and priorities. In other areas, MAiD services were deemed an essential service and continued unimpeded. Some colleagues announced online that MAiD requests had gone quiet where they worked. In contrast, most said that they were especially busy. Were fear and anxiety driving requests, or was this continued expected growth?

As the president of the professional MAiD organization CAMAP, I felt a responsibility to help support the assessors and providers of this care. It was of paramount importance that medical and nursing staff remain safe and healthy so they could continue to provide all kinds of health care during the COVID-19 pandemic. There were many factors to consider for clinicians providing MAiD: the level of personal protective equipment that might be required; the number of people who could attend an event; the safest location of the procedure; and what to do about our patients who could no longer transfer out of a nonparticipating facility because there was no longer any ability to transfer anyone anywhere. CAMAP lobbied for the increased use and acceptance of telemedicine for patient assessments and request form witnessing. We recognized that for those patients dying from COVID-19, MAiD was not likely a viable solution. The eligibility process takes time. Ideally, timely, quality palliative care that included sufficient levels of sedation were most appropriate in an emergency to facilitate a peaceful death while not exposing additional staff to infectious agents. CAMAP produced three new guidance documents to address these issues and more.

For most providers, the biggest change during COVID was the feel of the event. We started wearing gloves and a mask when providing MAiD, and so did the gathered family members. Physical contact with the patient became more limited and distant. Explanations to families took place outside on the balcony, porch, or patio from at least six feet away, so we could consider removing our masks in an effort to be heard. The MAiD procedure became somewhat less intimate. But it was still possible.

CAMAP UPDATE

As for CAMAP, our organization now has over four hundred members nationwide. We've produced twelve guidance documents, hosted three national conferences, developed a standardized national training workshop that has been used in multiple provinces and is now also available in an online format. We run frequent high-quality educational webinars for our membership. We've partnered with both provincial and national organizations, facilitated a significant body of published research, and—due entirely to the ongoing day-to-day work of our committed, diverse membership—become the country's leading clinical experts on medical assistance in dying. In my role as president, I was invited to give testimony at both the House of Commons and the Senate when lawmakers were debating proposed legislation.

LAST WORDS

Over the years I have compiled many of the final words spoken by my patients and think this list makes a fitting end for this book.

Thank you all for being here
I'm so ready
Take care of each other
Fire!
I did it my way
Goodbye, my sweet
Let's get going already
I need this to happen
Thanks for your support
Here we go . . .
Now, please
Take care of yourselves
I love you
Let 'er rip!
Bless you
Thanks for the memories
My only regret was . . . [*fell asleep*]
I'm ready now
See ya, suckers!

I love you all
I'll be watching you
See you on the other side
I'm so glad you're here
Give it to me . . . let's go!
[*Looking at me*] I love you

AUTHOR'S NOTE

EARNING AND HOLDING THE TRUST of a patient is something I never take for granted. It is the cornerstone of a therapeutic relationship and nothing I would intentionally put at risk. My obligation to respect an individual's privacy means that throughout this book, other than where I have obtained express consent to describe real events, characters and cases have been purposefully altered—including name, age, gender, ethnicity, profession, familial relationship, place of residence, and diagnosis—and in some instances reflect fictional composites.

Similarly, I am deeply committed to respecting the confidential nature of the CAMAP online community, so specific quotes are only provided with permission of the CAMAP board of directors and in conjunction with those to whom they are attributed, or have been altered to protect the forum's integrity.

Aside from these necessary changes, this story is an accurate reflection of what I witnessed and experienced with my colleagues, patients, and their families.

For the greatest amount of clarity, I remind you that all views expressed in this book are entirely my own and do not necessarily reflect those held by my colleagues or any association, including the College of Physicians and Surgeons of BC, the Canadian Medical Association, the Vancouver Island Health Authority, or the Canadian Association of MAiD Assessors and Providers. And nothing in this book should be taken as legal or medical advice on the requirements for medical assistance in dying or any other aspect of health care.

ACKNOWLEDGMENTS

WHILE I LIKE TO PRETEND I had the idea of writing about my clinical experiences long before this book project began, it's just as true that it may not have happened without Catherine Porter of the *New York Times* (and Cory Ruff, who facilitated our meeting). Her beautifully written article about the extraordinary John Shields was a watershed moment that captured the hearts and minds of a great many around the world. Thank you, Catherine, for taking the time to get to know John and his story; for honoring him, his family, and their intimate journey; and for your craft in sharing it so vividly.

The piece was so compelling that Neeti Madan of Sterling Lord Literistic reached out from across the continent to ask if I was interested in writing a book. Neeti, thank you for your vision of the potential of this project. It never wavered, and I am indebted to you for your trust in me to eventually get this right.

Valerie Steiker, your letter of offer to acquire this project for Scribner remains on my desk as inspiration. For two years you encouraged me to rise to your standards, and I eventually learned to listen. This book would not exist without you.

Eve Claxton, what words can I use for the talented book doctor who helped me find order to my flow? You made it all make so much more sense, and with your help, I was able to win over Kara Watson, my final editor at Simon & Schuster, who grabbed on to the manuscript and threw it across the finish line with the gusto I'd been craving.

Those are the big names, but just as important were the lesser known.

Shelley Flam, Pamela Medjuck Stein, Beverley Merson, and Kimberly Lurie, your honest feedback on my earliest drafts was invaluable in helping me shape the story I wanted to tell.

Thaddeus Pope, Jocelyn Downie, Lonny Shavelson, and Joshua Wales, your expertise in some of the minutiae was greatly appreciated.

Agnes Van der Heide, Kenneth Chambaere, and Rob Jonquiére, you supplied some of the data and the references I required, but more than that, I want to thank you for your presentations in Amsterdam. You captured my intellectual curiosity, you convinced me there was rigor and research behind the work, and you unknowingly cracked open the door to my career change.

I would not likely be doing this work today were it not for the early and ongoing support of the entire team of compassionate professionals working throughout the MAiD community. You are far too many to name, but I must offer particular recognition to my fellow CAMAP cofounders for their extraordinary, pioneering work: Dr. Tanja Daws, Dr. Jesse Pewarchuk, Dr. Jonathan Reggler, Dr. Konia Trouton, and Dr. Ellen Wiebe. Paul Schachter and Ashley Hall rounded out our original board of directors and helped create the organization that CAMAP is today. To the entire membership and current board, know that you sustain me, inspire me, and constantly challenge and teach me.

And finally, I am grateful for the friends and family who have somehow found the patience for me and this project over the years it took to complete. I promised not to single anyone out, but how can I not? Sam and Sara: I love you both, deeply and dearly. Alexandra McPherson: for no particular reason except any and every reason that really matters. Jean-Marc: my rock, my partner, my love. Thank you for *providing me* the gifts of reassurance, support, and empowerment.

To my patients over the past three decades, thank you all for sharing your lives and entrusting me with your care. I believe you have assisted me as much as I may have assisted you.

RESOURCES

ASSISTED DYING CONTINUES TO BE an emotional issue fraught
with ethical, legal, and practical conundrums. I am certain it will continue
to be debated, adopted, and adapted in a growing number of jurisdictions
in the world. For readers who are interested in seeking more information
on the topic, I have compiled a few graphs of recent data on MAiD in
Canada, a short list of reputable resources—a mixture of government sites
and patient advocacy groups, and a few books on related issues.

Total Reported MAiD Deaths in Canada, 2016–2020

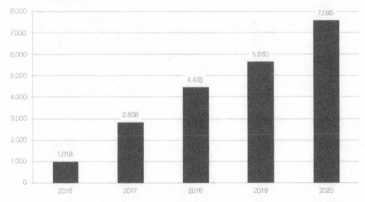

EXPLANATORY NOTES:
1. MAiD cases are counted in the calendar year in which the death occurred (i.e., January–December 31) and are not related to the date of receipt of the written request
2. For 2016, Quebec data begins December 10, 2015, when its provincial act respecting end-of-life care came into force. Data for the rest of Canada begins June 17, 2016
3. Previous years' reporting has been revised to include corrections and additional reports.
4. This chart represents MAiD deaths where a report was received by Health Canada by January 31, 2021 (7,384 deaths), as well as additional MAiD deaths reported by the jurisdiction (221 deaths), where the report was not yet received by Health Canada, for a total of 7,595 MAiD deaths in 2020.
5. Cases of self-administered MAiD are included in this chart. They are not identified by year or jurisdiction in order to protect confidentiality.

MAiD by Main Condition, 2019–20

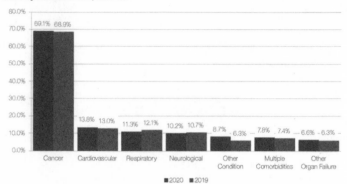

	2020	2019
Cancer	69.1%	68.9%
Cardiovascular	13.8%	13.0%
Respiratory	11.3%	12.1%
Neurological	10.2%	10.7%
Other Condition	8.7%	6.3%
Multiple Comorbidities	7.8%	7.4%
Other Organ Failure	6.6%	6.3%

■2020 ■2019

EXPLANATORY NOTES:
1. This chart represents MAiD deaths where the report was received by Health Canada by January 31, 2021. For 2020, this represents 7,384 MAiD deaths.
2. Providers were able to select more than one medical condition when reporting; therefore, the total exceeds 100%.
3. Data adjustments has resulted in the revision of 2019 results, which are presented here for comparison purposes with 2020 data.

MAiD Deaths as % of Total Deaths, 2020

(Bar chart with values by region: Newfoundland-Labrador, Prince Edward Island, Nova Scotia, New Brunswick, Quebec, Ontario, Manitoba, Saskatchewan, Alberta, British Columbia, TOTAL CANADA, Oregon, Netherlands, Vancouver Island)

UNITED STATES

Death with Dignity: a national advocacy group:

www.deathwithdignity.org

Compassion and Choices: a national advocacy group:
www.compassionandchoices.org

American Clinicians Academy on Medical Aid in Dying: supporting the professionals who do the work in the U.S.:
www.acamaid.org

CANADA

Government of Canada: information on medical assistance in dying:
www.canada.ca/en/health-canada/services/medical-assistance-dying.html

Dying With Dignity Canada: a national advocacy group:
www.dyingwithdignity.ca

Canadian Association of MAiD Assessors and Providers (CAMAP): supporting the professionals who do the work of MAiD in Canada:
www.camapcanada.ca

End of Life Law and Policy in Canada, Health Law Institute, Dalhousie University: answering questions on law, policy, and practice concerning end-of-life care in Canada: http://eol.law.dal.ca

WORLD FEDERATION OF RIGHT TO DIE SOCIETIES

wfrtds.org

CHILDREN'S GRIEF RESOURCES

A number of resources can provide more information about kids' grief. Two I recommend are:

Kidsgrief.ca, offered by Canadian Virtual Hospice. In particular, parents can
refer to Module 2, "Talking about Dying and Death," chapter 7, "Preparing for a medically assisted death" (Canada).

The Dougy Center: The National Grief Center for Children & Families (U.S.):
www.dougy.org

RELATED READING

Being Mortal, Atul Gawande
Knocking on Heaven's Door, Katy Butler
The Inevitable, Katie Engelhart
Physician-Assisted Death: What Everyone Needs To Know, Wayne Sumner
A Good Death, Sandra Martin

NOTES

CHAPTER 4

46   *A national poll had recently found that 84 percent:* "Dying with Dignity Public Perception Survey," https://d3n8a8pro7vhmx.cloudfront .net/dwdcanada/pages/47/attachments/original/1435159000 /DWD_IpsosReid2014.pdf?1435159000.

50   *Both the American Academy of Pediatrics and the Canadian Paediatric Society:* American Academy of Pediatrics, "Circumcision Policy Statement," https://pediatrics.aappublications.org/content/pediatrics/130/3/585 .full.pdf; and Canadian Paediatric Society, "Newborn Male Circumcision," https://www.cps.ca/en/documents/position/circumcision.

CHAPTER 5

56   *"The most recent data suggests ninety-three percent":* Tweede evaluatie Wet levensbeeindiging op verzoek en hulp bij zelfdoding (Second Evaluation of the Termination of Life on Request and Assisted Suicide Assessment Act), pp. 82 and 86.

56   *"Of all cases of assisted dying in the Netherlands":* Regional Euthanasia Review Committee—Annual Report 2015, https://www.euthanasiecom missie.nl/binaries/euthanasiecommissie/documenten/jaarversla gen/2015/april/26/jaarverslag-2015/Jaarverslag2015ENG.pdf.

NOTES

57   *I had assumed that people requested assistance in dying:* "Oregon Death with
       Dignity Act: 2015 Data Summary," https://www.oregon.gov/oha/PH
       /PROVIDERPARTNERRESOURCES/EVALUATIONRESEARCH
       /DEATHWITHDIGNITYACT/Documents/year18.pdf.

CHAPTER 12

138   *One report from the Netherlands showed that in 2015:* Tweede evaluatie
       Wet levensbeeindiging op verzoek en hulp bij zelfdoding (Second
       Evaluation of the Termination of Life on Request and Assisted Suicide
       Assessment Act), p. 195.

139   *Assisted dying remained illegal in the Netherlands:* Regional Euthanasia
       Review Committees, "Due Care Criteria," https://english.euthanasie
       commissie.nl/due-care-criteria.

139   *By contrast, in Canada, our eligibility criteria read "a patient must":* Parliament
       of Canada, Bill C-14, https://www.parl.ca/DocumentViewer/en/42
       -1/bill/C-14/royal-assent. See Eligibility section 241.2.

CHAPTER 14

153   *the World Health Organization's definition of palliative care:* Frequently quoted:
       WHO 2013—third bullet point, https://palliative.stanford.edu
       /overview-of-palliative-care/overview-of-palliative-care/world-health
       -organization-definition-of-palliative-care/. For a newer definition in
       2018 (see p. 5, tenth bullet point), https://apps.who.int/iris/bitstream
       /handle/10665/274559/9789241514477-eng.pdf?ua=1.

159   *This approach has been widely accepted by the Belgian public:* Jan L. Bernheim
       et al., "Questions and Answers on the Belgian Model of Integral
       End-of-Life Care: Experiment? Prototype?" *Journal of Bioethical Inquiry*
       11 (2014), 507–29, https://link.springer.com/article/10.1007/s11673
       -014-9554-z.

159   *even the Brothers of Charity, a religious order:* Francis X. Rocca, "Catholic Hospital Group Grants Euthanasia to Mentally Ill, Defying Vatican," *Wall Street Journal,* October 27, 2017, https://www.wsj.com/articles /catholic-hospital-group-grants-euthanasia-to-mentally-ill-defying-vati can-1509096600.

159   *Just as important, data suggests that since the legalization of assisted dying:* Kenneth Chambaere and Jan L. Bernheim, "Does Legal Physician-Assisted Dying Impede Development of Palliative Care? The Belgian and Benelux Experience," *Journal of Medical Ethics* 41, no. 8 (August 2015): 657–60; DOI: 10.1136/medethics-2014-102116 OR http://jme.bmj .com/ (first published online on February 3, 2015).

CHAPTER 15

174   *But I do think we can find:* Jocelyn Downie and Stefanie Green, "For People with Dementia, Changes in MAiD Law Offer New Hope," *Policy Options Politique,* April 21, 2021, policyoptions.irpp.org/magazines /april-2021/for-people-with-dementia-changes-in-maid-law-offer-new -hope.

CHAPTER 20

217   *I suggested resources they could tap:* Kidsgrief.ca, offered by Canadian Virtual Hospice (in particular, parents can refer to Module 2: "Talking about Dying and Death," chapter 7, "Preparing for a medically assisted death" [Canada]); and the Dougy Center: The National Grief Center for Children & Families (U.S.), https://www .dougy.org.

CHAPTER 23

241   *Transition is the "passage from one state, stage, subject, or place to another":*
       Merriam-Webster Dictionary, https://www.merriam-webster.com
       /dictionary/transition.

244   *For all his emotional availability:* Catherine Porter, "At His Own Wake, Cel-
       ebrating Life and the Gift of Death," *New York Times,* May 25, 2017.

246   *over a thousand Canadians:* Government of Canada, Second
       Annual Report on Medical Assistance in Dying in Canada 2020,
       https://www.canada.ca/en/health-canada/services/medical
       -assistance-dying/annual-report-2020.html.

EPILOGUE

258   *"taking into account all of their medical circumstances": A.B. v. Canada*
       (Attorney General), 2017, https://camapcanada.ca/wp-content
       /uploads/2018/12/ABDecision1.pdf.

258   *Justice Baudouin of the Quebec Superior Court agreed: Truchon c. Procureur général*
       du Canada, 2019, https://www.canlii.org/en/qc/qccs/doc/2019/2019
       qccs3792/2019qccs3792.html?searchUrlHash=AAAAAQANdHJ1Y2
       hvbiBnbGFkdQAAAAB&resultIndex=1.

260   *Bill C7 became law in March 2021:* Parliament of Canada, Bill C-7,
       https://parl.ca/DocumentViewer/en/43-2/bill/C-7/royal-assent.

261   *a recent review of the various assisted dying laws in the U.S. by legal scholar*
       Thaddeus Pope: Thaddeus Mason Pope, "Medical Aid in Dying: Key
       Variations Among U.S. State Laws," *Journal of Health and Life Sciences*
       Law 14, no. 1 (2020), 25–59, https://papers.ssrn.com/sol3/papers
       .cfm?abstract_id=3743855.

264   *As for CAMAP:* www.camapcanada.ca

RESOURCES

271   *Assisted dying continues to be an emotional issue:* "Second Annual Report on Medical Assistance in Dying in Canada, 2020," https://www.canada.ca/content/dam/hc-sc/documents/services/medical-assistance-dying/annual-report-2020/annual-report-2020-eng.pdf.

INDEX

American Academy of Pediatrics,
position statement on
circumcision, 50
amyloidosis, 122, 243
amyotrophic lateral sclerosis (ALS)
or Lou Gehrig's disease, 43
Arvay, Joe, 165
assisted dying, 151–52
arguments against, 43, 47
author's view of, 7, 50–51, 54,
60, 87, 96, 241, 254–55
Canadian model, 138–39
clinicians' support system, 121
compassion and, 6, 47, 48, 160
countries where it is legal, 5, 45
dementia or patients with mental
disorders, 172–74, 201–2,
259–60
demographics of patients, 196
different names for, 5
done under the guise of
appropriate pain control, 171

eligibility for, in Canada, 4–5, 6,
13–14, 20, 81, 135–36 (see also
assisted dying eligibility)
empowering the patient, 1, 7,
21–22, 45, 50, 120, 140–41,
159, 183, 250–55
finding a practitioner, 62,
229–30
holidays' effect on requests,
165–66
in a hospital setting, 77–88
medical community's response
to, 50–51
medical conditions commonly
leading to (cancers), 2, 56, 66,
77, 140, 152–53, 167, 208,
214, 228, 229, 230, 231, 250
medical professionals' training,
53–59, 90, 96
motives for choosing, 7, 13, 19–20,
21, 22, 57, 67, 68–69, 81–82,
84, 179, 231, 243, 250, 251

assisted dying (*cont.*)

opponents to, 78, 133–34, 153

overturning the legal ban on in Canada, 4, 11, 41–51

palliative care vs., 21, 57, 127, 130, 151–52, 168

patients' choices: memorable playlists and scenarios, 2, 100–101, 140–41, 253–54

people's emotional reactions to, 78–79

planning in advance for the end, 249–54

as a rights-based issue, 138, 139

updates to Canadian law, 257–60

updates to global laws, 262–63

updates to U.S. laws, 260–62

what to call an assisted death, 89, 96

what to say at the end, 59

assisted dying cases

Anne, tension with daughter and last words unfinished, 233–36

Bev, an aged mother bids farewell to dying daughter, 208–12

Charlie, assisted dying in a hospital setting, 77–88

Ed, choosing to remain a free spirit and clown, 1–4, 246

Edna, a family's religious objections to the patient's choice, 177–83

Gordon, unable to give final consent, 166–72, 174

Harvey, first assisted dying case, 16–23, 31–40

Helen, grandson and unfinished family business, 107–11

John Shields, legacy of sharing his story with the public, 242–45

Katie, memories shared by her family, 102–5

Liz, emotional death of a mother with a young family, 214–22

Louise, assisted dying at remote location and assessment by telehealth, 67–76

Ray, assisted dying after a "total pain crisis" in hospice, 152–55, 157–60

Richard, leaving in his wife's embrace, 249–54

trio of urgent referrals, 228–31

assisted dying eligibility (in Canada), 4–6, 13–14, 20, 81, 135–36

author's approach to, 119–20

eligibility criteria, 4–5, 6, 13–14, 20

example, Anne, uncommon neurological disease, eligible, 233

example, Charlie, pancreatic cancer, eligible, 78–81

example, Edna, neurodegenerative disorder, eligible, 179–80

example, Harvey, end-stage liver failure, eligible, 20

example, Louise, metastatic breast cancer, eligible, 68–69

example, Nevin and Suzanne, possible legal ramifications, questionable eligibility, 121–31

example, ninety-four-year-old patient, not eligible, 11–15

example, Ray, "total pain crisis" in hospice, eligible, 158–59

example, Richard, metastatic prostate cancer, eligible, 249–51

foreign visitors to Canada as not eligible, 135–36

patient's reaction to approval, 120

qualification of "advanced state of decline," 5, 14, 125, 126, 128, 135, 172, 251, 257

qualification of "decline as irreversible," 5, 125–26

qualification of "grievous and irremediable condition," 20, 48, 120, 124, 125, 126, 139, 258

qualification of "intolerable suffering," 7, 45, 96, 126, 130, 135

qualification of "natural death as reasonably foreseeable," 5, 13, 14, 126, 128, 135, 199, 257–59

regulatory guidelines, 19

risk of criminal penalties for not meeting the criteria, 120, 128, 129

assisted dying protocols and procedures, 99, 121–31

addressing patient fears, 34–35

administration of drugs, 39–40

aftercare, 66

assessment by telehealth, 67–68

"choreographing" of the event, 59, 180

duplicate set of medications, 59

Dutch protocol, 57–58

example, Harvey, steps in the assisted dying of, 31–40

final consent, 22, 34, 67–68, 72–73, 108, 166–72, 259

finding a pharmacy to fill the prescription, 22, 32, 70–71, 98

assisted dying protocols and
procedures (*cont.*)
initial consultation and
determination of eligibility,
4–5, 6, 11–15, 19, 20, 67,
68–69, 78–81, 99, 119–31,
249–50
legal counsel and, 23
legal ramifications and, 23, 120,
121–31, 170–71
medical credentials for, 61
official request, 22, 82, 123, 139,
168, 172, 179, 182, 215, 251,
252
opting for oral medication or
intravenous, 22
paperwork after the death,
74–75, 86, 189, 222
patient signature on the final
form, 36
patient's medical history
reviewed, 16, 69, 121, 178,
195, 199, 230
physician reimbursement,
69–70, 100
pronouncement of death, 40,
190
second clinical opinion required,
22, 82–83, 103
steps in, 82
support for the practitioner
during, 59

waiting period, 22, 168, 259
what to say at the end, 75–76
witnesses for request forms, 99,
168, 264
assisted dying resources, 271–74
Canadian organizations, 273
children's grief resources,
272–73
global right to die societies, 273
graphs of recent MAiD data,
271–72
related reading, 273
U.S. advocacy groups, 272–73
assisted suicide or physician-
assisted suicide, 5, 136–37
difference from euthanasia, 5
Sue Rodriguez and, 44
Australia, VAD legalized in
Victoria, Tasmania, South
Australia, and Queensland,
262
Austria, overturns law against
assisted death, 262

Baudouin, Justice, 258–59
BC Civil Liberties Association
(BCCLA), 47
Belgium
assisted suicide or physician-
assisted suicide in, 5
doctor-administered care vs. self-
administered drink, 138

eligibility for assisted dying in, 137

euthanasia in, 6

integrated end-of-life care, 159

religious orders' response
euthanasia, 159

Beuthin, Rosanne, 83–84

Bill C7, amended legislation on
assisted dying, 259–60

Bill C14, legislation on assisted
dying, 11, 49, 135, 258–59

CAMAP (Canadian Association
of MAiD Assessors and
Providers), 163–65, 239, 242

creation of, 163–64

first national conference, 165

goals and accomplishments, 164,
246–47

Health Canada's recognition of,
247

online forum, issues addressed
and, 164, 171–72, 183–84,
192–93

updates on membership and
accomplishments, 264

Canada, 4–5, 6

assisted dying model benefits,
138–39

assisted suicide or physician-
assisted suicide in, 5

Bill C7, amended legislation on
assisted dying, 259–60

Bill C14, legislation on assisted
dying, 11, 49, 135, 258–59

date of assisted dying becoming
legal, 49

early lack of assisted death
providers, 66–67, 70

eligibility for assisted dying, 4–5,
13–14, 19, 137 (see also assisted
dying / eligibility)

foreign visitors not eligible for
assisted dying, 135–36

framework for assisted dying as
patient-centric, 139

increase in assisted dying
patients in, 213–14

number of assisted dying
patients, first year, 246

overturning the legal ban on
assisted dying, 41–51

PharmaCare and coverage of
medication costs, 32

public support for assisted dying,
46, 60, 133

resources for assisted dying
organizations, 273

Thanksgiving in, 111

updates to national assisted
dying law, 257–60

See also MAiD

Canadian Medical Protective
Association (CMPA),
121

Canadian Paediatric Society,
position statement on
circumcision, 50
Carter, Kay, 45
Carter v. Canada, 4, 42, 45–47, 135,
165, 258
arguments presented, 46
Justice Smith pens the lower
court decision, 46
Supreme Court of Canada
decision on, 47–48
Taylor joins the lawsuit, 46
when filed, 46
circumcision of infant males, 50
author providing in addition to
maternity care, 50, 60
decision-making about, 50
clinician self-care, 58, 101–2, 119,
147–48, 177, 225–28
College of Physicians and Surgeons
of British Columbia (CPSBC),
22–23, 52, 61
dealing with complaints, 123–24
professional practice standard on
MAiD, 124
Colombia, euthanasia in, 6
COVID-19, 263–64

Daws, Tanja, 65, 66, 163
death
of the author's father, 111–15
author preparing a shiva as a
teenager and, 25–28
case of a stillborn baby, 93–96
discussions about, 134
end-of-life decisions, 113–14,
115, 144, 150, 236–38
family's bereavement and,
185–93
home deaths vs. dying in
institutions, 45
Jewish community and chevra
kadisha, 114
John Shields's journey with
assisted dying and, 244
as a medical challenge,
extending life, 45
palliative care and, 45
reality of loss and, 85
unfinished business and, 14,
107–11, 150
witnessing of assisted dying, 87,
96, 99
witnessing of natural death,
Mr. King, hospital setting,
90–93
witnessing of natural deaths, 87
See also assisted dying
death certificates, 99
dementia patients, 172–74, 259–60
Dying With Dignity Canada
(DWDC), 61, 99, 164

author as keynote speaker for,
2017, 239, 242

euthanasia, 5–6
difference from assisted suicide, 5
eugenics movement and, 6
Nazis and, 6
what it is, 5
where it is available, 5–6
Euthanasia 2016 conference,
Amsterdam, 53, 55–59
Canadians at, 55–56, 57
closed-door session with
experienced providers of
medically assisted dying, 58–59
presentations at, 56
program of, 56

family of patient
author's accessibility for, 84–85
bereavement resources, 185, 189
clinician's relationship with,
185–93
at consultations, 16–22, 72–76,
81–82
end-of-life decisions and, 113–
14, 115, 144, 150, 236–38
example, Anne, resolution of
family problems and, 233–36
example, Bev, her mother's
farewell to, 208–12, 225

example, Edna, family's religious
objections to her choice and
legal threats, 180–84
example, Harvey, family's
presence, 16–23, 34–40
example, Helen, unfinished
family business, 107–11
example, Joseph, wife's concerns
about his being dead, 186–93
example, Katie, memories
shared, 103–5
example, Liz, mother with a
young family, 214–22
example, Louise, son's difficulty
with her death, 72–76, 192
explaining administration of
drugs, 36–37
explaining likely visual events,
37–38
the gift of their support, 85
how to say goodbye, 185–86, 210
meeting people where they are,
191
a member's objection to assisted
dying, ramifications of, 123–24
preparing for what to expect,
36–38
presence at the death, 34, 38–40,
84–85, 140–41, 181
pronouncement of death as a
beginning for, 186

family of patient (*cont.*)

    reactions of, 40, 79, 115, 185–
      86, 192

    religious ideology of, 180

    spousal abuse and, 193

    what to say at the end to them,
      75–76

    witnessing a natural death,
      Mr. King, 90–93

Germany, assisted suicide legalized
    in, 262

Gladu, Nicole, 258–59

Green, Stefanie, 6, 254–55

    average age of assisted dying
      patients, 140

    CAMAP creation and, 163–65

    cautious approach to assisted
      dying, 60, 87, 124, 170, 174

    childhood and education, 25–29,
      111, 145–47, 205

    circumcision practice by, 50, 60

    contemplating her own death,
      103–5

    demeanor and approach to
      assisted dying, 33, 212

    early experience with death and
      mourning, 25, 27–28

    emotional responses to assisting
      in death, 65, 140–41, 160–61,
      205, 211–12, 222, 225, 226

    entering medicine, 27–28

    expansion of her assisted dying
      practice, 213, 226, 228–30

    father's death and, 111–15

    fellowship in palliative care,
      155–56

    first assisted death, 15–23,
      31–40, 62, 65

    first assisted dying patient in an
      institutional setting, 77–88

    first consultation, ninety-four-
      year-old Peggy, 11–15

    first four months, patient
      statistics, 151

    first month of assisted dying
      practice, 66

    first natural hospital death
      witnessed, 90–93

    growing community of
      supportive colleagues, 97–100

    guiding the conversation and,
      14

    home life and children, 16, 31,
      41–42, 45, 60–61, 105, 165,
      204, 226–27

    how assisted dying patients
      found her, 62, 66

    husband, Jean-Marc, 16, 41,
      42, 46, 49, 52, 54, 60, 65, 66,
      113, 165, 202, 203, 227,
      230

    introducing herself to a patient,
      17–19

introspection and insights about herself and her relationships, 115, 208, 236, 237

learning about the field of assisted dying, 53–59, 155–56

learning from her MAiD patients, 105

legal ramifications for mistakes and, 121–31

maternity case, birth of a colleague's baby, 239–41

maternity case, birth of a stillborn baby, 93–96

maternity practice of, 6, 33, 41, 44, 45, 48–50, 59, 105, 155–56, 165, 212, 239–41

mother's relationship with and debilitating condition, 112, 143–50, 203–8, 233, 236–38

New York Times article and, 242

nurse practitioners working with, 23, 33, 109–10, 188, 209, 212, 219, 221–22, 252, 253

office manager for, Karen, 14–15, 61–62, 71, 96, 133, 199, 227, 230

parallels between maternity practice and assisted dying, 212, 239–41

practice changed from maternity to assisted dying, 6–7, 41, 49, 51–54

public talks by, 133, 140–41, 166–67, 239, 246, 250

questions confronted by, 8, 87

radio interview by, 89–90

role of, for assisted dying patients, 7, 96, 156, 160, 183, 241, 255

routine on days she assists in dying, 119

safety protocols created after consultation with mentally ill patient, 196–202

"see one, do one, teach one" medical school saying, 33

self-care by, 119, 147–48, 177, 200–201, 225–28, 230

seminar at the United Church, 134, 140–41

setting parameters on her availability, 105, 225–27

setting up an assisted death practice, 61–62

support system and email group, 121, 160–61, 163, 164, 171

telehealth consultation, 68–69

Green, Stefanie, assisted dying cases

Anne, resolution of family problems and, 233–36

assisted dying cases, trio of urgent referrals, 228–31

assisted dying requests of Nevin and Suzanne, possible legal ramifications, 121–31

Green, Stefanie, assisted dying
cases (*cont.*)

Bev, emotional scene as her
aged mother bids farewell to,
208–12, 225

Charlie, first in a hospital setting,
77–88

Ed, attending a free spirit and
clown, 1–4, 246

Edna, dealing with a family's
religious objections and legal
threats, 178–84

Gordon, a patient unable to give
final consent and legal stop to
assisted dying, 166–72, 174

Harvey, first assisted death
to proceed on Vancouver
Island and among the first in
Canada, 15–23, 31–40, 62, 65

Helen, patient confronting her
grandson, unfinished family
business, 107–11

John Shields, willingness to share
his death and *New York Times*
coverage, 343–45

Joseph, wife's concerns about
the finality of his death and
possibility of abuse, 186–93

Katie, family's spontaneous
sharing of memories at her
death, 103–5

Liz, emotional response to
mother with a young family,
214–22, 225

Louise, helping her in a remote
location and dealing with her
son's grief, 67–76, 192

Ray, first assisted dying patient
in hospice after a "total pain
crisis," 152–55, 157–60

Richard, witnessing his intimate
leaving in his wife's embrace,
250–54

hospice or palliative care, 21, 57,
127, 130, 131, 151–54, 167,
229, 230

assisted dying and, 153, 154,
215, 219

assisted dying case, John Shields,
243–45

assisted dying case, Ray, "total
pain crisis," 152–55, 157–60

in Belgium, 159

"continuous palliative sedation
therapy" (previously known
as terminal sedation), 157–58,
169

"forced transfers," 154

patient, Gordon, unable to give
final consent, 168, 174

reducing suffering and, 157

World Health Organization's
definition of palliative care,
153
hospitals
assisted dying case in a hospital
setting, 77–88
bereavement program, 85
clinical nurse leader (CNL),
83–84, 86
DNR (do not resuscitate) order, 91
MAiD in, 78
MAiD staff debriefing, 83–84, 86
staff reactions to assisted dying,
79–80, 83–84, 86–88

Kevorkian, Jack, 44, 129
Kopetsky, Darren, 55

last words, 4, 36, 103, 110, 160,
221, 254, 255
compilation, 265–66
unfinished, 235
living wakes, 7, 23, 230–31, 244
Living Well, Dying Well public
workshop, 243
Luxembourg
assisted suicide or physician-
assisted suicide in, 5
doctor-administered care vs. self-
administered drink, 138
euthanasia in, 6

MAiD (medical assistance in dying)
access for mature minors,
172–73, 260
administered provincially, 53,
98–99
assessments, variation in
duration of, 249
assisted death in a hospice
setting, 152–55, 157–60
assisted death in a hospital
setting and, 77–88
author's group in British
Columbia, 65, 96–100
bereavement resources, 185
Canada's law allowing use of, 4
Canadian health insurance, an
eligibility requirement, 136
clinical teams attending each
event, 219
clinicians' mental grounding
before and after, 101
clinicians reluctant to get
involved, 82–83, 98
conditions triggering a request
for, 251–52
as controversial, 60
COVID-19 and, 263–64
creation of a national body for
(CAMAP), 163–65
December 2016 and MAiD
requests, 166

MAiD (medical assistance in
dying) (*cont.*)
demographics of patients, 196
difficulty for the public to find
information and, 166, 171
difficulty sourcing medications
or finding willing pharmacists,
70–71, 98
early challenges and creation of
procedures, 96–100
effects of, 120
first assisted death, 15–23, 31
goal of, 171
graphs of recent data, 271–72
issues slated for further study,
172–73
lack of knowledge about, 83
legal criteria, consensus needed,
121–31, 163
mental health disorders and
requests, 196–202, 259–60
mixed reception to, religious
communities and, 148
need for increased number of
clinicians, 97–100
in Ontario, 98–99
palliative care physicians and,
154
as patient-centered care, 78
people coming too late, 229–30
physician reimbursement,
69–70, 99–100
problems with final consent
criteria, 166–74, 259
prosecution risk to clinician, 124,
128
public support for physician-
assisted death, 133
question of advanced requests,
171–74, 260
rules of eligibility for, 4–5, 6,
135 (*see also* assisted dying
eligibility)
springtime and increase in
requests, 213
two methods of assistance
allowed, 4, 5, 6, 137–38
types of medical professionals
allowed to assist, 4, 98
updates to national law, 257–60
why the term is used in
Canada, 6
"MAiD in the back pocket," 251,
255, 260
Malleson, Roey, 65
medications used in assisted dying,
137
air travel and, 71
duration of process, 37
finding a pharmacy to fill the
prescription, 22, 32, 70–71
intravenous drugs, 36–37
lidocaine, 36–37
midazolam, 36

oral drug(s): barbiturates, 5, 137–38
physiologic pathway of, 190
propofol, 37
rocuronium, 37
Morgentaler, Henry, 129

Netherlands
AIDS crisis and assisted dying,
138–39
assisted suicide or physician-
assisted suicide in, 5
doctor-administered care vs. self-
administered drink, 138
due care criteria in, 139
eligibility for assisted dying in, 137
Euthanasia 2016 conference,
Amsterdam, 53, 55–59
euthanasia in, 6
framework for assisted dying as
physician-centric, 139
history of laws allowing assisted
dying, 138–39
medical professionals support of
physician-assisted death, 56
primary care health system, 56
public support for physician-
assisted death, 55
statistics on assisted dying in, 56
New York Times
Porter's article on assisted dying
in Canada and patient John
Shields, 242–45, 246

New Zealand, VAD law passed in,
262

Oregon Death with Dignity Act,
44, 136, 214

pain
assisted dying case, Ray, "total
pain crisis," 152–55, 157–60
defined, 156
emotional pain, 156
individual reactions to, 156
MAiD qualification of
"intolerable suffering," 7, 45,
96, 126, 130, 135
reassurance, empowerment, and
reduction in suffering, 156–57
suffering and, 156
women in labor and, 156
palliative care. See hospice or
palliative care
Park, Grace, 55, 65
Perell, Justice, 257–58
Pewarchuk, Jesse, 53, 55, 61, 65, 163
PharmaCare, 32
Pope, Thaddeus, 139, 261–62
Porter, Catherine, 242, 244

Reggler, Jonathan, 65, 66, 163
right-to-die movement, 44, 46
Rodriguez, Sue, 42–44, 48
assisted suicide and, 44

Rodriguez v. British Columbia, 44, 45, 46, 135
Royal Jubilee Hospital, 68, 78, 188

sailing truism, 219
sanctity of life, 43
Scotland, debate on assisted dying legislation, 263
Shields, John
  amyloidosis and, 243
  assisted dying of, 244
  ceremony at death of, 244
  living wake of, 244
  Living Well, Dying Well public workshop, 243
  New York Times article and, 243–45
Smith, Madam Justice Lynn, 46
Spain, assisted dying legalized in, 262
suicide, 131, 198–99
  assisted suicide or physician-assisted suicide, 5, 44, 136–37
  decriminalization of, 44
Supreme Court of Canada, 41–42
  assisted dying as a rights-based issue, 138, 139
  Carter v. Canada, 4, 42, 45–48, 135, 165, 258
  Rodriguez v. British Columbia, 44, 135
  signing a decision by "the Court," 48

Switzerland
  assisted suicide or physician-assisted suicide in, 5
  eligibility for assisted dying in, 137
  foreigners receiving end-of-life care in, 45, 138

Taylor, Gloria, 45–46, 47
Toronto, number of assisted dying providers, 66
Trouton, Konia, 53, 55, 61, 65, 83, 163–64, 230
Truchon, Jean, 258–59

United Kingdom, Scotland, debate on assisted dying legislation, 263
United States
  advocacy groups, 272–73
  assisted dying medication self-administered as drink and problems of method, 5, 137, 139, 261–62
  assisted suicide or physician-assisted suicide in, 5, 136–37
  eligibility for assisted dying in, 136–37
  laws changed by voter ballot initiatives, 139
  onerous eligibility requirements and safeguards, 139

Oregon Death with Dignity Act
as template for statutes in, 44,
136–37, 261
public support for physician-
assisted death, 44
updates to assisted dying laws
and states allowing, 260–62
University of British Columbia,
164
University of Toronto, 28

Vancouver Island, British
Columbia, 7, 11
first assisted death, Harvey,
end-stage liver failure, 15–23,
31–40, 62, 65
Island Health Authority, 53, 166,
195
MAiD program on, 61, 163
need for increased number of
clinicians, 97–98, 214
number of assisted dying
providers, 66
Vass, Dr., 177–78

Victoria, Australia, 262
Victoria, British Columbia
about, 11, 165, 213, 249
assisted dying patient, Ed, choice
to be a free spirit and clown,
1–4
autumn in, 119
as home to Canadian Navy's
Pacific fleet, 165
hospitals serving, 78
number of assisted dying
providers, 66, 226
palliative care in, 226
Rodriguez legal challenge to the
ban on assisted dying, 42–44
Victoria Hospice Unit, 151, 154,
244
voluntary assisted dying (VAD), 262

Whitmore, Dr., 151, 152–55,
158–59
Wiebe, Ellen, 55, 65, 164
World Federation of Right to Die
Societies, 53